C. W Bibb

Polished Stones and Sharpened Arrows

A collection of scripture texts and illustrations for the Christian worker and the

home

C. W Bibb

Polished Stones and Sharpened Arrows
A collection of scripture texts and illustrations for the Christian worker and the home

ISBN/EAN: 9783337288877

Printed in Europe, USA, Canada, Australia, Japan

Cover: Foto ©Lupo / pixelio.de

More available books at **www.hansebooks.com**

POLISHED STONES

AND

SHARPENED ARROWS

𝔄 Collection of
SCRIPTURE TEXTS AND ILLUSTRATIONS FOR
THE CHRISTIAN WORKER, THE HOME,
AND THE PRAYER MEETING.

BY

C. W. BIBB

NEW YORK
THOMAS Y. CROWELL & CO.

TO

My Beloved Father,

WHO FOR NEARLY SIXTY YEARS SO FAITHFULLY PREACHED THE

GOSPEL OF JESUS CHRIST,

AND WHOSE UNWAVERING FAITH HAS DONE MUCH TOWARD
STRENGTHENING MY OWN LIFE,

This Volume

IS RESPECTFULLY DEDICATED BY

THE AUTHOR.

PREFACE.

It was our Lord's favorite method of teaching, to bring into use some familiar figure to illustrate the truth he wished to impress upon the hearts of his hearers; and we, his followers, will often find an apt illustration the best means of touching the secret spring of the heart, and causing its door to swing open to receive the same truth at our hands.

Doubtless some of the illustrations in this collection are already familiar to many into whose hands this little work will fall; but as our aim is not for originality, it is hoped that they may prove not less useful than those which are entirely new.

The reader will observe that some of the selections are not intended to be confined to the texts of Scripture under which they are placed, but may appropriately be used under numerous other headings.

This volume has been prepared with a threefold purpose in view. *First*, To serve as a handbook of illustrations for the preacher, the teacher, and the Christian worker, that they may abound more and more in every good word and work. *Second*, That it may be the means of arousing some sleeping Christian to a higher sense of his duty to himself, his fellow-men, and to his God. And last, but not least, that some unsaved soul may be directed to the "Lamb of God that taketh away the sins of the world." If in either of these purposes I have been successful, my labor has not been in vain.

C. W. BIBB.

MINNEAPOLIS, MINN., Dec. 1, 1888.

CONTENTS.

CHAPTER		PAGE
I.	THE CHRISTIAN LIFE	1
II.	TRUST IN CHRIST	37
III.	STAGNANT POOLS	55
IV.	POWER OF CHRISTIAN INFLUENCE	63
V.	TEMPTATION	81
VI.	SECRET SINS	91
VII.	SERVING GOD OUR FIRST DUTY	101
VIII.	PERSONAL WORK	111
IX.	PRAYER	141
X.	CHARITY	149
XI.	THE CHRISTIAN'S REWARD	161
XII.	THE BIBLE	167
XIII.	GOD'S LOVE TO MAN	177
XIV.	CHRIST THE ONLY WAY	191
XV.	CHRIST'S WILLINGNESS TO SAVE	219
XVI.	CHRIST INVITES ALL MEN TO SALVATION	239
XVII.	ONLY BELIEVE	263
XVIII.	NOW	277
XIX.	DANGER IN DELAY	291
XX.	PERSONAL APPEALS	319
XXI.	TRYING TO SAVE YOURSELF	333
XXII.	SATAN'S DEVICES	343
XXIII.	THE BLOOD	353

INTRODUCTION.

The value of illustration in speaking and in writing cannot be over-estimated. But if illustration passes into mere ornamentation, it may be a hinderance rather than a help. "Illustrations are the windows of thought." If they are stained windows, which color the light rather than transmit it, they will inevitably attract the thought to themselves rather than reveal that thought to us. How can we make illustrations interpret the truth to the hearer, instead of diverting the hearer from the truth? If they can be so employed as to throw their light upon Scripture, and so to irradiate the word of God that it shall become luminous while the illustration is quite forgotten in the higher glory of the text, the end is attained. Illustration is the John the Baptist preparing the way of the truth, saying evermore, "I am not that light, but am sent to bear witness of that light."

The aim of the excellent volume which we hereby take pleasure in introducing to the public is just this which we have above indicated. May it throw its illustrative light on many a gospel message of preacher and worker for Christ.

A. J. Gordon.

Clarendon Street Church,
   Boston, Feb. 1889.

CHAPTER I.

THE CHRISTIAN LIFE.

"HE THAT SAITH HE ABIDETH IN HIM OUGHT HIMSELF ALSO SO TO WALK, EVEN AS HE WALKED."
1 John ii. 6.

THE CHRISTIAN LIFE.

"*Looking unto Jesus.*" — HEB. xii. 2.

Two boys were playing in the snow one day, when one said to the other, "Let us see who can make the straightest path in the snow." His companion readily accepted the proposition, and they started. One boy fixed his eyes on a tree, and walked along without taking them off the object selected. The other boy set his eyes on the tree also, and, when he had gone a short distance, he turned, and looked back to see how true his course was. He went a little distance farther, and again turned to look over his steps. When they arrived at their stopping-place, each halted, and looked back. One path was true as an arrow, while the other ran in a zigzag course. "How did you get your path so true?" asked the boy who had made the crooked steps. "Why," said the other boy, "I just set my eyes on the tree, and kept them there until I got to the end; while you stopped, and looked back, and wandered out of your course." Just so is the Christian life. If we fix the eye of our hope, our trust, and our faith upon Jesus Christ, and keep them continually fastened thereon, we will at last land at the desired haven, with flowers of immortal victory at our feet.

Many Christians stop in their course, and take their eyes from the objective point, and look back over their course, brooding over the crooked places they have made. Oh! that we could learn to let the past take care of the past, and we press forward "toward the mark of the high calling," fixing our gaze on the adorable Jesus, whose light will shine around us, and guide us in our straight pathway.

> "Would you lose your load of sin?
> Fix your eyes upon Jesus.
> Would you know sweet peace within?
> Fix your eyes upon Jesus."

"*He shall sit as a refiner.*"— MAL. iii. 3.

"Some years ago, in Dublin, a company of ladies met to study the Holy Scriptures. One of the ladies observed a peculiarity in the words "He shall *sit* as a refiner." After some discussion, a committee was appointed to call on a silversmith, and learn what they could on the subject, and report at the next meeting. They called at the silversmith's, who readily showed them the process. "But, sir," said one, "do you *sit* while the refining is going on?" — "Oh, yes, madam!" he said, "I must sit with my eyes steadily fixed on the surface, for if the time necessary for refining be exceeded in the slightest degree, the silver is sure to be injured." At once the ladies saw the beauty and the comfort, too, of the passage. As they were leaving the shop, the silversmith called them, and said that he wanted to still further mention that he only knew when the process was complete *by seeing his own image reflected on the silver.*"— MACKNIGHT.

How glorious to be so refined by Christ that his blessed image will be reflected in our lives, and attract and win those about us to him.

"*And this is life eternal, that they might know thee, the only true God, and Jesus Christ, whom thou hast sent.*"

Jno. xvii. 3.

It is said of Dr. Fisher, Bishop of Rochester, who was cruelly condemned to be beheaded by Henry VIII., when he came out of the Tower, and saw the scaffold, he took from his pocket a small testament, and, turning his eyes heavenward, said, "Now, O Lord, direct me to some passage which may support me through this awful trial"; he opened the book, and his eyes fell on these words: "This is life eternal, to know thee, the only true God, and Jesus Christ, whom thou hast sent"; he closed the book, and, looking to God, said, "Praise the Lord! this is sufficient, both for me and for eternity."

Thrice blessed is he who seeks to know "God and Jesus Christ, whom he has sent"; and doubly thrice blessed is he who, when he has been made acquainted with God, tries to bring others to the like relationship. Dear reader, are you doing this? Does Christ's love flow through you, unto lost souls? Does your walk in life lead any soul to Christ?

"*There is a friend that sticketh closer than a brother.*"

Prov. xviii. 24.

In the city of Baltimore, not long ago, two Christian young ladies set out to do missionary work in the suburban districts of the city. They soon came to a small cottage, standing on the edge of a field, where they found in one corner of the only room. the poor wasted form of the husband. At a glance they saw he was in the last stages of consumption. They began conversing with him, but, seeing he was disturbed, they soon left the house. As they were leaving, one of the ladies handed the sick man a gospel tract. He glanced at it, and threw it from him; it lay beside his pallet until it became soiled and worn. One day his eye rested upon it, and he read the title, "Do you want a friend?" He thought of his condition, and said to himself, "Surely, if any one needs a friend, it is I." He asked his wife to hand him the soiled paper, and he again read, "Do you want a friend?" "There is a friend that sticketh closer than a brother." He read the tract through, and requested his wife to bring him her Bible. The Spirit opened the eyes of his understanding, and revealed to him the unsearchable riches of Christ; and he was led to believe in Christ unto salvation. I doubt if either of the young lady missionaries ever knew what precious fruit the tract yielded, and they probably will never know until the poor consumptive greets them in heaven, and tells them how they rescued him from the verge of hell, and led him to the blessed Saviour.

One word to you, Christian reader: "In the morning sow thy seed (the word of God), and in the evening withhold not thine hand." Sow! sow! sow! "Cast thy bread upon the waters, and it shall return unto you after many days." It may be after your soul has been admitted to the bliss of heaven, but it will return, bearing fruit.

"Whosoever, therefore, shall be ashamed of me and of my words in this adulterous and sinful generation, of him also shall the Son of Man be ashamed, when he cometh in the glory of his Father with the holy angels.

MARK viii. 38.

In the "Confessions of St. Augustine" he relates a story of Victorinus, an eminent man at Rome, who had won the respect of a large number of his countrymen, among whom were many heathen. When the spirit of God dawned upon his heart, and the light of Christ therein shone, he went direct to one of his friends, and told him that he was a Christian. The friend replied, "I will never believe it until I see you openly profess your new faith in the church." The above text came to him with such force that he went back to his friend, and boldly and openly confessed Christ as his Saviour.

My friends, how is it with you? Do you shirk your duty? are you afraid, ashamed of Christ? Remember, there may come a time when you will need his strong arm to support you, and it will be withdrawn: "When ye call, I will not answer."

"*Blessed are those servants, whom the Lord when he cometh shall find watching.*"— LUKE xii. 37.

An Arctic explorer found, floating helplessly about among the icebergs of that cold, lonely country, a ship. Going on board he found that the captain was frozen, and sat dead at his log-book, while the helmsman stood at his post, and the men on watch still on duty, but cold in death. What happiness will it be when our Lord doth come to know we have done our duty, and can welcome our Saviour as he bids us "come up higher." "Blessed are those servants whom the Lord, when he cometh, shall find watching." Reader, are you ready? Are you ever watching and waiting the coming of your Lord?

"*I have no pleasure in you, saith the Lord of hosts. Neither will I accept an offering at your hand.*"

MAL. i. 10.

Miss J. F. Willing says that in the church of Ara Cieli in Rome, there is always a large wooden doll, the Holy

Bambino, which represents to its worshippers the child Christ. "When we went to see it," she says, "the priest unlocked and opened doors and drew aside bolts and bars, as if he had to keep his treasure with the utmost care. And well he might; for, ugly bit of wood that it was, its clothes were ablaze with precious stones. Its reputation for miracles and getting up thunderstorms, etc., would hardly have hindered a burglar from helping himself to its wealth had a chance been given." People who wanted to show their love for the Saviour had brought these worthy gifts, and laid them upon the shrine of this wooden representation of his babyhood. Such foolishness God has declared an abomination in his sight, and that such acts of praise are honoring the devil and not God [Deut. xxxii. 17] who declares, "To do justice and judgment is more acceptable to the Lord than sacrifice."

"But whosoever shall deny me before men, him will I also deny before my Father which is in heaven."
MATT. x. 33.

In the city of Boston, some years ago, lived a lady who was known as the most beautiful woman in the vicinity. One day the house in which she lived was found to be on fire, the flames spread rapidly; the lady rushed into the burning building to rescue her infant daughter. The flames sadly disfigured her once beautiful features, and she became a hideous cripple, but she saved her daughter. Years passed, the daughter grew to be a beautiful woman; one day she and a companion were walking down the street when they met a poor cripple woman; as they passed her, the companion asked the daughter, "Who is that hideous creature?" The ungrateful daughter did not say it was the dearest friend on earth to her; that she had sacrificed her earthly joy and beauty to rescue her from an awful death. No! no! She simply said, "I don't know who she is." Methinks I hear the reader say, "ungrateful wretch!" But, dear friend, multitudes of us are doing ten thousand times worse than this ungrateful child; we are denying the one who rescued us from the gaping jaws of endless torment, and gave his own life to save us; the gay world asks us who he is; we answer "I don't know." Did you ever think what it is to be denied by the great judge? The denial comes when we most need the support of his strong arm, when all earthly support has left us, and we stand trembling before the bar of justice. But there is in the darkness of this scene a ray of light, for the same judge says, "Whosoever shall confess me before men, him will I confess before my Father which is in heaven." Happy are we if our daily walk confesses Christ before the world. And we have the Son of God to stand before the Father confessing us.

"*If ye abide in me, and my words abide in you, ye shall ask what ye will and it shall be done unto you.*"
Jno. xv. 7.

A few years ago George Muller, the superintendent of the great orphan asylum of Bristol, England, paid this country a visit. In a lecture delivered in one of our cities, he told upon what basis the Society was conducted. On many occasions, said he, we do not know at one meal where food for the satisfying of the hundreds of little mouths is to come from for the next meal, and in such cases we always assemble and lay our case before God, and we have never yet been disappointed. It always happens that some Christian's heart is moved to bring or send a contribution just in the hour of need, and during all these years of the institution's existence we have never once been disappointed, because we trust in God to supply and care for the army of little unfortunates, which seems almost beyond the power of human efforts to do. Neither will the child of God ever go away empty handed, provided he abides in Christ, which insures the abiding of Christ in him, and through whom "we can do all things." We ofttimes marvel because our prayers are not answered; but my friend, if you would halt and examine the Spirit in which the prayer was uttered, you would the more marvel if your prayer was answered. Here is the assurance of answer to your prayers "*If ye abide in me* ask what ye will and it shall be done unto you." By faith our hearts must be interlinked to the blessed Christ, which will insure our earnestness in asking. In Christ, we cannot ask wrong, out of Christ, we cannot ask right. "Therefore I say unto you, What things so ever ye desire, when ye pray, *Believe* that ye receive them, and ye shall have them."

Too many prayers are uttered in a half-hearted way, and which never ascend to the Father for want of zeal to fire them on their flight. Many rise no higher than the tide waters of this world can waft them, because they are uttered in the spirit of worldliness which can not ascend unto spiritualness.

My dear young friend, profit by the experience of past ages, and when you pray "enter into thy closet" and when thou hast shut out every form and thought of worldliness, open thy heart's door and pour out thy soul to God. Then you will realize the truthfulness of our text. "If ye abide in me, and my words abide in you, ye shall ask what ye will and it *shall* be done unto you."

"*And Jesus came and touched them, and said, Arise, and be not afraid.*" — MATT. xvii. 7.

During our late war, a poor widow received a despatch saying her only son was severely wounded. Immediately, the sorrowing mother started to the front to care for her son. When she reached the hospital, the surgeon at first refused her permission to see him, saying, "He is now sleeping, and the sudden surprise of your presence may prove fatal." But the mother plead, and promised not to wake her wounded boy. As she sat in silence by the bedside, she gently laid her hand upon the forehead of her sleeping son, and that moment he opened his eyes, saying, "O! Mother! I am so glad you have come." How unmistakably similar is the presence of Christ in the heart of one of his trusting children. Like an electric flash the wires of his heart are set in motion, and he sweetly communes as "friend with friend." The child of God knows the touch of its Master, and rests in security in his presence.

"*For I have given you an example, that ye should do as I have done.*" — JNO. xiii. 15.

It was the custom among the ancient Romans on important occasions to bring the images of their departed citizens, who were noted for their good citizenship, before the people, that the thought of the original might inspire the people to emulate their virtues.

So the image of the wonderful character of Christ, so plainly portrayed in the Scriptures, should arouse us to activity in following the example he has left for us.

When we consider what he accomplished during his life in three and a half short years, ought it not to inspire us to imitate him as far as possible. He went about continually doing good. Should we not make that our motto? His great heart throbbed with sympathy, for the fallen around him. Should not the same spirit find lodgment in our hearts and aid us in helping those around us to lighten their burdens, and to learn to lay all on the shoulders of the Strong One?

Such a life never dies; we may pass away and be forgotten, but our lives live on and on through all eternity.

"*Blessed is that servant, whom his Lord, when he cometh, shall find so doing.*" — MAT. xxiv. 46.

It is said of Sir Henry Havelock, that one day he was going over London Bridge with his son Harry; he said to him, " Stop here, Harry, till I return."

The father completed his business and returned home alone. After a short time his wife asked, "Where is Harry?" "Why bless me," replied Sir Henry, "I left him on London Bridge, and I am sure he will remain there until I return." He hastened to the bridge, to find his son waiting his return.

There comes to the child of God, hours when it seems as if he must give up all efforts to labor for his master. Dark hours come, hours of discouragements fall upon him, and he feels as if not only earthly friends had forsaken him, but that Christ Jesus had withdrawn his presence. Dear reader, such scenes come to us all, but thanks be to God, for his uplifting promises, such as: —

"He that endureth to the end shall be saved."

"I will never leave thee nor forsake thee."

"Lo, I am with you always."

"My grace is sufficient for thee."

Shall we not then go forth with renewed vigor, pleading the precious promises of God? His great, strong arm is sufficient to bear us up, and then, too, his willingness to help us; no sooner do we make room for him in our hearts than he fills us.

Oh, what encouragement we have to watch and work and wait, because we know he is with us and will not forsake us.

"*Ye also shall bear witness.*" — JNO. xv. 27.

When the late Commodore Foote was in Siam, he had upon one occasion the king upon his vessel as a guest. As every true Christian should do, he did not hesitate in the presence of his royal highness to ask a blessing as the guests took their places at the table.

"Why, that is just as the missionaries do," said the surprised king. "Yes," said the godly Foote, "and I am a missionary too."

What a golden truth this godly man uttered. Every one born into the kingdom of Christ is in duty bound to become a missionary, and every true child of God is a missionary because he is laboring to sow the seed of the gospel in the hearts of those around him. It is not necessary to go to some dark, unexplored continent in order to be a missionary; we have work to do at home, some of us under our own roofs, in leading souls to Christ.

Would to God we had more of the missionary spirit in our hearts, that we become more earnest and active in leading souls, with whom we daily associate, to the foot of the cross.

Christians will find it helpful to frequently ask themselves, — what kind of a witness am I? and to whom am I bearing witness?

These two questions should ring in our ears until our

hearts become on fire with the missionary spirit, and we find ourselves daily seeking to lead souls to Christ.

"*Verily, I say unto you, inasmuch as ye have done it unto one of the least of these my brethren, ye have done it unto me.*" — MATT. xxv. 40.

There is a legend which says it was the custom of St. Gregory, after he became pope, to entertain every evening at his own table twelve poor men, in memory of Christ's twelve apostles. It is said that one evening there were thirteen instead of twelve — he summoned his steward and asked how it happened. The steward counted and could make but twelve. At the end of the meal St. Gregory asked the unbidden guest who he was. "I am the poor man whom thou didst relieve. My name is *Wonderful*, through whom God will give whatsoever ye ask." St. Gregory knew he had been entertaining the Lord Jesus.

And so may we entertain him too if we only open our hearts and bid him come in. "Behold I stand at the door and knock, if any man open, I will come in unto him."

On the other hand, we can never entertain Him until we empty our hearts of selfishness and give him complete sway.

"*Without controversy, great is the mystery of godliness.*"
1 TIM. iii. 16.

An old Hindoo story says, that Ammi one day called his son to him and said, "My son, bring me a fruit of that tree and break it open. What is there?"

The son replied, "Some small seeds."

"Break one of them, and what do you see," said the father. "Nothing, my lord," said the son. "My child," said Ammi, "where you see nothing, there dwells a mighty tree."

So it is in our experience; at times we allow Satan to cast over our eyes a film darkening the preciousness of God's word, and while we may fail to see the exquisite beauty therein, it contains a mighty truth whose end is eternal life.

"If ye have faith as a grain of mustard seed, . . . nothing shall be impossible unto you." — MATT. xvii. 20.

It is said of Dr. Charles Pitman, that as he stood before an immense audience one afternoon to preach to perishing men, the sky became dark and a terrible storm threatened to disturb the services. Lightnings flashed thick and fast, loud thunders rolled, the congregation became frightened. The godly man knelt down and poured out his earnest soul to God to hold back the storm for one hour and let him go forward with the services, and that souls might be saved. Three times he repeated his petition. A member of the congregation, who took note of the time, said afterward that it was difficult to say which produced the greater effect, the signal answer to prayer or the zeal and pathos of the preacher. As Dr. Pitman closed the services of the hour, he said, "Go to your tents and fall down before God and thank him for this glorious privilege we have enjoyed together." As the last of them entered their tents, the elements broke forth from their pent-up prison, and a terrible tempest raged; it is said that over five hundred were converted to Christ.

Oh, my Christian friends, how oft do we come to the Throne of Grace with our petitions, and plead for our needs in a half-way manner, and then wonder how the words of our text can be true. Christ's promises to us are, "Ask what ye will, *believing*" and it shall be granted us. Oh, how many of our prayers are never heard by the Father, how many of them are too worldly to ever be allowed into heaven's record, and how we wonder and pine at our unfruitfulness; and at times murmur at the galling yoke of Christ. Friend, our hearts are not right. They are filled with something else.

"*If ye abide in me, and my words abide in you, ye shall ask what ye will, and it shall be done unto you.*"
JNO. xv. 7.

A modern novelist tells us of a great bell which was made to vibrate by the note of a slender flute. The flute had no influence upon the bell, except when a certain note was sounded; then the great mass of metal breathed a responsive sigh.

So it is only when our wills are in accord with God's will that we experience an answer to our prayer, and the feeble human cry seems to elicit a divine response. There is a pre-established harmony between the voice of the Shepherd and the hearts of the sheep. "If ye abide in me, and my words abide in you, ye shall ask what ye will, and it shall be done unto you."— EDWARD JUDSON, D.D.

"*Who will render to every man according to his deeds: To them who by patient continuance in well-doing seek for glory and honor and immortality, eternal life.*"— ROM. ii. 7.

When Scarron, the wit and ecclesiastic, as poor as he was brilliant, was about to marry Mme. de Maintenon, he was asked by the notary what he proposed to settle upon Mademoiselle; he replied, "Immortality. The names of kings' wives die with them; but the name of the wife of Scarron will live forever."

So Christ is pleased to bestow on him who by a life of patient service, merits honor, glory, immortality, life eternal. "He that overcometh, I will give to eat of the tree of life, which is in the midst of the paradise of God"; and he who by patient endurance holds out to the end shall be made a partaker of that immortal glory, hid with God in Christ Jesus our Lord.

"*Take, therefore, no thought for the morrow, for the morrow shall take thought for the things of itself.*"
MATT. vi. 34.

"I compare the troubles," said Mr. John Newton, "which we have to undergo in the course of a year to a great bundle of fagots, far too large for us to lift. But God does not require us to carry the whole at once. He mercifully unties the bundles, and gives us a stick which we are to carry to-day, and another which we are to carry to-morrow, and so on. How much easier life would be if we could learn to carry each day only the burdens appointed for that day, and not take up yesterday's trouble, and add it to to-morrow's cares.

William Jay very beautifully says on the same thought: "We consider the year before us a desk, on which lay 365 sealed letters — one for each day, prescribing its duties. We much desire to unseal each one, which would only add to our burden," while it would violate the will of our Maker, who expressly commands not to let the weight of one day's cares trespass on that of another.

"*For he doth not afflict willingly, nor grieve the children of men.*" — LAM. iii. 33.

As Mr. Cecil was walking one day in the Botanical Gardens of Oxford, his attention was arrested by a fine pomegranate tree, cut almost through the stem, near the root. On inquiry the gardener said: "Sir, this tree used to shoot so strong that it bore nothing but leaves. I was therefore obliged to cut it in this manner; and, when it was almost cut through, it began to bear plenty of fruit."

There are times in our Christian experiences when it becomes necessary for God to sorely afflict us to bring us back to the post of duty: it may be the taking away of an idolized loved one, reverses in business, or something else that is infringing on the time that belongs to our Christian duties.

He may be compelled, for our good, to cut us to the very quick to bring us back to bearing fruit. Whatever it may be, rest assured it is for our own good and his glory.

"*Not unto us, . . . but unto thy name give glory.*"
Ps. cxv. 1.

After the battle of Agincourt it is said of Henry V. that he wanted to acknowledge the divine interposition, he ordered the chaplain to read a Psalm of David, and, when he came to these words, "Not unto us — not unto us, O Lord! but unto thy name give glory and praise," the king dismounted, his officers dismounted — the cavalry all dismounted, great hosts of officers and men fell on their faces in reverence to their Great Deliverer.

When we contemplate what great victories we have attained over sin, through Christ, how fitting to fall before God in thanksgiving and praise, crying, "Not unto us, but unto thy name be the praise." "For thou hast redeemed us to God by thy blood, which was shed for the sins of many."

"*I will guide thee with mine eye.*— Ps. xxxii. 8.

A blind boy sat one day by the wayside begging. A Christian gentleman, passing by, halted, and began talking to him, and offering his sympathy in his misfortune. "Ah, my poor boy! your case is very sad indeed."— "Not so very sad, sir," replied the boy. "While it has pleased God to deprive me of my outward sight, he has given me a sight far more precious. He has given me the sight to see his Beloved Son; he has opened the eyes of my understanding, and I behold, written in letters of gold, his great and precious promises. He has opened the eyes of my soul, and I behold my sinful life made white through the blood of the Lamb. And, while I have no physical sight, he comes to me, saying, 'Son, be of good cheer. I will guide thee with mine eye.' What more, sir, can I ask or wish for?"

Oh, the preciousness and comfort of that soul which is so lighted by devotion to Christ that the infirmities of the body can be forgotten!

"*Without controversy, great is the mystery of godliness.*"
1 Tim. iii. 16.

"A great banquet was given by King Edwin in honor of his nobles. A discussion arose as to how they should receive the Christian missionary Paulinus, who had just arrived from the continent. Some argued the sufficiency of their Druid and Norse religions, and voted the death of the invading heretic; others were in favor of hearing his message; finally, the king, to quiet the discussion, asked the opinion of his oldest counsellor. The venerable sage arose and said, 'Oh, king and lords, you all observed the swallow which entered this festal hall to escape the chilling wind, and how it vanished through an opposite window. Such is the life of man. Whence it came and whither it goeth no one can tell. Therefore, if this religion brings light on this great mystery, it must be diviner than ours, and should be welcomed.'

"The advice of the venerable sage was adopted."

"*Let us therefore fear, lest a promise being left us of entering into his rest, some of you should seem to come short of it.*" — HEB. iv. 1.

A gentleman who was present at the death of an aged man describes the scene as follows: "The dying man had a large family of grown-up sons and daughters, part of them sons and daughters by a former wife. The gentleman noticed some coolness existing between the two factions as they stood around the bedside of the dying father, who soon peacefully passed away. Kind friends took charge of the remains and tenderly prepared them for interment. While doing so they heard loud words in an adjoining room, and one of the party went in unannounced; on the floor lay the dead man's papers and documents, while the brothers and sisters were eagerly examining the contents of a large desk, hoping to find the last will of their deceased parent; each anxious to know what part of the estate would fall to him. And so intense was this desire that they overlooked the solemnity of the occasion."

My friend, there is a last will and testament in which your name is mentioned as one of the legatees. The blessed word of God has for you "great and precious promises," whereby you may escape the lusts of the world and find life eternal. Will you heed the command of the Lord Jesus to "search the scriptures" and find that portion of the eternal inheritance that is bequeathed to you?

"*Almost persuaded.*" — Acts xxvi. 28.

There are certain places along the Alpine Mountain ranges, where the snow piles up so high on the lofty peaks that the crack of a whip, or a loud cry, will cause the vibrations of the air to start the snow and prove sudden death to the traveller.

From this some Christians can learn a much-needed lesson in advising those convicted of sin. Their salvation hangs by a slender cord — a sensitive pivot; one word may turn the balance and send it headlong to eternal death. Every Christian should, in such cases, ascertain as far as possible the state of the inquirer's heart before he begins to give him advice, and ever keep his eyes fixed on the Holy Spirit to speak through him those words that may undermine the false props of the inquirer's trust, and lead him to the feet of Jesus Christ.

"*Let your light so shine.*" — MATT. v. 16.

In South America there is a tree called the "Rain Tree." During the wet season it absorbs the moisture, and when drought sets in, it gives forth the moisture in drops of water, refreshing the thirsty traveller, and feeding the vegetation around it.

The traveller soon learns to look for these green spots in the parched wastes of the desert. So should be every Christian life. It should absorb the love of Christ to such a degree that those around him might be attracted by the pleasant atmosphere, and be led to the Fount, giving forth the true water of life. Reader, this is your duty as a follower of Christ — this is your privilege as one of the *blood-washed* — this is your portion as the heir of eternal life. *Are you doing it?*

"*Hold up my goings in thy paths, that my footsteps slip not.* — Ps. xvii. 5.

On a bright July morning, some years ago, a gentleman, famous for his learning in science, started with two companions to ascend Piz Morteratsch — a steep snow mountain of Switzerland. Their experienced guide took a strong rope and tied it around the waist of each man. "Keep carefully in my steps, gentlemen," said the guide, "for one false step may start the snow and send us down in an avalanche." Hardly had his words left his lips when, by a sudden misstep of one of the party, the great mountain of snow began to move and carry the struggling little party with it. Down, down, down they sped, faster and faster, until presently the guide cried. "Halt! halt!" and with almost superhuman energy drove the sharp nails of his great boots into the ice, and saved his party from the terrible death that awaited them. He entered upon his journey well shod, and came off victor. So it is in life, if we start out without being shod we are in constant danger of being tripped on the many slippery places, and carried along until at last we find ourselves on the verge of a great precipice, with eternal death staring us in the face. Oh! my young friend, how hard it is to stop when you once start on the downward grade without any sharp nails in your shoe heels to hold you! Take unto yourself Christ. "Put on the whole armor of God, that ye may be able to stand against the wiles of the devil." For we "wrestle not against flesh and blood, but against principalities, against powers, against the rulers of the darkness of this world, against spiritual wickedness in high places. Wherefore take unto you the whole armor of God, that ye may be able to withstand in the evil day, and having done all to stand. *Stand*, therefore, having your loins girt about with truth, and having on the breastplate of righteousness; and your feet shod with the preparation of the gospel of peace. Above all, taking the shield of faith, wherewith you shall be able to quench all the fiery darts of the wicked. And take the helmet of salvation, and the sword of the spirit, which is the word of God." This, my friend, is what is meant by beginning life "well shod." This is the only way you can ever over-ride the slippery places that Satan will throw in your life's pathway; this is the only remedy by which you can be able to stand against "the wiles of the devil." And one word more to you that are not thus *shod:* your pathway may become so slippery that it will carry you down and over the precipice ere you can secure this remedy, and land your soul in eternal death. Such cases are numbered by the thousand; therefore, let me entreat you now, to take unto yourselves the means of resistance, which lies in your acceptance of the Lord Jesus Christ. This alone insures your safety in this life, and your immortal soul's safety in the life to come.

"*Do not they blaspheme that worthy name by the which ye are called?*—JAS. ii. 7.

It is said of Alexander the Great, that among his army was a soldier named Alexander. One day the great general, after noting the slothfulness with which the soldier performed his duty, went to him and requested that he either change his name or become a better soldier, and cease to dishonor the name of his general.

Every professed lover and follower of Christ carries the name Christian, ofttimes to bring dishonor and shame to that name that is "above every name."

Reader, did it ever occur to you that your actions,

your thoughts, your life, bring dishonor to the name of Jesus?

Do you stop before performing any doubtful deed, and consider if the same will honor or dishonor Christ? "He that is not for me, is against me." If your life is not for the honor of Christ, it is decidedly against him.

Oh, that we may more closely guard our lives, our thoughts, and our actions, that each will be made to glorify Jesus, and leave to the world a monument that shall shine through the ages of time.

He that meditates before performing any act, and asks himself the question, "In what will this act glorify Christ," will seldom dishonor his Lord. The experience of almost every life is to desire to recall many steps in the past, and make them straight. The crooked pathways of the past, are, in the majority of instances, made on the impulse of the moment, without regard to the consequences, and without halting to see if they will honor or dishonor God.

"*The Lord also will be a refuge in times of trouble.*"
Ps. ix. 9.

In the history of the Israelites, we read of "Refuge Cities" located here and there as the safety of the people demanded. If a man murdered or killed, even accidentally, a fellow-man, the next kin to the deceased could avenge the death of his relative. As a protection, these cities of refuge were built, and whenever the slayer of a man got inside the walls of one of these refuge cities he was safe. His pursuers could come to the entrance, but no farther. That moment the gate was passed, he was safe.

So with the Christian. Satan is daily watching to

find him outside the city of refuge, which is Christ Jesus — and then he pursues his attack, ofttimes resulting in success. But, dear reader, Satan never can pass the entrance of your Refuge. As long as you live in Christ Jesus, his attacks will be fruitless and your safety a surety.

"*Make thy face to shine upon thy servant.*"
Ps. cxix. 135.

Dr. Clemance said, "One day I was climbing one of the Alpine range of mountains, near the boundary line between France and Switzerland. By and by we came upon snow and icicles, and all the usual attendants in the train of winter; but when we got higher we found delightful flowers blooming, in all the beauty of floral loveliness. I said to myself, 'how is this?' Down yonder are icicles and snow, up here are those exquisite flowers. The secret of it was, that this part of the mountain *faced the sun,* while the other was turned from it.'" So not unlike this is the change in the heart of him who turns from the cold world of sin to the warming rays of the Sun of Righteousness, and casts his lot in his service.

How exquisitely satisfying are the warming rays of that Sun whose foundation is the Light of the world. Oh! what a wonderful transposition from the cold, friendless world, into the flowery paths leading unto life eternal.

"*God resisteth the proud, but giveth grace unto the humble.*" — Jas. iv. 6.

An old legend tells of an emperor who won in battle from a pagan king the true cross, and with great pomp returned to Jerusalem with it. When he arrived at the city's gate, he found it walled up and an angel standing guard. "Thou," said the angel, "bringest back the cross with pomp and splendor; he that died upon it had shame and mockery for his companions, and bore it upon his bare back, barefooted, to Calvary." Then the emperor dismounted, cast off his garments, and barefooted approached the gate which swung open, and he passed in.

Just what amount of truth is embodied in the illustration it is impossible to say, neither does it concern us; but this we do know, that "God resisteth the proud, but giveth grace unto the humble," and delights in their pure devotion. Is not a mere glance at the story of the cross, the shame it laid upon the Son of God, the humiliation it brought on the King of Heaven, the sorrow and anguish it caused him that was God and man, the pain he bore, that spake as never man spake, — I ask is not this sufficient to incite in us a desire to meekly and humbly take up our cross and DAILY follow him?

"*Teach me, and I will hold my tongue.*" — Job vi. 24.

"The wasp's sting is provided with a barb, and when he feels particularly vicious and drives the sting into the flesh, it becomes so firmly imbedded that the only way for him to escape is to leave the sting behind. This, however, is sure to cause his death. He receives himself such a wound that he cannot recover. We sometimes forget that when we hurt others by stinging words and treacherous acts, we ourselves, in the long run, are generally the greatest sufferers." — DR. JUDSON.

It ofttimes transpires that when we dig a pit for others to fall into, we ourselves fall into it. The inspired penman says, "The tongue can no man tame." Oh! the pain and suffering caused by an unguarded tongue. Oh, that the prayer of Job, "Teach me, and I will hold my tongue," and the brief petition of the Psalmist, "Keep my tongue from evil," would daily ascend to the throne of grace, that our tongues would be kept from such evil.

"*I the Lord search the heart ; I try the reins, even to give every man according to his ways, and according to the fruit of his doings.*" — JER. xvii. 10.

In Japan the followers of Shinto place in the centre of many of their churches a large mirror of the finest plate, and gorgeous carvings, designed to represent to the worshippers that in like manner as their personal blemishes are therein displayed, so are their secret evil thoughts laid bare by the all-searching eyes of their immortal gods.

So the Scriptures teach us to "examine ourselves." "For man looketh on the outward appearance, but the Lord looketh on the heart."

Self-examination, then, should be prominently placed upon our list of duties, and we should be careful to attend the secret faults, for God knows human nature so well that he looks at the seat of secret sins first.

"*For whom the Lord loveth he chasteneth, and scourgeth every son whom he receiveth.*" — HEB. xii. 6.

In Southern Europe grow the larches. When they were first introduced into England, the gardeners took it for granted that they needed warmth to cause them to grow; so they were placed in the hothouses, and at once began to wither and droop. The gardeners became disgusted, and threw them out of doors. They at once began to grow, and became trees of great beauty. So it ofttimes becomes necessary for Christ to throw us out of doors into the cold of reverses, disappointments, sorrow, and pain, that our Christian characters may be developed.

It becomes at times necessary that God bring upon us sore trials and bereavements that we may be brought back to him and his service. God does not willingly afflict his people; but in order to bless us it is often necessary to put us in a position to receive and to appreciate his blessings, though it may be through severe trials and galling crosses.

"*So likewise, whosoever he be of you that forsaketh not all that he hath, he cannot be my disciple.*"

Luke xiv. 33.

In the year 1695, Madame Guyon was, by the order of the king, imprisoned in the Castle of Vincennes, on her refusal to abandon her religious convictions, and cease to preach Christ to her friends. To her brother, who besought her to throw off her religion, she wrote, "If your house, my dear brother, had been made of precious stones, and if I could have been treated and honored in it as a queen, yet I should have forsaken all to follow after God." "So likewise, whosoever he be of you that forsaketh not all that he hath, he cannot be my disciple." This is the kind of service that pleases and honors Christ — a service that costs us something. We are commanded to forsake, if necessary, our brightest hopes on earth, our dearest friends; commanded to sever the ties of nature, to forsake all, if needs be, to serve our Master.

"*I will make darkness light before them.*" — Isa. xlii. 16.

It is said of Cowper, while laboring under the influence of mental derangement, he believed that he was ordered of God to drown himself in the river Ouse. One evening he called for a hackman to drive him to the spot. The driver missed his way, and, after wandering about for several hours, admitted that he had lost his way. Cowper returned to his home, sat down, and wrote that wonderful hymn, "God moves in a Mysterious Way," acknowledging his interference with his planned self-destruction.

God's ways are to us, at times, veiled in mystery: many time we look upon his rulings as the opposite of our needs, but they work out for our good and his glory. We oftentimes feel that he is putting upon us a great cross when it proves to be a blessing. It is our sweet privilege to possess that blessed degree of faith that we can say, Come what may, *I will* cling to my Saviour; and, "though he slay me, yet will I trust him."

"*Give and it shall be given unto you; good measure, pressed down, and shaken together, and running over.*"

LUKE vi. 38.

A pastor went one day to call on a member of his church, who was a farmer. During the conversation the work of Christian benevolences was touched upon, and the farmer proudly alluded to the fact that out of his few acres of ground, he always set aside one acre to the Lord's use. The pastor, hoping to here get the material for an illustration in his own work, asked the farmer brother, "Which acre do you set aside?" This was a question that came very unexpectedly, but the farmer was honest enough to tell the truth, and replied, "When it is a dry season, I select one up there," pointing to a field on the hillside; "and when it is a wet season, I choose one down there," pointing to a field of very low land which lay at the foot of the hill. I give this illustration not on account of its rarity, but because it is a true picture of thousands of professed Christians, who give to God's service that part of their time and means that is left, after first satisfying their own personal selfish ends.

God demands of us the first fruits of our hearts and hands. What right, then, have we to strain his words, and twist his commands, and make them read, *the last*, and what is left after we have satisfied our desires?

It was said, many years ago, that "what the cause of Christ needs is not only converted hearts, but converted pocket-books." And it is no less true now than ever before. Oh, the selfishness of the human heart! Self! self! self! it cries from morning till night, and from night till morning; and when it enjoys the privilege of service for the Master, it cries, Sacrifice! sacrifice! Would to God we could learn and realize that all we have and are belongs to God, and that the first duty enjoined on us is to "Seek first the kingdom of God and his righteousness, and all these things shall be added."

"*Christ also suffered for us, leaving us an example, that ye should follow his steps.*" — 1 Peter ii. 21.

"The great and noble-hearted Livingstone visited his native land after an exploring tour; his friends praised him much for the sacrifices he had made. The godly man turned to them and said, 'People talk of the sacrifices I have made in spending so large a portion of my life in Africa. Can you call that a sacrifice, which is only a small payment on the great debt to God, which can never be fully discharged? Say rather that it is a privilege; I have never made a sacrifice.'

"Christ also suffered for us, leaving us an example, that ye should follow his steps."

I doubt very much if the beloved Livingstone realized what a wonderful truth he had spoken, and while his great true heart throbbed with God's love, the truth he uttered was more wonderful than he thought. How often do we mistake sacrifices for privileges? Christ says, "follow me," and though the path may lead through places of suffering, he also travelled there, and it is our duty as his followers to unflinchingly bear them, and to accept them as grand privileges, and not as sacrifices. And he that accepts his Christian race as such will realize that the sufferings and sacrifices of this life are nothing to be compared to the glory that shall be revealed in him when the race is over, and when he is called on to "come up higher."

"Then spake Jesus again unto them, saying, I am the light of the world, he that followeth me shall not walk in darkness, but shall have the light of life." — JNO. viii. 12.

It is said of St. Wenceslaus, a Bohemian king, that one bitter cold night, as he was going to his devotions in a distant church, his servant Redivivus, barefooted in the ice and snow, but who was trying to imitate his master's example of piety, fainted on the way. The king bade him follow him, and set his feet in the footsteps that he would make for him. He found in this a remedy, and he without discomfort followed his master.

So the blessed Jesus never sends us alone, but says "follow me," I will open up the road and you follow in my footsteps. Some Christians start out to walk alone, and soon the stony points of sin lacerate their feet, and they fall by the wayside in despair. Friend, Christ never intended for you to walk alone. If he says go, he says also, "Lo, I am with you." He says follow and place your feet in my footsteps, and "I will guide you with mine eye."

"Train up a child in the way he should go: and when he is old he will not depart from it." — Prov. xxii. 6.

A man, distinguished for his learning, in an unguarded moment took the life of a fellow-man, and, being asked why he did such a thing, said, "In my childhood I was never taught to obey my parents. I am irritable and passionate; my uncontrollable temper has been the great sin of my life. I was an only child of indulgent parents, who never required of me the control of my temper. The result is I stand before you, a murderer."

Oh! loving parents, let not the satanic film grow over your eyes and blind you to the neglect of your children's early training. Such neglect will not only bring to your eyes bitter tears, to your head premature gray hairs, to your heart piercing pangs, but when you stand before the throne of God Almighty, you will be required to answer for such neglect. "Train up a child in the way he should go: and when he is old he will not depart from it."

"Whosoever he be of you that forsaketh not all that he hath, he cannot be my disciple." — Luke xiv. 33.

It is said of Nebridius that he left his native country, where he lived in great luxury, forsook friends and kindred to go into a foreign city to live, in the most ardent search after truth and wisdom.

He forsook all to become a disciple of wisdom. So must we do when we take upon ourselves the Lord Jesus Christ. We must make everything else of a secondary nature; we must give him the first fruits of our hands, hearts, and hopes. We must first seek the kingdom of God and his righteousness, and these objects of a secondary nature will be added unto us. Reader, are you doing this? If you are, may the Holy Spirit this moment help you. If you are not, may the Holy Spirit this moment help you to make a resolution from now ever more to do so.

"*Thou hypocrite!*" — MATT. vii. 5.

A traveller in Russia tells the following of a lady who, leaving a party of companions in St. Petersburg, called a hack and directed the driver to take her home. Instead of following her directions, he drove her to a deserted part of the city, murdered her, and taking her jewels, threw her body into the canal. As he returned to the city he was hailed by a gentleman who proved to be the husband of the murdered lady, he recognized the cloak, and had the murderer arrested. The murdered lady had with her a basket of pie; when asked why he did not eat that, the murderer replied, "It was Lent. How could I think of eating that, it may contain meat, and I am, thank God, a good Christian."

We sometimes express an abhorrence of insignificant things when our hearts are set on the vilest of things.

"*No man can serve two masters.*" — MATT. vi. 24.

I remember when I first left home to seek my fortune in the world, I engaged my services to a large mercantile establishment, and was assigned certain duties. The firm consisted of four members. One would come to me and say, "You do so and so" — presently, another member would come and tell me to do it another way as I was wrong, and the third would say — "I fear you cannot fill the place, as you are continually performing your work wrong and require too much of my time in looking after you." Finally, one day I went into the main office and laid my resignation on the desk, fully convinced of the truth of our Saviour's words, — "No man can serve two masters." How many of us to-day are following Satan six days and God one. How many of us are letting the god of this world have the best part of our time and talents, and making our service to God Almighty a secondary object. "Seek ye first the kingdom of God and his righteousness, and all these (lesser) things shall be added unto you." "No man can serve two masters."

"*Be thou faithful unto death, and I will give thee a crown of life.*" — REV. ii. 10.

"It is told of Mr. John Maynard, a well-known and God-fearing seaman, that one day his steamer was on fire some distance from shore and loaded with a cargo of tar and rosin. There was no hope of saving the vessel; the passengers, men, women, and children, were crowded to the edge of the forward part of the ship. The brave pilot stood firm at his post, surrounded by fire and smoke. The captain called through the speaking tube. 'John Maynard.' 'Ay ay,' responded the brave man. 'Head her southeast and run her to shore.' As they drew nearer and nearer to shore, the captain again called out. 'John Maynard,' 'Ay sir,' came the response almost in a smothered voice. 'Can you hold on five minutes longer?' 'By God's help I will.' The brave man stood at his post until the vessel reached shore and every passenger safely landed, while he perished at the wheel, though faithful unto death." Oh what grand reward Christ offers those that remain faithful unto death, Oh, the glory in a crown of life!

One day, one of the pupils of that eminent German scholar, Bengel, wished to know how his teacher prayed.

So he followed him that evening to learn what proved to him to be a lifelong lesson.

The godly Bengel, after spending several hours in studying and meditating upon God's word, quietly folded his hands, and as if looking up into the very face of Christ, said, "Lord Jesus, thou knowest me; we are on the very same old terms," and his weary eyes closed in sleep.

How much lighter would life's cares be, how much more fruitful would our lives be, how much happier would our hearts be, and how much more pleasing would our service be, if we would only learn to sink deep into the rich storehouse of God's Word and approach Christ in the familiar terms a constant communion insures.

If we would rightly follow Christ, we must make Christ our intimate friend, and out of this intimacy will bloom a deep, ardent love that will shine in our lives to the glory and honor of his name, and the salvation of souls. The two go hand in hand and cannot be separated, for the love of Christ cannot be imprisoned in so small a space as the human heart, but will shine out and touch others.

CHAPTER II.

TRUST IN CHRIST.

'IN THY PRESENCE IS FULNESS OF JOY.'
PSALM xvi : 11.

TRUST IN CHRIST.

"*Though I walk through the valley of the shadow of death I will fear no evil, for thou art with me: thy rod and thy staff they comfort me.*" — Ps. xxiii. 4.

The case of Charles the First beautifully illustrates the Christian's blessed trust in the hour of death, and his fearlessness in facing its dreaded hand. It is said that when he lay in his cell he could clearly see the workmen preparing the scaffold upon which he was condemned to die, each stroke of the hammer could be distinctly heard, yet these combined could neither interrupt his conversation by day nor disturb his sleep at night. On the morning of his execution he arose at dawn, and bade his attendant exercise unusual care in the arrangement of his dress, befitting, as he termed it, such a great and happy solemnity — the close of his earthly sorrows and the beginning of his eternal bliss. He knelt and committed his soul to God; with a brave step he ascended the scaffold, saying, "I will soon be tenderly wafted to the Great Judge."

"*For I reckon that the sufferings of this present time are not worthy to be compared with the glory which shall be revealed in us.*" — Rom. viii. 18.

Margaret Wilson, a young lady of eighteen, living in Wigtown, Scotland, was cruelly condemned by James II. to be drowned for her faith in Christ. She was taken to the seashore and tied to a stake so that the rising tide would slowly overflow her, and give her an opportunity to recant her faith. Calmly she awaited the approaching tide. Some one asked her if she had any fears of the future. She calmly replied, "Christ is my stay." As the waves came up to her mouth she repeated these lines: "For I am persuaded that neither death, nor life, nor angels, nor principalities, nor powers, nor things present, nor things to come, nor height, nor depth, nor any other creature, shall be able to separate us from the love of God, which is in Christ Jesus our Lord."

"Let us therefore come boldly unto the throne of grace, that we may obtain mercy, and find grace to help in time of need." — HEB. iv. 16.

An old Scotchman was one day on his way to some mission week services. The old pilgrim was poor and ill clad, and partially deaf, but he trusted in the Lord whom he served, and rejoiced in his kind providence. On his way to the meeting he fell in with another Christian brother; a younger man, bound on the same errand, and they travelled on together. When they had nearly reached the place of meeting it was proposed that they should turn aside and have a little prayer. They did so, and the old man, who had learned in everything to let his requests be known unto God, presented his case in language like this: "Lord, ye ken weel enough that I'm deaf and that I want a seat on the first bench if ye can let me have it, so that I can hear thy word; and ye see that my toes are sticking through my shoes, and therefore I want ye to get me a pair of new ones; and ye ken I have nae siller, and I want to stay during the meetings, and therefore I want ye to get me a place to

stay." When the little outdoor prayer-meeting was finished, the two Christians arose and resumed their journey. As they walked along, the young brother said to the Scotchman that he thought his prayer hardly so reverential as seemed proper in approaching the Supreme Being. "Why, my son," said the Scotchman. "He's my Father, and weel acquainted with me, and I take great liberties with him." They soon arrived at the church in which the meetings were to be held, and the old Scotchman took a position in the rear of the church, and placed his ear trumpet to catch the words of the speaker: pretty soon a gentleman motioned him to come forward and occupy the front pew where he could better hear. At the close of the service a lady noticed his ragged shoes, and asked him if they were the best ones he had. "Yes," said he, "but I expect my Father will get me a new pair soon." — "Come with me," said the lady, "and I will get you a new pair." — "Shall you stay to the end of the meeting," asked a Christian lady. "I would," said the Scotchman, "but I am a stranger here, and have nae siller." — "You shall be made welcome at my house," said the good lady. The old man thanked the Lord that he had given him all that he had asked for; and while his younger brother's reverence for the Lord was right and proper, it is possible that he might have learned that there is a reverence that reaches higher than the forms and conventionalities of human taste, and which leads the believer to come boldly to the throne of grace, and to find all needed help in every trying hour."
— *Selected.*

"*There is no fear in love.*" — 1 Jno. iv. 18.

A little girl lay dying, surrounded by loving parents and friends, who readily saw that the fair bloom was fast withering, and as the bereaved hearts watched the beautiful light going out, she looked up, and said, "Papa, mamma, why do you cry so, I am not afraid, what can harm me? Jesus has hold of my hand — fear is all gone." She passed away, her love to Christ had conquered the dread of the cold-handed messenger of death.

Reader, this is a scene through which you and I must pass — have you that sweet trust in Christ that dispels all fear for that trying moment? and makes you cry out, "Oh death! where is thy sting? oh grave! where is thy victory?"

Have you any assurance that when such a time comes, you will have his arm to support you?

"*In thy presence is fulness of joy.*" — Ps. xvi. 11.

A gentleman riding abroad one day perceived a hare, hunted almost to death, running toward him, and crouched betwixt the legs of his horse; he dismounted, and took the poor frightened and fatigued creature in his arms, where it laid its head, and ceased to tremble with fear; but, rather, it showed fulness of joy in finding a rescuer. — *Cyclo. Bible Ill.*

So it is with us: we may sometimes wander away from Christ, and try to struggle against old Satan, who is watching us; but the moment we turn to the Saviour, our pursuer stops, and he gently takes us in his strong arms, and cares for us. Reader, can you trust him? Are you trusting him? Would that I could impress upon you the importance of this trust. Rest assured you will be attacked by the evil one, and can never resist him in your own strength, but simply in the strength Christ will give you of his own fulness.

"*The secret of the Lord is with them that fear him.*"
Ps. xxv. 14.

There is a safe and secret place,
  Beneath the wings divine,
Reserved for all the heirs of grace;
  Oh, be that refuge mine!

The least and feeblest there may bide,
  Uninjured and unawed;
While thousands fall on every side,
  He rests secure in God.

He feeds in pastures large and fair
  Of love and truth divine;
O child of God! O glory's heir!
  How rich a lot is thine!

A hand almighty to defend;
  An ear for every call;
An honored life, a peaceful end,
  And heaven to crown it all!

Christian Worker.

"*For I trust in thy word.*" — Ps. cxix. 42.

A poor man, depending on his daily labor for food to supply the needs of his large family, found it necessary to go to the city, some miles from his home, to find employment.

He came home on Saturday evening, and went away early the following Monday morning. His custom was to bring home his weekly earnings every Saturday evening, which went to the support of his family until his return. One Saturday his employer told him that, owing to his inability to collect some outstanding debts, he was unable to pay him his wages that day. The poor man well knew what embarrassment this would cause him, but he saw it was useless to press his claim. As usual, he went home, and found the children all neatly clad in their clean garments, and the faithful wife busily engaged in preparing for the evening meal, which she expected her husband to purchase on his way home. With tears in his eyes he told his wife that he had failed to collect his earnings, as usual, and that he did not know what to do. They knelt down, and laid their case before the "Giver of every good and perfect gift," and sought His aid. Hardly had their prayer ended before a sharp rap was heard at the door. The father opened it, and a kind lady handed them a large loaf of bread, saying she had made a greater quantity than she could use, and thought it would be acceptable to them. Again they fell on their knees, and thanked God for his deliverance. When the meal was finished, the father went to some friends, and stated his case. They secured a week's supplies at the store, and promised to see that his family did not suffer in his absence.

God promises us his care: his word is unchanging. May we not then learn to trust him more fully — wholly rely on his word, so fraught with precious promises?

"*Put on the whole armour of God, that ye may be able to stand against the wiles of the devil.*" — EPH. vi. 11.

It is said of the Archbishop of Canterbury, as he was passing along the highway one day, he met a boy with a bird, to which he had tied a cord. The bird was trying to fly away to its freedom, but, when it got a little way in the air, the boy would pull the cord, and drag it back.

So it ofttimes befalls Christians, who attempt to walk

alone. When they think they are progressing fairly well, Satan draws the cord, and they find themselves at the point of starting. Not so with him who starts out trusting solely in the blessed Christ for help. The cord is cut asunder, and he is "free indeed." My friend, the Christian warfare is a happy warfare, when we enter it properly armed. Victory is certain, when we set out with the armor that God has provided. On the other hand, it is a continual struggle, resulting in frequent defeats, because our human forces are inadequate to resist the mighty forces of Satan. This one point I would press upon you in starting out: Put on the "Whole armour of God," and simply trust him to guide you.

"*Take unto you the whole armour of God.*"
Eph. vi. 13.

We are told that the mother of Achilles dipped him, when an infant, in the river Styx to prevent danger that might ensue by reason of the Trojan war. His enemies having learned that he was invulnerable in every part of his body, except his heel, where his mother held him while dipping him, took advantage of this information, and shot him in the heel, killing him instantly.

So with Christians: unless we are wholly covered with the cloak of Christ's love, Satan will find our unprotected part, and attack us there. When we make Christ our *all*, then we are safe: for he that is for us is greater than he that is against us.

"*He leadeth me.*" — Ps. xxiii. 2.

It is said of the Rev. Mr. Needham that he and his wife were once landed in a strange city, without money or friends. They refused to go to a hotel and order accommodations without the means of paying for it. They walked the streets and prayed, expecting the Lord to open up the way for them. As they were slowly walking along, a gentleman who knew Mr. Needham, and had heard him deliver one of his stirring discourses, met him and invited him to spend the night with him at the hotel. The pressing invitation was accepted without the kind man ever knowing his friend's circumstances. Oh, the sweet trust in the adorable Lord! Oh, that we each had more to ease life's burdens! "Cast your care upon *him*, for he careth for you," is a lesson, though simple, yet how hard for weak mortals to learn.

"*Because thou hast made the Lord . . . thy habitation; there shall no evil befall thee, neither shall any plague come nigh thy dwelling: for he shall give his angels charge over thee, to keep thee in all thy ways.*" — Ps. xci. 9–11.

"A lady in England told the following illustration of the blessedness of having Jesus Christ betwixt us and danger. She said, 'I was weary with the cares of the day, and went to my chamber to gain a much-needed rest; I laid down on my bed, and was soon fast asleep. My rest was disturbed by a continual tapping on the window pane, which so annoyed me I got up and went to the window to see what it meant. I saw a butterfly flying back and forth on the inside of the window, and, outside, a sparrow pecking and trying to get inside. The butterfly did not see the glass, and expected every moment to be devoured by the sparrow. The sparrow, too, did not see the window glass, and expected to get the butterfly for its dinner.'"

And so it may be likened of the Child of God who puts Christ between him and danger. So far can come the evil designer, and no farther. In the shadow of thy wings will I hide, saith the Christ-loving soul, and the gentle answer comes back, "I will deliver thee." "In the day of trouble," saith the trusting soul, "I will call upon thee." "I am a very present help in time of trouble," comes the reply. "Deliver me from the enemy." "Because thou hast made the Lord thy habitation, there shall no evil befall thee." Oh, that we could more fully learn to put Christ between us and everything else; how much lighter life's burdens! how much easier would grow the cares of life! how much stronger our faith! how much plainer the road to eternal glory! how much brighter the dark valley of death when we are holding on to Christ with all our might, mind, soul, and strength!

"*My sheep hear my voice and I know them, and they follow me. And I give unto them eternal life: and they shall never perish; neither shall any man pluck them out of my hand.*" — JNO. x. 27, 28.

A gentleman who has travelled in the East tells us that about the hour of noon he halted at one of the wells to watch the shepherds water their flocks. They assembled and drew water, not each for his own flock, but in common, they drew until enough was drawn. Then the shepherd would lead the way, and call to his sheep to follow him; they knew the voice of their master, and followed after him. The gentleman asked one of the shepherds to let him put on his mantle and take his crook, when he would call out to the sheep to follow him; the shepherd gave his consent, and when the gentleman called to the flock to follow him, they turned and ran from him, and only when they heard the true shepherd's voice did they follow.

The true child of God knows the voice of his master, and at his loving call follows after him. Strange voices will he not follow, but fleeth away, and so too the Great Shepherd knows his sheep, and with his unerring eye he ever watches over them, and no power can pluck one of them out of his strong hand. Though a thousand forces assail him, he fears no evil, for in the hollow of the great shepherd's hand he is hid. The ungodly are not so, for they wander about on the bleak desert of sin, and are hunted down by the evil one, pressed hard by the enemy, and in despair they yield to his power. Blessed is he that trusteth in the Lord. Is he thy trust, oh, thou soul that readest these words?

"The Lord knoweth how to deliver the godly out of temptations." — 2 PETER ii. 9.

It is related of Augustine that, as he was journeying to a certain city to teach the people, he took a guide with him to point out the way. The guide took him out of the usual road, and along a by-path, by which means he escaped death at the hands of the bloody Donatist, who, knowing his intentions, waylaid him to kill him. "Blessed is he that trusteth in the Lord." The same shall be delivered from the hands of the enemy, and all the fiery trials of the evil one.

"He that believeth . . . shall be saved." — MARK. xvi. 16.

During a severe storm at sea, it seemed that the vessel could last but little longer, and that the precious cargo of human freight would soon find their graves in the raging billows. The waves were already coming over the deck, and passengers were rushing hither and thither, wringing their hands and weeping, each one expecting every moment to be their last. In their midst sat a young man, who unconcernedly watched the mad waves as they dashed against the vessel. Some of the passengers asked him how he could be so calm in such an hour, when his life hung by a very slender cord; he replied, "I feel no fear whatever; why should I? My father is commanding the vessel, and he knows what he is doing. I trust him — he will bring us through safely." Fellow-traveller, when danger, trouble, disaster, and reverses overtake you, how much easier it will be to trust all to our Heavenly Father. "Though he slay me, yet will I trust in him."

"*For thus saith the Lord God of Israel, the barrel of meal shall not waste, neither shall the cruse of oil fail.*"
1 KINGS xvii. 14.

"A poor prisoner, confined for the causes of Christ, was given only bread and water to eat and drink. When ridiculed because she had no meat, she replied, 'If you take away my meat, I will trust God to take away my hunger.'" Happy trust in him who hath said, "I will never leave thee nor forsake thee." How easy self-denial would become, did we but exercise such simple trust in Christ to remove the desire far from us.

"*Neither murmur ye, as some of them also murmured, and were destroyed of the destroyer.*" — 1 COR. x. 10.

"A man carrying a valise filled with money was overtaken by a severe rain storm, which caused him to complain bitterly of the weather. Reaching a forest, a robber waylaid him and attempted to shoot him, but the rain had dampened the powder, and his gun missed fire. 'How wrong was I,' said the man, 'in not patiently enduring the rain sent by Providence, which saved my life and property.'"

How often we are found murmuring and upbraiding God, for what seems to our human minds a great affliction, but which proves to be a real blessing in disguise.

Oh, that our trust in God was more complete, and that we could learn to commit our ways unto him and be willing to say at all times, "Thy will be done." "Though he slay me yet will I trust in him."

"*I can do all things through Christ, which strengtheneth me.*" — PHIL. iv. 13.

When the illustrious Oliver Cromwell lay upon his death bed, he rejoiced that, although he had been a man of war, the strong arm of Christ had reached out and had drawn his heart into a penitent faith in the Redeemer. He requested his wife to read to him Paul's letter to the Philippians. When she came to the words, "I can do all things through Christ," the dying man exclaimed. "Oh! St. Paul, you are entitled to speak thus, and he who is your Saviour shall also be my Saviour too. Oh! what love; to descend so low and take hold of the hand of such a mortal as I."

After a brief prayer for those about him, the great man said, "I pass to my Father."

"I can do all things through Christ, which strengtheneth me," and "Without me ye can do nothing." Would to God that you, and that I, reader, would learn to "go in the strength of the Lord God." Would that I could learn to regard not the strength of my puny, weak self, and learn that "through Christ I can do all things." Oh, what remorse and sorrow our own efforts often bring us, because we try to do too much in proportion to our strength and often end in miserable, humiliating failure. Not so with him "who goes in the strength of the Lord God," for then "he can do all things through Christ." Our Saviour delights to have us seek his aid even in temporal, as well as in spiritual things, and is ever ready to bless us and cause the guiding rays of his light to shine upon us, and direct us in our daily cares.

"*Examine yourselves ; whether ye be in the faith.*"
2 COR. xiii. 5.

Sextus had a custom which every Christian would do well to follow, and which when rightly considered, teaches an important truth. He asked himself, every night before closing his eyes in sleep, "What evil hast thou done this day? what wrong hast thou amended? what vice hast thou shunned? what good hast thou done? In what part art thou bettered?"

How much easier would life's burdens grow, how much lighter the cares of life would be, how much worry and vexation of heart would we save, did we but daily examine our lives and profit by our experiences, and not be burdened with our past sins and shortcomings. Happy is he who lays the weight of his load of misgivings on Him who so graciously invites us to "Cast all our care upon Him, for He careth for you (us)."

"*Therefore I take pleasure in infirmities, in reproaches, in necessities, in persecutions, in distresses for Christ's sake ; for when I am weak then am I strong.*"
2 COR. xii. 10.

John Huss, the martyr, for his opposition to the errors of Rome, and his unceasing efforts to revive

Christianity, was sentenced to be burned. Surrounded by eight hundred soldiers, he was led to a small meadow as the place of execution. When he came to the stake he turned his face toward heaven and prayed, " Into thy hands, oh Lord, I commit my spirit; thou hast redeemed me; assist me with a firm mind, by thy most powerful grace, that I may undergo this most awful death, to which I am condemned for preaching thy most holy gospel,—amen!" Bundles of straw and wood were placed about him; a heavy chain was put upon his neck, he said, " Welcome this chain for Christ's sake," and as the flames leaped around him he sang a hymn with a loud voice.

Such is the power of Christ, in the heart of the true trusting Christian, that he will glory in the persecutions and reproaches of man, for when the strength of human nature can no longer bear us up, Christ makes us able and willing to endure them, and we come out of the fiery trials, strong in the Lord.

"*Fear not them which kill the body, but are not able to kill the soul: but rather fear him which is able to destroy both soul and body in hell.*—MATT. x. 28.

When Queen Mary of Scotland was crowned, in order to gain more power with the classes which exercised the greater influence, and to show her attachment for the cause of the Pope, she ordered that the Calvinist, Anne du Bourg, an heroic adherent to the Protestant faith, be executed. When the eventful day arrived, she bravely ascended the scaffold, and in a gentle but clear voice, said, " Six feet of earth for my body, and the infinite joy of heaven for my soul, is what I shall soon have." What more could mortal crave, than the last part of the utterance of brave, Christian Anne du Bourg?

"Casting all your care upon him, for he careth for you."
1 PET. v. 7.

Payson, on his death bed, said to his daughter, "My child, you will avoid much pain, care, and anxiety if you will early learn to trust your every concern into the hands of God."

Fellow Christian, why all this fretting? why all this anxiety? why all this disquietude? why all this concern? why all this solicitude about the petty cares and trials of life? "Cast all your care upon him, for he careth for you."

Even the very hairs of your head are numbered; your heavenly Father knoweth your every care, your sympathizing Saviour knoweth your every anxiety, and with a pitying eye looks down on you, and says, "Oh, thou of little faith," "Call upon ME in the day of trouble and *I will* deliver thee."

"Cast thy burden on the Lord, and he shall sustain thee."

"Have we trials and temptations,
Is there trouble anywhere,
Are we weak and heavy laden,
Take it to the Lord in prayer."

"Though he slay me, yet will I trust in him."
JOB. xiii. 15.

A gentleman passing a poor beggar that sat by the wayside, said to him, "Good morrow, my poor man." "I never had a bad morrow," replied the beggar. "You are a poor miserable man, nearly naked, no friends to help you, still you tell me you never had a bad morrow."

"I'll tell you," said the beggar, "whether I am sick or well, cold or warm, clothed or naked, fed or hungry, I bless God for all."

"But friend," said the gentleman, "what if Christ should cast thee to hell?" "If he should, I would be content; I have two arms, the one of faith, the other of love; I would lay such hold on Christ that I would have him with me, and wherever he is, there will be heaven."

"Though he slay me, yet will I trust in him." Happy state is that which can make the child of God, through his great faith in the Lord Jesus Christ, say, Come whatsoever will, God is my refuge and my stay. I will trust him in all things. "Though he slay me, yet will I trust in him;"— though he take all my worldly possessions, still will I cling to him;— though he deprive me of my loved ones, yet will I hold fast his precious promises to again meet them in the glorious reunion of heaven;— though he take my health from me and cause me to languish on beds of sickness, yet will I pour out my heart to him in praise and thanksgiving;— though he make my heart to sorrow and be sad, I plead his own promise, "Blessed are they that mourn, for they shall be comforted";— though he take my very life, I shall trust his guiding hand to lead me "through the valley of the shadow of death, and I will fear no evil."

CHAPTER III.

STAGNANT POOLS.

"WELLS WITHOUT WATER."
2 Pet. ii. 17.

STAGNANT POOLS.

"*And when he came to it, he found nothing but leaves.*"
MARK xi. 13.

In my father's orchard stood a large and beautiful apple tree, and one to which he had devoted a great deal of attention; he spared no pains to make its growth thrifty, expecting to reap a bountiful harvest of fruit. At harvest time he went through the orchard gathering the fruit, and when he came to this tree he found it fruitless.

He pruned it again and gave it extra care, expecting the next autumn to find it laden with fruit. Imagine his chagrin when he went to it and found "nothing but leaves."

Not yet caring to give up such a promising tree; he cultivated it with care the third time, only to reap as before a harvest of "nothing but leaves." He ordered it taken out root and branch, and hauled to the woodyard and burned with the refuse sticks that had been gathered from time to time.

Christian friend, how is it with you? Are you among the number that have long trespassed upon the patience of the living God, and bear "nothing but leaves?" Take these words of Christ to your heart, "Every tree that bringeth not forth fruit shall be hewn down, and cast into the fire." How cowardly the thought to take only so much of Christ into our lives as will barely land us into heaven. How painful the sentence will be when **Christ** comes, "Cut it down, why cumbereth it the ground?"

"I know thy works, that thou art neither cold nor hot. I would that thou wert cold or hot." — REV. iii. 15.
"I will kindle a fire in thee." — EZEK. xx. 47.

An old Scottish doctor got on board a train one day, and became very fidgety because the train did not start. "What is the matter," he said, "isn't there plenty of water?"—"Oh yes," some one replied, "there's plenty of water, but it isn't boiling."

This is the trouble with a great many professing Christians, they have plenty of water, but it is kept too far from Christ's love to make it boil. How many thousand Christians to-day are idle because they have no motive power to propel them; they are so far from Christ that there is no fire to heat the water and produce steam to move them in Christian work. Oh! thou cold soul, fall on thy knees and plead the promises of thy God to kindle a fire in thee, and move thee to Christian duty. "Rescue the perishing" that are on the right and left, crying, "What must I do to be saved?"

"Freely ye have received, freely give." — MATT. x. 8.

On my father's farm was a pond or lake by which I had occasion to frequently pass. During several months of the year the surface was covered with a greenish substance which produced an unwholesome odor. The birds cast not their feathery forms in it to bathe. The fishes seemed not at home in its impure depths. Much of the sickness of the vicinity was attributed to this stagnant pool. During the rainy spring season the swollen stream near by would flow into it, and for a time it would be again pure, and so long as the water flowed through it, was as clear and cool as other streams.

Not unlike this pool is the Christian who takes in the love of Christ and never lets it out. He only, is a successful and true Christian who allows the stream of Christ's love to flow into his heart, and he sends it forth again unto some other heart. And in order to retain true Christianity we must pay as much attention to the outlet as we do to the inlet of our hearts, or in order to be pure we need to let the stream of God's love flow through our hearts constantly. The heart is a little member, and if we bar the outlet what little love it is capable of holding becomes stagnate, and we become a misery to ourselves and a stumbling block to others.

Oh, thou sin-cleansed heart! open wide thy doors and let the river of Christ's love flow through thy domains, and on to thy neighbor.

"*Therefore, my beloved brethren, be ye steadfast, unmoveable,* ALWAYS *abounding in the work of the Lord.*"

1 COR. XV. 58.

On my father's farm was a field, one part of which was on the hillside, while the other part lay in the level valley below. That portion in the valley never failed to produce a bountiful yield; while it was necessary each season, before seeding, to apply fertilizers to make the hillside yield any crop. When the showers came, the nutriment would wash to the valley below.

How truly this represents Christians. While one class is "always abounding in the work of the Lord," the other class sit still and wait for the annual revival to stir them up to the proper spiritual point of work. Eleven months of the year they sit idle, and the showers of heavenly blessings pass by them, and they must be themselves preached back to the kingdom of spiritual working grace before they can work with sinners. Christ's intention in establishing the beautiful Christian religion was to make it a religion of everyday life, and not a fitful, periodical religion. We are to "take up our cross *daily* and follow him."

The one that makes the best Christian character is he who lives every moment so near to Christ that Satan has no chance to put in a word and ensnare him in his web of temptations too strong for human nature to resist.

Reader, art thou a periodical Christian? You are poorly honoring him whom you profess to love, and who you confess has taken away the guilt of a sinful heart and saved you from eternal doom.

"*All unrighteousness is sin.*" — 1 JNO. v. 17.

A company of ladies and gentlemen went one day to view the destruction of property a swollen stream was making.

As they stood there, and watched the rapid torrent, they saw three little girls playing near by, each trying to see how near the edge of a high bank they could go, and not fall into the raging waters below. Presently a cry of distress was heard: looking over the steep bank, they saw one of the little girls being carried down by the rapid stream.

Just so with a great many Christians: they try to see how near the world they can live, and still be safe. They seem to try to live just near enough to Christ to squeeze in at heaven's gate at the end. A very dangerous ground, indeed, on which to rest a hope of eternal life. A very low estimation to place upon the religion of Christ. Would it not, my friend, be wiser to serve him from a sense of love to him in giving his life for us?

"*Tell them how great things the Lord hath done for thee.*" — MARK v. 19.

The question was asked not long since, why the Dead Sea took the name it bears.

Among the answers, one advanced a very appropriate one: "because it is always receiving, and never letting out," or because it has an inlet and no outlet. Water to be pure must be kept flowing; stagnant pools are those that have no outlet. No one can be a Christian, and live all to himself. The love of Christ cannot be kept pent up. When it enters a heart, it makes that heart active, and anxious to tell others of its wondrous joy.

"*From me is thy fruit found.*" — Hos. xiv. 8.

It is said of the olive tree that it enriches the soil upon which it feeds; while the stately sycamore draws sustenance therefrom, and gives nothing in return.

So there are two classes of men: while one class strive to serve the Hand that created them, the other recognizes not such a power, but lives solely for that which renders momentary pleasure. Oh, that we all could recognize that "every good gift and every perfect gift is from above, and cometh down from the Father."

"*By their fruits ye shall know them.*" — MATT. vii. 20.

In Palestine there is a counterfeit olive tree, called the wild olive, or *oleaster*. It is in every way like the genuine olive, with one exception: it bears no fruit. Mr.

Bowes says, "When I see a man taking up a large space in Christ's spiritual orchard, and absorbing a vast deal of sunlight and soil, and yielding no real fruit, I say, "Ah, there is an oleaster!"

There is a certain class of professed followers of Christ who bear a very striking resemblance to the oleaster, but "by their fruits ye shall know them."

CHAPTER IV.

THE POWER OF CHRISTIAN INFLUENCE.

"YE ALSO SHALL BEAR WITNESS."
JNO. xv. 27.

THE POWER OF CHRISTIAN INFLUENCE.

"*We are his witnesses.*" — ACTS v. 32.

The sweet gospel singer, Mr. Peter Bilhorn of Chicago, who was at one time a well-known saloon concert singer, was passing by a gospel service a few years ago. When he came opposite to the gathering of Christians, the testimony of a young man, "Christ saves the worst of sinners," fastened itself on his heart, and led him to Christ.

He never saw the young man afterward — never has been able to find him, but his words so came home to him that he changed his course, and is now devoting his life to God's service.

Oh! the power of a life that is not ashamed to make Christ known to the world. How beautiful the feet of them that never tire of witnessing before the world the riches of eternal life in Christ Jesus! What glory awaits the soul that daily walks so near to Christ that others see Christ through him!

"*For thou wast slain, and hast redeemed us to God by thy blood.*" — REV. v. 9.

"A little girl of eight years was sent on an errand by her parents. On her way she was attracted by the singing at a Gospel meeting in the open air, and drew near. The conductor of the meeting was so struck with the child's earnestness that he spoke to her and told her about Jesus. When she returned home her father asked her what had detained her. She looked up in his face and told him where she had been; he beat her, and forbade her ever again going to such a place.

Some weeks later she was sent on another errand; she passed the same spot and saw the same gentleman, who again told her of Jesus. She became so deeply in earnest that she quite forgot her errand, and, returning home, told her father that she had forgotten what she was sent to bring, but that she had brought Jesus. The enraged father kicked and beat the poor little creature until the blood trickled down her face and fell upon her dress. She was put to bed by her kind mother, never to recover from her father's ill treatment. Just before she died, she called her mother and said, 'Mamma, I have been praying to Jesus to save you and papa.' Then, pointing to the dress, she said, 'Mamma, cut me a bit out of the blood-stained part.' The mother did so. 'Now,' said the dying child, 'Christ shed his blood for my sake, and I am going to take this to Jesus to show him that I shed my blood for his sake.' The trusting child passed away, not, however, before she had sown the seed that in after years ripened into the fruit of salvation to her father and mother." — *Selected.*

Reader, what are you doing for him who shed his blood to redeem you to God and life eternal?

Does his love fire your heart, and send you to lost men and lead them to him?

"*What ye hear in the ear, that preach ye upon the housetops.*" — MATT. x. 27.

A poor, ignorant man became converted, and was in the habit of holding religious meetings in the loft of an

THE POWER OF CHRISTIAN INFLUENCE. 67

old barn. Prince Albert, the husband of England's queen, chanced to hear one of the rude discourses, which so opened the avenues of his heart that it afterwards led him to Christ.

Simply the result of telling of Christ's love, and what he has done for us. And simply the duty of every professing Christian. And simply a duty that is neglected more than almost any other by Christians.

The moment we take Christ as our Saviour, that moment our duty as preachers of Christ begins, and he only does his duty who makes use of every opportunity to preach Christ to those around him. Testify of his love, confess his saving power, and seek to draw men unto him.

"*Wherefore come out from among them, and be ye separate, saith the Lord.*" — 2 Cor. vi. 17.

A Christian Chinaman, paying a visit to our country, at once noticed the nearness to the world to which many professing Christians were living. Later on, when alluding to the matter, he said, "When the disciples in my country come out from the world, they come *clear out.*"

It is a low estimation of Christianity we possess who try how near to the world we can live and yet be Christians. We are commanded to come out and be separate from the world when we take upon ourselves the duties of a Christian. Furthermore, we cannot rightly serve God and yet love and cling to the frivolities of the world; but our lives should so shine with the illumination of the light of Christ's love that the world would not have to examine us closely to see if we were Christians. The true Christian reflects the light of Christ in his daily walk in life, and never finds it necessary to go through the world sounding a trumpet and crying out, "A Christian! a Christian!" One question that is sometimes asked me is indeed very humiliating, though meant for my good, and that is, if I am a Christian? Oh, I do so want to reflect Christ in my life that wherever I go I may hear on my right and on my left, "*there goes a Christian.*"

Friend, it is well to remember that the eye of the world is constantly upon us, and that our crooked paths are noticed far and near; the voice of the world cries out, "Hypocrisy! hypocrisy!" and unbelief forges another link in its strong chain. "We ought also so to walk even as he walked."

"*And every one that hath forsaken houses, or brethren, or sisters, or father, or mother, or wife, or children, or lands, for my name's sake, shall receive an hundredfold, and shall inherit everlasting life.* — MATT. xix. 29.

A wealthy infidel had a lovely daughter, on whose education he had bestowed much care and pains. The father was attending a session of the legislature, of which he was a member. In his absence, the daughter stole away and attended a revival service, held in the village in which they lived. The Spirit aroused her to a true sense of her lost condition, and she wept aloud. Going home, she told her mother all. She became very angry, and said, "Just wait till your father comes home." The next evening she went again to the house of God, and found that sweet peace of Christ. Word reached the father that his daughter had professed Christianity, and he hastened home. The daughter met him at the gate. As she ran to him to kiss him, he rudely seized her by the arm, and severely beat her with his riding-whip, bidding her begone, and never return.

She walked down the road, not knowing where to go, until she met a poor widow, who took her to her own home, and cared for her. There she spent the night in prayer. Early next morning the father sent, in great haste, for his daughter, and met her at the gate, saying, "I give you my heart and hand to go with you to heaven." The mother followed, and all rejoiced in the saving power of Christ.

A firm stand for Jesus did it all. Oh, that we would get a firmer grasp on Christ, and make our prayers and love melt those around us to the same sweet trust in Jesus.

"*O sing unto the Lord.*" — Ps. xcvi. 1.

During the days of fierce persecutions of the Christians by the Catholics of Ireland, a small company met in a barn to hold their meeting. One of the most violent opposers secreted himself in the barn in order to open the door, and let in his comrades. As the earnest voices joined in singing praises to God, the Holy Spirit touched the spring of his heart, and his evil designs came up before him as a great mountain, and he cried out from his hiding-place for mercy.

How true the words of him who said, "A hymn is a singing angel that goes walking through the earth, scattering the devils before it."

Many of us fail to realize that we can worship God by singing from the heart, songs of devotion. It is a form of worship that we can attend or partake of as we go about the busy cares of life. "O sing unto the Lord."

"*Let the redeemed of the Lord say so.*" — Ps. cvii. 2.

At the breaking out of the late war an old woman started out with a shovel in her hand. When asked what she intended to do, she replied, "I can't do much, but I can show which side I am on."

How little do Christians realize the necessity of confessing Christ by their everyday life. In that memorable sermon of our Lord, he commands that we "let our light so shine before men that they, seeing our good works, may glorify our Father which is in heaven." Beloved, the eye of the world is ever gazing at you. If you deny your Saviour, you may cause another to deny him also, and at the last be denied of him.

Let us be more faithful in making our life show that we are on the Lord's side.

"So shall my word be that goeth forth out of my mouth; it shall not return unto me void, but it shall accomplish that which I please, and it shall prosper in the thing whereto I sent it." — ISA. lv. 11.

Mrs. A. C. Morrow relates of a lady who, looking out from a window upon a river, was attracted by the strange appearance of a gentleman walking excitedly up and down the banks of the stream. She suspected he was meditating suicide, and determined to make an effort to save him. Walking toward the river, and passing quietly by him, she said softly, as if speaking to herself, "There is a river the streams whereof make glad the City of God."

She returned home. Years went by, and the incident was forgotten. Attending a religious meeting, the gentleman spoke to her, and told her how the words she had quoted were the means of saving him, both soul and body. "Then there is a happiness to be found, and I will seek it," thought the man, and he turned from the river which he had determined to make his grave. So many Christians sow too little of the word of God, and worry too much about the growth of that already sown. Would to God we would only do that which it is our duty to do, and let God make the growth as seemeth best in his sight. What a great ingathering of lost ones, if every Christian would plant the word of God into the hearts of those around him, and trust God's promise: "I will not let my word return unto me void."

"*And let us consider one another to provoke unto love and to good works.*"—HEB. x. 24.

I remember reading of a traveller who was crossing the Alps, being overtaken by a severe snowstorm, he became drowsy by his long exposure to the cold, and lay down in the snow to rest. Just then he saw another traveller approaching from an opposite direction. The poor, unfortunate man seemed even in a worse condition than himself. He collected his strength, and managed to crawl to where the traveller was, and, taking his hands in his own, he began to rub them with all the strength left him. His companion soon began to revive, his powers were restored, and he was able to resume his journey. The exercise bestowed upon the traveller had started the first traveller's blood into circulation anew, and they reached shelter in safety. So it is in our Christian life: by helping others heavenward, we also walk in the same direction, and render pleasing service to our God.

"*Evil communications corrupt good manners.*"
1 COR. xv. 33.

It is told of a sweet-voiced canary that it forgot how to sing by having its cage hung outside where it was constantly surrounded by sparrows. It gave up its once sweet notes, and learned to chatter the meaningless, tuneless notes of the sparrow. The constant association with the Christless is apt to make our hearts Christless. What a heaven-sent blessing are our church homes, that we may from time to time have the fire of Christian love kindled into a new blaze, and have our strength renewed to serve Christ, and withstand the wiles of the evil one.

"Let your light so shine before men, that they may see your good works, and glorify your Father which is in heaven." — MATT. v. 16.

Some years ago a minister was invited by a pastor in another neighborhood to come and aid him in a revival service. He accepted the invitation, and spent several days laboring for souls. The day of his departure came, and as he was leaving, the pastor walked with him some distance, and when they arrived at the edge of a beautiful grove, they knelt down and prayed for each other. A man was at work in a field near by, and saw the servants of God on their knees praying. He began to meditate on his own condition, and soon saw what a great sinner he was. He attended the meetings, and publicly confessed Christ, dating the first impression to the influence of the two godly men in their little outdoor prayer-meeting.

May God use this little illustration in bringing us to a truer realization of the importance of living for Christ in such a way that our daily lives will influence sinners to turn to God's service.

"A little leaven leaveneth the whole lump." — GAL. v. 9.

In one of our western cities, high up on a very tall building, is a large clock. It registers what is called "electric time," and known to be very accurate because it is regulated by the calculations of scientific instruments. On a large sign is painted, "Correct city time," and when one has any doubts about having the exact time, he sets his watch by this clock.

Great mills, railroads, manufactories, run by its time. Should it lose or gain an hour the whole city would be thrown into confusion. Let us remember, one watch set right will do to set many by; while, on the other hand, the watch that goes wrong may be the means of misleading a whole multitude of others. So it is with life. A wholly consecrated person may become the example for many, and a wicked life of sin may too be the means of entangling a whole community of associates. "Examine yourselves."

"*And whosoever shall offend one of these little ones that believe in me, it is better for him that a millstone were hanged about his neck, and he were cast into the sea.*"

MARK ix. 42.

A fashionable lady passing down one of the streets of a great city one day saw two men quarrelling; they soon came to blows, and suddenly one drew a pistol and shot his antagonist dead. The lady fainted at such an awful sight, and was at once conveyed to her elegant home, and tenderly cared for by kind friends.

When the poor unfortunate murderer came to the bar of justice to answer the charge of taking the life of his fellow-man, the lady was summoned as a witness for the State. The evidence was conclusive. The jury said he was guilty, and must suffer the penalty in such cases. The day of execution arrived. The condemned man sent the lady a request to visit him. Hardly had she entered his cell when the poor man pointing his finger at her, said, "Madam, I was raised by praying parents, early was I taught to reverence everything sacred. Well do I remember a sainted mother who taught me to lisp the name of Jesus. Years ago, you invited me, then a young man, to attend a card party at your residence. There you handed me the first glass of wine that ever passed my lips. Madam, it was on that occasion, and at your earnest entreaties, I took the step that placed me where I now am. There it was I learned to love that which made me an outcast in life, and my disgrace at death. What ever part of this deed you shall be called upon to answer for, I must not say." The officer led the man to his doom, and the lady returned home with a heavy heart, knowing she had heard the truth. Great God! awaken us and help us to see the responsibility our actions bring upon us. Every child of God is but a signboard, as it were, whose life should point the world heavenward. How careful should we be that Satan does not creep in unawares, and cause us to point in the wrong direction.

"*But let all those that put their trust in thee rejoice: let them ever shout for joy.*" — Ps. v. 11.

A lad was converted at a revival service. On his way home the thought came to him that his parents would be sore displeased with him, and his brothers and sisters ridicule him. He knelt down and poured out his soul to God in prayer.

The new-found joy beamed forth and manifested itself in every movement.

A few days later, the pent-up love of Christ could no longer be bound, and he went to his brother and told him that he had found such wonderful joy. The brother replied, "Henry, I've been watching you lately. I saw in your life something unusual. Do you suppose God will do for me what he has done for you?"—"Yes, Tom, and even greater things; only come to him trusting." The result was that the lad's example led to Christ the entire family, — father, mother, brother, and sisters, all were made to rejoice with him. My dear friend, the religion of Jesus Christ is a religion of joy and peace; and no one who basks in the sunshine of his love has a right to a downcast countenance. Then, again, if we have joy in our religion, it casts a ray of influence around us, and creates a desire on the part of our friends and associates to seek and find a like peace and joy.

"*Like as a father pitieth his children, so the Lord pitieth them that fear him.* — Ps. ciii. 13.

A gentleman was standing one morning on the platform of a railroad station, holding by the hand his little seven-year-old daughter. As they stood there waiting the arrival of the train, they heard on the platform the tramp of a dozen or more heavy feet coming up the walk. The little girl turned, and saw a sight such as she had never seen before. Six great, giant-like policemen marching two abreast, guarding a fierce, wicked-looking man, with great chains on his limbs. They were taking him under this heavy guard to prison for some great crime he had committed.

The little girl thought how sad must be that heart. She pitied him from the depth of her soul.

When the company had gathered opposite the little girl, the fierce eye of the prisoner turned and looked at her, and suddenly turned from her to almost immediately turn and glance back at her pitying eyes — he once more turned his face from her, as if her presence annoyed him. The child rushed forward, and nearly came to the prisoner. She looked at him, and said, "I did not mean to plague you, poor man; I am so sorry for you, and Jesus is sorry for you, too." The father led the child quickly away; no one seemed to hear the simple words but the prisoner, whose heart was cut to the quick. He carried the picture of that innocent child with him along his weary ride, and even to his gloomy cell. As the guards delivered their charge, the warden expected to have a great deal of trouble with such a noted criminal. But as time passed on, to the surprise of the prison officials, he grew more kind and obedient day by day. One day the chaplain asked how it was that he had turned out to be such a different man from what they expected of him. "It is a very simple story," said the man. "A child was sorry for me — she sympathized with me, and told me Jesus was sorry for me, too; her pity and his broke my heart of stone."

How Christ pities poor lost humanity! but we can never win them to salvation in Christ unless our hearts are so filled with him that we show his pity and love.

"*Blessed are the dead which die in the Lord.*"
Rev. xiv. 13.

"A Jew going into the house of a brother Jew, who had lost a dear child, saw him in uncontrollable agony. He tore his hair, and beat his head against the wall, and would not be consoled. He soon went into another bereaved home, where the inmates were Christians.

"Very calmly they led him to the room where the loved one lay in her coffin. There were no outbursts of grief there. Pinned upon the breast of the departed one were the words, "She sleeps in Jesus." He was so profoundly impressed with the love and faith of one who could so quietly look upon the face of the dead, that he too embraced Christianity."

"*Remember the Sabbath day, to keep it holy.*"
EXODUS xx. 8.

A servant who had recently experienced the blessedness of faith in Christ was ordered by his master to perform a certain piece of work on the Sabbath day. "But," said the servant, "it is the Sabbath day." "Does not Christ say, if a man have an ox or an ass that falls into a pit on the Sabbath day, he may pull him out," replied the master. "Yes," said the servant, "but if the ox has a habit of choosing the Sabbath day to fall into the pit, then the man should either fill up the pit or sell the ox."

How many unbecoming deeds Christians do on the Sabbath under the cloak of our Lord's words. "Ye have perverted the words of the living God," and placed a strained construction upon the Scriptures to make them apply to your deeds of unrighteousness.

"*For none of us liveth to himself, and no man dieth to himself.* — ROM. xiv. 7.

Of Pontitianus, a high officer in the court of the emperor, a story is told which runs as follows: He and a friend were walking one day in the gardens near the city walls, when they came to a humble cottage, occupied by a poor servant. In order to see more of the life of the poor, they went in and asked for a drink of water. As they sat there, one of them found on the table a small book — the life of Antony — he began to read and to admire; as he read a little farther he began to meditate upon abandoning such a life as he had lived, and take up such an one as he was reading. As the spirit of God began to loose the scales from his eyes, he turned to Pontitianus and said, "Tell me, I pray thee, what will we finally attain by all these labors of ours? What aim we at? Can our hopes rise higher than to become the Emperor's favorites? And in this, what is there that is not brittle and full of perils? And by how many perils arrive we at even greater perils? Now, if I desire, I can become the friend of God?" After reading a little more he exclaimed, "Now have I broken loose from these, our former hopes, and am resolved to serve God, and from this hour and from this place I begin; if you desire not to imitate me, do not oppose me." The friend replied, "I will cleave to you, and partake of so gracious a reward, and labor in so glorious a service."

Both led to saving faith in Christ by reading the good deeds of a Christian life. Dear reader, bear in mind our breath may leave this mortal body, but the character we have made will forever live and build up or pull down the travellers along the path we have trod. May we from this incident take new courage, and leave along the path of life only that which will build up our fellow-man in a godly life, and eventually lead him into the portals of heavenly bliss.

"*My son, if sinners entice thee, consent thou not.*"
Prov. i. 10.

One bright Sabbath morning, several years ago, eight young men were walking along the banks of the river not far from Washington city. They were on their way to a shady grove to spend the day playing at cards, and each carrying in his pocket a bottle of wine. They forgot the praying mothers they had left behind them. As they strolled along, amusing each other with their idle jests, the sound of the village church bell two miles away attracted their attention. Presently, one of their number suddenly halted, and, addressing the friend nearest to him, said, "I will go no further, but must return and go to church." His friend called to his companions, who were a little way off, and told them to come back, George had a religious fit; "Come," said he, "let us immerse him in the river." They formed a circle around him, and informed him that if he persisted in breaking into the arrangements as planned, they would immerse him in the cold river. "I am very well aware that you have the power to do so, and to even drown me if you choose; but I will never go with you. You all know I am two hundred miles from home, but you do not know that my mother has been, before my earliest recollections, a helpless, bedridden invalid. I am her youngest child; my father is poor, and could not afford to pay my way at school; the teacher kindly took me as a free student. The morning I left home, my mother called me to her and said, 'My son, you do not know the agony of a mother's heart in parting with her youngest child. When you leave me to-day, you will have looked upon my face for the last time on earth. Your father is unable to pay your expenses to visit us, and I am very near the grave; my counsel to you is to seek the help of God in everything you do. Every Sabbath morning from ten to eleven o'clock, I will spend in silent prayer in your behalf. Wherever you may be during that hour, as the church bell rings, let your thoughts come back to this chamber, where your dying mother is praying for you.' I never expect to see my mother again on earth; by the help of God, I will meet her in heaven." As George stopped speaking, great tears rolled down the cheeks of the little company; the circle was broken, and George went his way to church; he had battled against great odds, and had won the victory. As he turned to see the direction his companions had taken, he saw them following him to church; they had thrown away their cards and flasks, never again to take them up — from that day forward they became changed men, and useful Christian workers.

CHAPTER V.

TEMPTATION.

"BLESSED IS THE MAN THAT ENDURETH TEMPTATION."

JAMES i. 12.

TEMPTATION.

"*Blessed is the man that endureth temptation; for when he is tried he shall receive a crown of life, which the Lord hath promised to them that love him.*— JAS. i. 12.

A gentleman on being asked for a remedy for temptation, replied, "Keep yourself so full of Christ, that sin can find no crevice in which to breed mischief."

Mr. Spurgeon says, "The sea can do the ship no harm until the water enters it."

Fill a bushel with wheat, and the chaff comes to the surface and is blown away.

No wonder we ofttimes find it hard to keep sinful thoughts from our hearts.

How easy it would be if we kept Christ there. The heart cannot remain vacant, and if we do not have Christ's presence to fill it, we cannot hinder Satan from taking up his abode within us.

"*Put on the whole armour of God, that ye may be able to stand against the wiles of the devil.*"— EPH. vi. 11.

A well-known Christian gentleman was returning, a few years ago, from a voyage to China. As the vessel was just about entering the harbor of New York, and he had arranged his toilet and was ready to step ashore, there came a stubborn wind which drove them again to sea, and for several days they were tossed about by the turbulent billows, in a more furious manner than they had been during the entire voyage from the other side of the world.

Now this is often the way with the Christian; when Satan sees that he is about ready to quit the voyage of life and enter the harbor of God's joys, he ofttimes turns his marshalled forces against him, and tries to drive him back by doubts and fears. But he who has donned the whole armor of God is able through Christ to battle with all these forces and come off victorious, and triumphantly enter the portals of peace. Then, too, the same drawbacks are met with by the sinner who seeks to unload his burden of sin at the feet of Christ. Satan in this case, also makes a special effort to heap up the high mountains of obstacles and prevent his coming. Many are the devices to which he resorts. "Too great a sinner," "Wait awhile," "I will, by and by," "I am afraid I won't hold out," "My faith is too weak," "God will save me, any way," and a thousand others equally inconsistent.

But friend, "greater is He that is for you, than he that is against you." All you have to do to cause such foes to vanish, is simply, "Fix your eyes upon Jesus."

"*We ought to obey God rather than men.*"

ACTS v. 29.

A Christian captain of a sperm whaler, refused to allow his boats to be lowered for the chase on the Sabbath day. His men, who were to receive a share of the oil taken, rebelled, and in order to quiet their threatening voices, he promised to give them so much of his portion of oil as would pay them for the loss of the day. The mate, more violent in his determinations said, "The owner will think nothing of losing his share of the oil,

I will however, see that you do not command any more of his vessels." By this time the mate saw the dignity of his captain's position, and began to apologize, when his eye rested on the barometer. He noticed the very sudden fall of the mercury; and ere the men could be summoned, a terrible hurricane had struck the ship. Had the crew gone off on a cruise, all would have been lost. For days the wind drove the ship before it, and when calm was again restored they found themselves in such a good fishing place, that they filled their ship in less than one third the usual time.

"*The devil as a roaring lion, walketh about, seeking whom he may devour.*" — 1 PET. v. 8.

"The world is Satan's bait. He seldom throws out a naked hook. Let murder, fraud, idolatry, or lying, be presented in their undisguised turpitude, and few of good education and morals can be taken captive by him. But he conceals the hook in a tempting bait, and like a skilful angler, he knows how to use that part of the world that is best suited to our tastes, and most likely to decoy. For one he has a golden bait; for another, pleasure; for another, fame; another, worldly honor, etc., etc.;— and his throne in our families and in our closets." — JACKSON.

What a world of truth this great man has given us, and how true to life. In scripture we are repeatedly commanded to "examine ourselves," that we may rid our hearts of that which Satan employs to ensnare us.

"When the hours are dark and drear,
When the tempter lurketh near;
By thy strengthening grace, out-poured,
Save thy tempted ones, oh Lord."

"*Cleanse thou me from secret faults.*" — Ps. xix. 12.

A gentleman who had spent some time in Italy said that while at Florence, one day his attention was attracted by the mournful notes of some birds, and he was led to inquire the cause of their sad twitterings: he found in a room a great number of birds in cages, and that the eyes of each had been put out by means of some pointed instrument. At night the owners of the birds took them outside the city, and hung the cages in trees that were varnished with a heavy coat of a kind of mucilage. These birds kept up their mournful songs, and attracted other birds to their cages; and the coating of mucilage so fastened them that the men could easily capture them.

How true to life is the illustration! Satan puts the spiritual sight from millions of poor mortals, and uses them to decoy others into his net. On every hand we see the effect of wicked men who are Satan's agents in alluring others into the net. It behooves every child of God to arm himself with the whole armor of Christ Jesus that he may be "able to withstand the wiles of the devil," and constantly keep his eye upon God who "will not suffer you to be tempted above that ye are able, but will with the temptation also make a way to escape, that ye may be able to bear it."

"*Resist the devil, and he will flee from you.*"
Jas. iv. 7.

A gentleman, who has spent many years of his life in capturing wild animals, says of the wolf, that, when attacked, he will first note the earnestness with which the enemy presses the attack, and, if he shows great determination, he scampers away. But if he detects the least fear in his pursuer's movements, he will defend himself with great bravery.

The same way with old Satan: he tempts us by first placing some trivial thing in our path; and if we offer no resistance, he suddenly attacks us with all his force, and overcomes us. Thanks be to God, through our Lord Jesus Christ, resistance through him can make Satan flee from us!

"*Take the helmet of salvation, and the sword of the spirit, which is the word of God.*" — EPH. vi. 17.

"During the career of Joan of Arc as a warrior, it is related of her that she never appeared before her men without her banner waving above her; and the enemy is credited with saying that, in battle, they could see angels hovering over it, which so dismayed them that they despaired of victory. What amount of truth is in the illustration, judge ye? but this remember, dear friend, that when Satan sees you carrying the banner of Christ with you, he never will attack you with sufficient force to cause you to yield. Arm yourself, therefore, with the "sword of the spirit, which is the word of God," wave thy banner above thee, and victory is thine.

"*Remember the Sabbath day to keep it holy.*"
EXOD. xx. 8.

Some years ago a prominent bank president summoned his confidential clerk into his private office, and handed him a large bundle of papers, telling him that they must be copied and ready for him early Monday morning. "Sir," said the young man, "this is Saturday; in order to have them ready for you at the hour named I must work all day Sunday." — "That may be true; but when I want my work, I want it," responded the president. — "But, sir, I cannot break God's commandment, and will not do so for my salary," he said. — "You can choose as you like, sir," said the banker. "You can give up your position, or accede to my demands." — "I choose the former, sir, without hesitation," said the clerk. He took his hat, and left the bank. Some of his friends called him a fool for being so particular. In a few days the banker was called on by some gentlemen who were just starting a bank. They asked him if he could tell them of a reliable, capable man to act as cashier. "I know just the man you want," said the banker. — "Where is he now?" — "He is not employed, having been discharged by his former employer." — "We don't want any castouts," replied the men. — "Wait," said the banker; "I discharged him because he refused to work on Sunday. I will be his bondsman for any amount." The clerk was called on by the gentlemen, and engaged at a handsome salary.

Whatever may be our inclinations, in whatever light the world sees us, we will find in the end it is "better to obey and honor God rather than man."

"*The devil as a roaring lion walketh about, seeking whom he may devour.*" — 1 PET. v. 8.

During the darkness of a heavy fog, Hannibal, the great general, secreted his forces, and waylaid the army of Flaminius as it passed through a narrow defile. In an unguarded moment he sprang from his place of concealment, and almost completely destroyed the Roman forces.

So it is with Satan: he delights to waylay us, and, when off our guard, pounce upon us, and drag us down.

Our Saviour laid an equal stress upon " Watch " as he did upon " pray." " Watch as well as pray." He is able to succor them that are tempted and tried, for " The Lord knoweth how to deliver the godly out of temptation." At the same time, gentle reader, it is your duty to watch and pray that ye enter not *into* temptation.

CHAPTER VI.

SECRET SINS.

"HE THAT COVERETH HIS SINS SHALL NOT PROSPER."
PROV. xxviii. 13.

SECRET SINS.

" Put on the whole armour of God, that ye may be able to stand against the wiles of the devil." — EPH. vi. 11.

It is said that Baldur the Good having been tormented with terrible dreams indicating that his life was in danger, told them to the assembled gods who resolved to conjure all things so as to avert the threatened danger from him. Then Frigga, the wife of Odin, exacted an oath from fire and water, from iron and all other metals, from stones, trees, diseases, beasts, birds, poisons, and creeping things, that none of them would do any harm to Baldur. Odin, not satisfied with all this, and feeling alarmed for the fate of his son, determined to consult the prophetess Angerbode, a giantess, mother of Fenris, Hela, and the Midgard serpent.

But the other gods, feeling that what Frigga had done was quite sufficient, amused themselves with using Baldur as a mask, some hurling darts at him, some stones, while others hewed at him with their swords and battle-axes, for do what they would, none of them could harm him. And this became a favorite pastime with them, and was regarded as an honor to Baldur. But Loki, who beheld this scene, was sorely vexed that Baldur was not hurt. Assuming, therefore, the shape of a woman, he went to Fensalir, the mansion of Frigga. That goddess when she saw the pretended woman, inquired of her if she knew what the gods were doing at their meetings.

She replied that they were throwing darts and stones at Baldur, without being able to hurt him. "Ay," said Frigga, "neither stones, nor sticks, nor anything else can hurt Baldur, for I have exacted an oath from all of them." — "What!" exclaimed the woman, "have all things sworn to spare Baldur?" — "All things," replied Frigga, "except one little shrub that grows on the eastern side of Valhalla, and is called Mistletoe, and which I thought too young and feeble to crave an oath from."

As soon as Loki heard this he went away, and resuming his natural shape, cut off the mistletoe, and repaired to the place where the gods were assembled. There he found Hodur standing apart, without partaking of the sports, on account of his blindness, and going up to him said, "Why dost thou not also throw something at Baldur?" — "Because I am blind," answered Hodur, "and see not where Baldur is, and have, moreover, nothing to throw." — "Come then," said Loki, "do like the rest, and show honor to Baldur by throwing this twig at him, and I will direct thy arm toward the place where he stands."

Hodur then took the mistletoe, and under the guidance of Loki, darted it at Baldur, who, pierced through and through, fell down lifeless. —*From Twelve Steps Heavenward.*

The mother thought this little insignificant plant too feeble to injure her son, yet the same became mighty in the hands of the enemy. How many of us are carrying in our hearts some little sins that we think unable to injure us, so small and insignificant that we deem ourselves in no danger on account of them? Satan may take hold of just that little thing and drag us down. How necessary to "examine ourselves" often, and not let such little sins creep upon us. It has been said that "he that despiseth little things shall fall by little and little." Surely, he that allows little sins to lodge in his heart will "fall by little and little," yet his fall may be as fatal as that of the open rebellious sinner. Satan always attacks us at an unguarded spot, and though however little, he forces temptations upon us, it then becomes necessary for us to put on the whole armor of God that we may be able to resist Satan.

"*He that covereth his sins shall not prosper.*"
Prov. xxviii. 13.

A gentleman living in the State of New York said not long since, that, one day when he was a boy he became angered at a command of his father, and as an act of revenge took an axe, and hacked a deep gash in a beautiful maple tree that stood in the yard.

The bark soon grew over the wound, and nothing more was thought of it until many years later the tree fell before the wind storm. The gentleman went to the tree, and found the hack he had made had gone to the heart of the tree, and the whole heart had become rotten.

So likewise is he that harbors in his heart some secret sin. In the course of time he may rest assured "his sins will find him out." In the course of time, his heart will become polluted, and he will fall.

"Ye cannot serve God and mammon" for the two cannot exist in one heart. Oh that we, like the Psalmist, would seek divine aid in cleansing us of our secret faults, that are sapping our very life blood.

Like the little vine that begins to wind around the tree, at first nothing is thought of it, but as time rolls on it climbs higher and higher until it completely covers it, choking life out. So is the result of these secret sins. "He that covereth his sins shall not prosper." But on the other hand, he who goes to Christ, and confesses his sins shall be as the "tree planted by the river of waters . . . and whatsoever he doeth shall prosper."

"But if ye forgive not men their trespasses, neither will your Father forgive your trespasses." — MATT. vi. 15.

Many years ago, Governor Oglethorpe of Georgia, and Mr. John Wesley chanced to take passage on the same vessel for a voyage across the ocean. One day the governor became very angry at one of his servants for some trifling inattention, and said to Mr. Wesley, "I will be revenged on him, the rascal should have been careful how he used me, for I *never forgive*."

Mr. Wesley turned to the angry man, and calmly said, "Then I do hope, sir, you never sin."

The passionate man grew calm and said no more about the servant. Some professing Christians nurse in their hearts just such a spirit, and expect to serve the blessed Saviour acceptably. My friend, such worship is, in the sight of God, as "sounding brass and a tinkling cymbal." Christ's own words condemn us. If we forgive not the insignificant little matter between man and man, how can God forgive our constant shortcomings?

"But I say unto you, Love your enemies, bless them that curse you, do good to them that hate you, and pray for them which despitefully use you and persecute you."

MATT. v. 44.

During the illustrious Washington's life, a Christian gentleman learned that one of his neighbors had been sentenced to death. The gentleman went to the general, and besought him to pardon his neighbor.

The general informed him that the sentence must be carried out, and that nothing could be done for him.

"He is my worst enemy," said the intercessor. Washington turned to the man, and said, "And you have walked sixty miles, through the snow, to ask pardon for him? and he your worst enemy? Your request shall be granted." The gentleman set out on his weary journey, satisfied.

How pleasing in the sight of God is such a spirit! But I hear one say, "It is impossible to love and forgive him who is injuring you." My friend, Christ commands us to do it, and he never requires of us an impossibility. True Christian love overrides all such difficulties, and enables us to say, with our adorable Saviour, "Father, forgive them, for they know not what they do."

Let us at the outset fix this fact in our minds — that we cannot serve Christ while such a spirit finds lodgement in our hearts. Jesus cannot forgive us when we go to him with unforgiven wrongs treasured in our hearts.

"*Let us lay aside every weight, and the sin that doth so easily beset us, and let us run with patience the race that is set before us.*" — HEB. xii. 1.

Canon Wilberforce said that one day, while walking in the Isle of Skye, he saw a magnificent specimen of the golden eagle, soaring upward. He halted, and watched its flight. Soon he observed by its movements that something was wrong. Presently it began to fall, and soon lay dead at his feet. Eager to know the reason of its death, he hastily examined it, and found no trace of gunshot wound; but he found that it held in its talons a small weasel, which, in its flight, was drawn near its body, and had sucked the life blood from the eagle's breast.

The same end befalls him who clings to some secret

sin; sooner or later it will sap his life blood, and he falls down, lost, lost. Therefore, brother, "let us lay aside every weight" and the pet sin that we are harboring, and that is drawing us down, and "let us run the race that is set before us," "Looking unto Jesus, the author and finisher of our faith." We can run this race only when we have laid aside the weight of our worldliness, and have been cleansed of the sin that doth so easily beset us, by the blood of Jesus Christ his Son, which cleanseth us from ALL sin.

"*A little leaven leaveneth the whole lump.*"
1 COR. v. 6.

Dr. Booth once told the following incident of some brittle gold being accidentally dropped into a quantity of well-refined and tough gold; and it was found to have rendered the entire mass brittle and unfit for coinage. The impurity consisted of only a fraction of an ounce, yet it rendered seventy-five thousand ounces useless for coinage.

He that harbors some secret sin in his heart, though he do a million of good deeds, is in danger of letting one sin pull him down, and render of no value his good acts.

"A little leaven leaveneth the whole lump," and "he that offends in one point is guilty of all."

"*For whosoever shall keep the whole law, and yet offend in one point, he is guilty of all.*— JAS. ii. 10.

A wealthy gentleman employed a workman to erect upon a lot in the cemetery a costly monument. After the stone had been erected, and the finishing touches put on the carving, the proud workman sent for the owner to come and inspect the work. With a smile of satisfaction the artist pointed to the monument. The owner glanced at it a moment, and turned away, saying, " You have left out one letter, which renders all the labor and anxiety you have spent on it worthless to me, and I cannot accept your work."

And so in carving the monument of our Christian characters: one pet sin may render the whole structure worthless, and cause it to crumble to dust. "All these things" we may have "kept from our youth up, yet one thing," a very necessary thing, "thou yet lackest." We need to be wholly purified and "cleansed from our secret faults."

CHAPTER VII.

SERVING GOD OUR FIRST DUTY.

"SEEK YE FIRST THE KINGDOM OF GOD."
MATT. vi. 33.

SERVING GOD OUR FIRST DUTY.

"And he said to them all, if any man will come after me let him deny himself, and take up his cross daily, and follow me. — LUKE ix. 23.

The Wagultzes, a heathen sect of Tartars, assemble once a year at public worship, which consists of sacrificing one animal of every species. After which they hang the skins on certain trees, under which they assemble, prostrating themselves before them. This festival concludes with a great feast, at which the worshippers eat the flesh of the sacrifices, and return home feeling that they have discharged all their religious duties for the current year.

Now a great many professed Christians think that if they attend divine worship once a week, or once a month, they are discharging their whole duty to God. My friend, the religion of Jesus Christ is a religion for every day and hour of our lives. And he who truly serves God is he who makes his own life conform to the will of God, and daily follows in the footsteps of the adorable Christ.

"I bear in my body the marks of the Lord Jesus."
GAL. vi. 17.

In Hindoostan, the followers of Vishnu distinguish themselves from other sects by painting their faces with a horizontal line. The followers of Siva use a perpendicular line, made with a peculiar clay. They are not afraid nor ashamed to let the world know and see them following their gods.

So it should be with God's children. No act of worship is more honored and acceptable to Jesus than that of daily bearing the marks of our Lord, and showing to the world that we are not ashamed to be found serving Christ. Then, too, we have a direct command to so live; for, says Christ, "Let your light so shine before men that they may see your good works, and glorify your Father which is in heaven." And "He that confesseth me before men, him will I confess before my Father in heaven."

"*But seek ye first the kingdom of God and his righteousness; and all these things shall be added unto you.*"
MATT. vi. 33.

David Livingstone, who did so much toward opening up the dark continent of Africa, told the following story. When he was a boy, a faithful Christian man called him to his deathbed and said, "My son, make religion the everyday business of your life, and not a thing of fits and starts." Livingstone's life shows that he followed the advice to the day of his death, even to his last hour, which was spent on his knees in prayer to him to whom he had so often gone for comfort.

There is no class of professors that God has so little respect for as those that serve him periodically. And there is no class that do so little in the cause as those that wait for the annual revival to fit the harness to them. God loves and honors him who strives to show, by his daily and hourly walk, that he bears branded on his body the marks of the Lord Jesus. We are to DAILY take up our cross and follow him.

SERVING GOD OUR FIRST DUTY. 105

"*If any man will come after me, let him deny himself, and take up his cross and follow me.*" — MATT. xvi. 24.

There is among the Scythians a legend about one of their hero gods, who, after he had destroyed great numbers of the human race, destroyed himself. So great was this god in the hearts of his people that it was by them considered a disgrace to die on a bed, and those that did not fall in battle frequently took their own lives, rather than not follow the example of their god, and thereby incur his displeasure. These poor heathen considered the privilege of dying as their god died, a great honor. We often call the service of our God a great sacrifice, when we should esteem it a privilege. We call it a sacrifice because it requires self-denial, which most of us are unwilling to practise. Oh! that we could learn to crucify self; put self in the background for the service of our Master.

"*But grow in grace, and in the knowledge of our Lord and Saviour Jesus Christ.*" — 2 PET. iii. 18.

Passing along the street one day, I saw a company of men digging a large hole through a bed of solid rock. A few days afterwards I had occasion to pass that way again, and saw the men laying the foundations of a magnificent building. After some months I again passed that street, and found the workmen busily engaged in laying course after course of brick. The last time I saw that building it was towering heavenward, and the men were still laying the brick, course after course.

Now, this is the way with the Christian life. No one can at once enter into all the fulness of Christ, and sit down with folded hands, but day by day he is brought closer and closer, day by day he may "grow in grace and the knowledge of the truth as it is in Christ Jesus," until finally at the end he may step into the joys of heaven. Christ, who knew our nature, compared our lives to a "warfare." While he is ever ready and willing to bestow on us that which will build up our Christian character, Satan is ever watching and pulling down; hence, the warfare. Then, again, some Christians never get above the foundation, while others keep on building until their characters tower to the very heavens, and when the message comes to them, they only step over the word death, and enter the pearly gates.

Let us, then, begin with a fixed determination to grow daily in grace.

"*It is good for me to draw near to God.*"
Psa. lxxiii. 28.

It is told of the late General Gordon, that each morning, during his journey in the Soudan country, for half an hour there lay outside his tent, a white handkerchief. The whole camp well knew what it meant, and looked upon the little signal with the utmost respect; no foot dared pass the threshold of that tent while the little guard lay there. "No message, however pressing, was to be delivered. Matters of life and death must wait until the little signal was taken away. Every one in that camp knew that God and Gordon were communing together." Sweet is the communion of that spirit that craves a nearness to its God. Powerful is the influence of that soul who daily and hourly longs to draw near to its God, and drink in the inspiring draughts of His presence.

Brother, we don't get near enough to God; it is good to draw near to God, but it is better to live daily and hourly near to him.

SERVING GOD OUR FIRST DUTY. 107

"*And the cares of this world, and the deceitfulness of riches, and the lusts of other things, entering in, choke the word, and it becometh unfruitful.*" — MARK iv. 19.

It is said of the Duke of Alva, that on being asked by Henry IV., if he had observed the eclipses of the year, replied that he had so much business on earth, he had no leisure to even look up to heaven.

How true that is with multitudes of men to-day, engrossed with worldly cares, to the shutting out of all heavenly light.

Happy is he who recognizes the bountiful hand of God in his daily life, as the provider of everything we enjoy.

Thrice happy the lot of him who seeks first, the kingdom of God and his righteousness. Keeping the tempting cares of life behind him as he presses toward the "mark of the high calling."

"*He that endureth to the end shall be saved.*"
MATT. x. 22.

The Duke of Wellington once plead with his friends, to be allowed to give up his position of honor in the army, and accept a low place, simply because he despaired of advancement. And the great Napoleon was tempted to end his own melancholy career, because he saw no ray of hope in gaining the honor he afterward attained. Oh, godly servant, thy way may seem dark; the yoke of the master may seem to gall your neck, it may look as if the hand of God was withdrawn; you may think your burden too heavy, the arm of flesh may be almost worn out, the sorest of temptations may crouch by your wayside, your power of resistance may seem all but exhausted, the hand of bereavement may have torn your heart;—let me say, "Endure to the end." I come to you with a great promise from Christ the Lord; oh, take courage, "He that endureth to the end " *Shall be saved.*"

"*I bear in my body the marks of the Lord Jesus.*"
GAL. vi. 17.

A gentleman was receiving some money at a bank one day, when he noticed a small, scarlet thread pending to one of the bills, he took hold of it to pull it out, but found it was woven into the very texture of the paper, and could not be withdrawn without doing serious damage to the bill. "Oh," said the banker, "you'll find all government bills made in the same way, at least those of recent issue. It is a private mark; then, too, it also makes the art of counterfeiting much more difficult."

Oh, friend, the glory in the thought, that the Lord Jesus hath so honored us as to place his mark upon us! "My sheep know my voice and they follow me." May not the thought inspire us to greater zeal in walking so near Christ, that the world may see him through us and be led to serve him.

"*Resist the devil and he will flee from you.*"
JAS. iv. 7.

Martin Luther said. "When the devil finds me idle and I do not think of God's word, then he tempteth my conscience. But when I get hold on God's word, then I have won the game; then I resist the devil and say thus, 'I know, and of God's word am sure, that this doctrine is not mine, but the doctrine of the Son of God.' Oh weak and puny soul, lay hold on the mighty promises of your heavenly Father. Carry His Word in your heart. 'Grow in grace and the knowledge of the truth as it is in Christ Jesus.' Remember, you war not against 'flesh and blood,' but against powers and principalities, and you will never overcome them in your own strength, but by the Word of God, which is 'sharper than any two-edged sword.' "

Our Saviour overcame Satan's entreaties by quoting God's word, and so may we overcome him.

"*For without me ye can do nothing.*" — Jno. xv. 5.

A lady, in order to teach her little girl the beauty and truth of this text, requested her to go to the flower-bed and pluck the most beautiful lily and bring it to her. "Now," says the mother, "just lay it down on the doorstep in the sunshine and let it remain five minutes." When the child went to bring the flower to her mamma, she exclaimed, "Oh, mamma, see the once beautiful flower is withered and dead."— "Just so, my child," said the mother, "would you be unless God was with you each moment; may this teach you a lesson, to rely on your heavenly Father for everything you are and have." The same with the Christian, let him be exposed to the scorching rays of sin, worldly cares, and the wiles of old Satan, without the dew of Christ's grace, and he cannot lead a godly life. But let him live in Christ's love, and he will "flourish as the Cedars of Lebanon," and in due time, ripen into exquisite beauty in that heavenly Paradise above, where the sunshine of God's countenance will ever fall, and where he shall bloom forever more.

CHAPTER VIII.

PERSONAL WORK.

"HE (ANDREW) FIRST FINDETH HIS OWN BROTHER SIMON, AND SAITH UNTO HIM, WE HAVE FOUND THE MESSIAS, WHICH IS, BEING INTERPRETED, THE CHRIST. AND HE BROUGHT HIM TO JESUS." —
JOHN i. 41-42.

PERSONAL WORK.

" *Go out into the highways and hedges, and compel them to come in.*" — LUKE xiv. 23.

A young man made application to a great mercantile establishment for a position as salesman. "Can you sell goods?" was the first question asked him. — "I can sell goods to a person who wishes to buy," answered the young man. — "So can any one," replied the merchant. "What we want is salesmen that can so influence our customers that they will buy goods, whether they want them or not."

In Christian work it is easy enough to tell a soul of Christ who is eagerly seeking him; but what the cause of God wants to-day is men and women to go out into the "highways and hedges" of sin and degradation, and, by their earnest life and prayers, compel them to come into the saving bounds of free salvation. Christ wants men and women who are so full of love for lost souls that their influence will melt the hearts of the most obstinate, and persuade them to take Christ as their Saviour. You may say, "I have not the power of speech," "I have a poor memory, and I cannot remember the Scriptures," "I am afraid I will say something I ought not to say," and a dozen other threadbare excuses.

Reader, if you lack these gifts had you not better fall on your knees, and, like Jacob of old, wrestle with God in prayer, until they come? This is the way to get them: this is the way to get your weapons to battle with.

Satan knows you, and he makes you believe you can't do these things, because it is trampling upon his domains.

God commands, and invites you to come to him, and he will supply all your needs and requirements; but so long as you do not use them, be sure he will never bestow them upon you. "If any of you lack wisdom, let him ask of God, who giveth to all men liberally, and upbraideth not, and it *shall* be given him." — JAS. i. 5.

"*For unto every one that hath shall be given, and he shall have abundance.*" — MATT. xxv. 29.

An eminent merchant of St. Petersburg supported, at his own expense, a number of missionaries in India. Some one asked him how he could afford to do so, to which he replied, "Before my conversion, when I served the world and self, I did it on a grand scale and at the most lavish expense; and when Christ called me out of darkness, I resolved that he should have more than I had ever given the world. At my conversion I promised I would give a certain per cent of what my business brought me. Since that time it yields double as much." So it is in our service for Christ. God never allows any capital to lay idle, and, if we do not use the talent given us, he takes it, and gives it to him who will use it. How often do we see poor, lean Christians fretting and fuming and praying for more faith and more strength, when they sit still, and will not use what they have.

My brother, sister, when God sees our desires and determinations to actively serve him with the first fruits of our lives, he will give us a great supply of the things needed.

First show your willingness, and he will show you what to do, and go with you in doing it.

"*If a man abide not in Me, he is cast forth as a branch, and is withered.*" — JNO. xv. 6.

The tree that bears the choicest fruit stands continually in the sunshine, without which the fruit can never evenly ripen and mature.

So he who bears heavenly fruit must continually live in the light of the "Sun of righteousness," without which he can never accomplish anything, but is as the severed branch, withering away.

"If ye abide in me and my words abide in you, ye may ask what ye will, and it shall be given you." "Without me, ye can do nothing."

Let us, then, be careful to go in the "strength of the Lord God," or our efforts to honor Christ and win souls will end in failure.

"*Behold how great a matter a little fire kindleth.*"
JAS. iii. 5.

Some years ago a lady was walking along a crowded street in a Southern city, and, as she passed the entrance of a variety theatre, she noticed a young man of unusual promise standing beside the door. She turned aside, and walked to where he stood, handing him a small gospel tract, with a gentle request to read it when an opportunity presented itself. The young man, not caring to insult the lady, glanced about him to see if any one was watching him, and quickly put the tract in his pocket, thinking he would throw it away when the lady passed out of sight. As he stood there, it seemed as if the little tract was burning his pocket. He removed it, and then his eyes rested on a verse of Scripture which refused to leave him. He went to his room, and read and re-read the tract, telling him of Christ's wondrous love, and he saw himself a lost sinner. The Holy Spirit came to him, and removed the scales from his eyes, revealing the loving Christ. He gave himself to the Master's cause, and has been the means, in God's hands, of leading scores of souls to the cross of Christ.

It was a very small act for the lady to hand the young man a piece of paper; yet, many souls have been led to Christ by her doing so. My friend, bear in mind God does not despise your little acts of service, your little deeds of love, but the same may be the means of bringing a soul to him, and that soul may bring others, until multitudes may rise up and bless the day you kindled the fire of love in their hearts.

God says, "My word . . . shall not return unto me void, but it shall accomplish that which I please, and it shall prosper in the thing whereto I sent it."

"*As the branch cannot bear fruit of itself, except it abide in the vine ; no more can ye, except ye abide in me.*"

Jno. xv. 4.

It is said of the Rev. Dr. Franklin, that his great passion was for fruitfulness. When about to pass to his eternal home, his son asked him for some word of wisdom as a remembrance when he was gone. Drawing his son close to him, he said in a faltering tone, "fruitfulness." The word was ever a great source of comfort to the son, and became the motto of his life.

Grand motto it is: would that we all might engraft it

on our hearts, and as our blessed Lord went about doing good, learn to "walk even as he walked."

"He that abideth in me, and I in him, the same bringest forth much fruit." The whole secret of our fruitfulness is *Christ* for "without me ye can do nothing" are his own words; but we can do all things through Christ which strengtheneth us.

While our success in bearing fruit is with him, the success of his cause on earth depends on our faithfulness to him. Let us then, kind reader, make "fruitfulness" our motto, and go forth with renewed energy bearing fruit for the master.

"*In the morning sow thy seed, and in the evening withhold not thine hand.*" — Ecl. xi. 6.

There is a custom among the older farmers of our country to plant certain vegetables at a particular sign of the moon, and it matters not how suitable may be the time or the condition of the soil, they will not plant until the "sign gets right." Now that is just the way with a great many Christians, they sit around with folded hands waiting for the sign to get right before they thrust in the sickle for Christ. And with many the sign has never become right, and never will. "In the morning sow thy seed, and in the evening withhold not thy hand."

With such an one the sign is always right. The power of God is always present.

Then, too, a great many Christians think that the sign is right only once in the year. At the annual revival the sign is right for them to work, and at any other season it is not their duty to do anything but listen from Sabbath to Sabbath to the pastor, as he labors in fanning the smoldering coals to keep them from dying out until the next revival.

Brother, sister, this is a low conception of the religion of a crucified Christ.

This is a wrong construction placed on the duties of a professing Christian.

This is the reverse of the Scriptural delineation of service in the Master's cause.

"Daily follow me." What the world needs is men and women to daily — hourly — live to him, and make their religion a part of their lives.

"*Be thou faithful unto death and I will give thee a crown of life.*" — Rev. ii. 10.

"Exert your talents," said Dr. Samuel Johnson, "and distinguish yourself. Do not think of retiring from the world until the world will be sorry that you retire. I hate a man whom pride, or cowardice, or laziness drives into a corner, and who does nothing while there but sit and growl."

Activity is the key to a useful Christian life. The key to activity is opening the doors of our hearts, and letting the river of Christ's love constantly flow through.

Our realization of Christ's love prompts us to love our fellow-man, and strive to lighten his burden.

Then, too, the best way to be active in God's service is to embrace every opportunity to do our fellow-man all the good we can, knowing that he that is faithful unto death shall be given a crown of life.

"*Thou shalt tell them. Thus saith the Lord.*"
Jer. xv. 2.

A minister in one of the Northern States was called, as pastor, to a church in a thrifty little town. When he arrived he was told that there was a tailor living in the town who was a noted infidel, and was ready to insult any one who introduced the subject of religion in his presence. The pastor went one day, and during conversation with the infidel introduced the subject of religion. The infidel said, "Sir, if your religion is what you tell me it is, and does what you claim for it, why do not your people believe it?"

"I do not understand you," said the pastor.

"Why, if your religion is so wonderful, do not your people believe in it?" said the tailor. "Here I have been wishing some one would come and talk with me, but not one has ever done so. I have waited, watched, and longed, but no one came."

Oh, my Christian friend, how do you know but some soul near you is longing to know Christ, and to lay the burden of his guilt on Him. How many souls would yield did you and I but do our duty, and personally strive with them.

How many convicted, seeking souls are haunted to despair, and no one comes to bring them to Christ. Oh! that we might awake to our personal duty, and make it a rule to inquire of those around us if they have a hope in Christ; show them that we have an interest in their eternal welfare; show them that Christ, and we too, love their souls, no matter how deep in sin they are. This is your duty, Christian friend, as a member of the household of the redeemed in Christ Jesus.

"*And every one that hath forsaken houses, or brethren, or sisters, or father, or mother, or wife, or children, or lands for my name's sake, shall receive an hundredfold, and shall inherit everlasting life.*" — MATT. xix. 29.

A few years ago a bright and wayward Cuban landed friendless and penniless in the city of New York.

After roaming about the streets for some days, he was

taken with fever, and conveyed to the hospital, where for weeks he was on the verge of the grave. A kind Christian lady, made it a point to go to the hospital, and while the physical ills were being treated, she pointed them to the Great Physician. She talked with this young Cuban, and she found that he was interested; before she left him she put into his hand a copy of the New Testament; he read it, and ere long, light dawned upon his dark heart, and he rejoiced in faith in Christ. When he recovered, so great was the love of Christ in his heart that he sailed for his native island to preach Christ to his kindred and friends. He endured all kinds of persecutions, but never shirked his duty, and preached Christ the more earnestly.

His own mother for months refused to speak to him. His dearest friends forsook him, but he kept on preaching, and after several months he saw one by one of his friends and countrymen melt under the spirit, and give their hearts to Jesus, until to-day nearly ten thousand have been converted.

Dear Christian friend, this is the spirit with which to serve Christ. Very seldom does it become necessary to sever family ties, but when it is so, we are commanded to do it, and in doing so we have this great promise from God Almighty, "*I* will not leave thee nor forsake thee."

"*Cast thy bread upon the waters; for thou shalt find it after many days.*" — ECL. xi. 1.

Dr. Bainbridge preached once in San Francisco. Some time afterward an officer of a vessel came to him and said, "Mr. Bainbridge, you do not recognize me, but I once heard you preach a sermon that went direct to my heart, and proved just the food for which my soul craved, and led me to the saving power of the Lamb of God. I want to personally thank you for that sermon." So the bread cast upon the waters had returned after many days. And so it is with our sowing the seeds of the Gospel; we may not live to see the result, but God will not let his "word return unto him void." It is not our office nor duty to attend to that, but it is our bounden duty to sow — sow — sow. "In the morning sow thy seed, and in the evening withhold not thy hand."

This is the one grand object of our earthly existence.

"*I will meditate also of all thy work, and talk of thy doings.*" — Ps. lxxvii. 12.

"A little boy, whose delight it was to sit on his mother's knee and hear the story of Jesus, one day went to his grandmother and said, 'Grandmother, why is it I never hear men talk of Jesus? I hear them talk of everything else, seldom ever did I hear them talk of Jesus, unless it was in the church or Sunday-schools; don't they love him?'"

Oh, what a stinging rebuke, brother! Can it be said truthfully of you? and do you delight, with the Psalmist, in "talking of thy doings?" Do you delight in the cross of Christ, and ardently long to make his glories known to those around you?

Remember how closely the world is watching you, and Satan uses your lack of enthusiasm in his arguments against God's cause.

Therefore, let the words of your mouth and the thoughts of your heart show forth the glory of your crucified and risen Lord. "Tell them what great things the Lord hath done for thee."

"*Whosoever, therefore, shall confess me before men, him will I confess also before my Father which is in heaven.*"

MATT. x. 32.

A Roman emperor said to a Greek architect, "Build me a coliseum — a grand coliseum, and if it suits me I will crown you in the presence of all the people, and I will make a great day of festival on your account." The architect did his work — did it magnificently, planned the building, and looked after its construction. The building was finished, the opening day arrived, the emperor and the architect were in the coliseum. Amid loud cheers, the emperor arose and announced that the day was set apart in honor of the Greek architect, and everything must be done to his honor. "Let us make merry and enjoy ourselves; bring out those Christians, and let us see the lions destroy them." A group of imprisoned Christians were led forth, and a number of half-starved lions turned loose among them. They were soon devoured, and the architect slowly arose, and in a firm though gentle voice said, "I, too, am a Christian." The howling mob seized him and flung him to the fierce beasts, who soon tore his limbs from his body.

This is confession, true and undefiled. It is easy enough to confess Christ before our own church and friends, but do we confess him among those that revile him? Do we go among men that despise his precepts, and by our very life tell of him? If we do not, we do not do our duty as his followers. The confession that pleases him is to "let our light so shine before men, that they will be led to glorify our Father which is in heaven."

"Whosoever shall deny me before men, him will I also deny before my Father."

"*Let us consider one another to provoke unto love, and to good works.*" — HEB. x. 24.

A man who was very sad, once heard two boys laughing, and asked them, "What makes you so happy?" "Happy," said the elder boy, "why, in making Jim glad, I get glad myself."

This is the true secret of a useful and happy life, to make others happy. To so direct our ways and aims that our example, our kind words, our pleasant smiles, and our sympathies, may fall on some one else and provoke him also to good works. To lead lost souls to the true happiness in Christ Jesus, and rejoice with them. To rescue from degradation, a fallen brother and rejoice with him in his new-found peace. There never was a truer saying than this, " He that makes others happy will himself not be unhappy." The magnetic key in Christ's journeyings in the world, " He went about doing good." Healing the sick, comforting the bereaved, opening the eyes of the blind, raising up the fallen, speaking peace to the distressed, guiding the seeker unto life eternal, giving the water of life to the thirsty. He loved the souls of men. Therefore "let us consider one another, to provoke unto love, and to good works."

How quickly a poor, fallen, degraded, sin-soiled soul, will melt under the influence of love. Convince him that with all his filth and sins, Christ loves his soul, and that you love his soul. My Christian friend, if you ever win a soul to Christ it will be through this word LOVE.

This is the flower from the Garden of God, and a flower that needs to be cultivated among Christians. Love made a full and free salvation, love redeemed you from eternal death, love will bear you over life's fitful sea and land you on the shores of the reality of heaven.

"Beloved let us love one another; for love is of God; and every one that loveth is born of God, and knoweth God," "and if God so loved us we ought also to love one another."

"*I will give unto him that is athirst, of the fountain of the water of life freely.*" — Rev. xxi. 6.

"A gentleman stopping at a noted watering-place, went one morning to one of the springs, for a draught of water. While there, a lady came also for a draught of the cooling, sparkling water; the aged Christian turned to her and asked her if she had ever drunk at the Great Fountain. The lady turned and walked away without answering the question. Not many months after, the gentleman was attending a meeting for religious conference and prayer; while there a request came for him to visit a lady in the town, who was dying. As he entered the dying lady's chamber, she fastened her eyes on him, and said with a smile, 'Do you recognize me?' The gentleman was forced to answer in the negative; when the lady said, 'Do you remember asking a lady last spring, if she had ever drunk at the Great Fountain?' 'Yes,' said the gentleman, 'I remember that.' 'Well, sir, I am that person. I thought at the time you were very rude, but your words rang in my ears and I was without peace or rest, until I found Christ; I now expect to soon pass to my Saviour. I wanted to encourage you by telling you, that under God you were instrumental in bringing me to Christ; be faithful to others as you have been to me.'"

There is a class of work which only a personal effort can accomplish. In this case, had not the godly man personally sown the seed of eternal life, the dying lady probably would have never been saved. Every converted man or woman, boy or girl, is a preacher, and bound by the ties of God's love to preach a personal Saviour, in a personal way, and urge a personal acceptance of him. This is a class of work the minister, the pastor, can never accomplish, and the responsibility rests on your shoulders and mine, dear reader.

"*Many shall come from the east and west, and shall sit down with Abraham, and Isaac, and Jacob, in the kingdom of Heaven.*" — MATT. viii. 11

Mrs. Stowe tells the following of a poor slave who was brought to this country and sold into a Christian family. One day she heard her mistress telling the children of Jesus, and said, "Me know him." The mistress asked in her surprise, "When did you know him?" "Fore me came here," was the reply, and she went on to tell her story, how years before, her husband and children were kidnapped, and torn from her humble home. For days she walked up and down the beach wringing her hands in grief; at last some one came to her and told her to kneel down and look up to the sky, and comfort would come to her broken heart. She did so, and peace came to her troubled soul. And when she heard the lady telling of Jesus, she knew it was he who so lovingly had taken away her burden.

It is our duty to sow the seeds of life eternal and trust God to so increase the growth, as seemeth good in his sight. The Christian who pointed this poor heathen to Christ probably never saw or heard of her again; but God, who will not let his word return unto him void, made it the power to win her to Christ.

What a glorious surprise awaits some of God's dear children, as the truth shall on that day be revealed, and the thanks of angelic hosts greet their ears as the means of bringing them to Christ. My brother, my sister, don't you want to be one of the number?

If so, spread the "glad tidings," make it the one theme of your life to confess Christ and tell of his love.

"*Now, therefore, go, and I will be with thy mouth, and teach thee what thou shalt say.*" — EXOD. iv. 12.

One afternoon Mr. Moody was being driven, by a Christian gentleman, to a town where he was to conduct revival services. They passed, on their way, a schoolhouse situated in the midst of a rich farming country; at the next farmhouse, Mr. Moody halted, and inquired of the lady if they ever held any religious meetings in the vicinity. She replied that they did not. Mr. Moody then said, "Tell everybody you see that there will be a prayer-meeting at the schoolhouse every night next week." The announcement was soon spread over the neighborhood. Mr. Moody's companion, knowing he had an engagement for every evening the following week, asked him who was to lead the meetings. "You are, sir," replied the great evangelist. — "I!" cried the astonished man. "I never did such a thing in my life." — "It is high time you commenced. I have made the appointment, and you must keep it." The timid man acquiesced, led the services, which resulted in a precious revival, and scores of souls were saved. My friend, we each have a work to do: how prone are we to shrink from duty. No man living could have taken the place of this Christian gentleman who stood in the Spirit before this people. No one living can do the work God says *you* must do; if you go to judgment with it undone, be sure an accounting will there be required for the talents entrusted to your keeping. I know what it is to be held back from duty by Satan. He is ever telling us, "Oh, you can't preach, or pray, or sing, or testify!" God will put words into our mouths, if we show a determination to preach Christ. "For I will give you a mouth and wisdom," and " I will give thee the opening of the mouth in the midst of them."

Dear reader, the word of God abounds in like promises; but to know their full meaning it is necessary that we first prove our desire for working for Christ before they will ever be made applicable to us.

"*Herein is our love made perfect.*" — 1 John iv. 17.

True love and childlike faith is beautifully illustrated by the following little incident: "A little girl, who loved her Saviour very much for having so loved her, came one day to her pastor with a dollar and a half for a missionary society. "How did you collect so much? Is it all your own?" asked the pastor. The little girl replied, "Yes, sir, I earned all of it." — "But how, Mary, did you do?" The child hung her head a moment in thought, and replied, "I thought how Jesus had suffered and died for me, and I wanted to do something for him. As I had no money, I earned this by collecting rain water, and selling it to a washerwoman at a penny a bucketful." — "I am thankful," said the pastor, "that your love for Christ has led you to labor so long and so earnestly for him." Friend, in just such deeds as this is our love made perfect. It is not necessary to do some great act in order to serve Christ. He will never despise any deeds, however small, provided we do them in the spirit of love; and in such a spirit only can our love be made perfect, and our service made acceptable unto him.

"*Tell them how great things the Lord hath done for thee.*"—MARK v. 19.

A young lady sat in her room one day reading her Bible, and came to these words: "Tell them what great things the Lord hath done for thee." The words rang in her ears, and refused to leave her, until she resolved she would speak to the first person she met on her way down town. Closing her book, she donned her wraps, and stepped into the street just as a young man, who was one of her particular friends, was passing. As they walked along together she tried hard to find courage to speak to him; but each time Satan would say, wait. When they came to the place of separation they lingered a moment, and she said, "George, I want to tell you about my friend,—one that has been so kind and good to me, and one whom you would enjoy to know, and whose influence you so much need." Her companion listened with unusual earnestness. "George, I want to see you under the care and influence of my Saviour. Won't you, now, just give up all, and take hold on him?"

The young man was deeply impressed, and promised to seriously meditate on such a step, at the same time informing his friend that he would leave town next day to be gone some time in the interest of his employer. The young lady passed on down the street to attend some business, thinking little more about the young man, until, a few days after, when a small note was handed her, bearing these words: "Mamie, I accepted your great Friend as my friend, too; am saved. Oh, how glad that you told me of him. Your friend, George." The words were written as he lay dying in a railroad wreck. O Christian brother, sister, how many unsaved that are daily going to perdition would be saved, if you and I would do our duty in telling them of Jesus, and of what great things he has done in saving us!

How many could be turned did we thrust the love of a crucified Lord in their pathway, and turn them heavenward.

"*Cast thy bread upon the waters : for thou shalt find it after many days.*" — ECL. xi. 1.

Some years ago a Christian lady making a missionary visit wrote these words, "The master is come and calleth for thee," upon a small slip of paper, and laid it upon the bookshelf of a poor family on whom she had called. Some time after her visit the mother was searching for something, when the slip of paper fell to the floor; she picked it up and read it, at the same time wondering where it came from.

Her son, a bright lad, in the bloom of youth, came in, and the mother handed the slip to him, telling him it had been found on the floor. The lad took it, and read, "The master is come, and calleth for thee." The call went direct to his heart. He found no rest until Christ came to him and took his burden away. He grew to manhood, embarked in mercantile pursuits, but louder and louder came the call, "The master is come, and calleth for thee." He disposed of his business, and became an earnest preacher of the gospel. One day the announcement was made that Mr. —— would preach at the village church on a certain Sabbath morning. The man of God chose for his text, "The master is come, and calleth for thee." The spirit came in great power. A gracious revival followed.

Among his hearers on that Sabbath morning was an aged lady to whose memory came the incident related, and who, years before, had laid the slip of paper upon the bookshelf, with an earnest prayer. Oh what exquisite joy must have come to the heart of that aged servant as the scene just related flashed over her mind. Trusting brother, sister, we may never know in this life, the result of our sowing. We may never see, this side of eternity, the ripening of our planting of heavenly fruits; but bear in mind that "The Lord thy God shall bless thee in thy works, and in all that thou puttest thine hand unto." And when we awake in Christ's glory there will be unfolded, to our now clouded vision, the unspeakable glory of a life of service for Christ.

> "Though scoffers ask, where is your gain?
> And mockers say your work is vain,
> Such scoffers die, and are forgot;
> Work done for God, it dieth not."

> "Press on, press on, nor doubt nor fear,
> From age to age, this voice shall cheer:
> Whate'er may die, and be forgot,
> Work done for God, it dieth not."

"The Lord God hath given me the tongue of the learned, that I should know how to speak a word in season to him that is weary." — Isa. l. 4.

It is said of Mr. John Vassar, that he could not be in the company of a man half an hour without trying to bring him to Christ.

On one occasion he visited a town, some distance from his home, to aid in a gospel meeting. As he and the pastor were walking from the station to the latter's residence, they passed a blacksmith shop on the way. "There," said the pastor, "is a scoffer, and one of the most wicked of men. I would be glad if you would talk

with him before you leave town." — " Dear man," said
Mr. Vassar, " I will go now. Where is the blacksmith ? "
The pastor led the way to the shop, and found the smith
very busy, and customers waiting to get work done. Mr.
Vassar walked direct to the smith, who left his work, and
listened very earnestly to the godly man's words ; in a
few moments they went behind the forge, and both knelt
down. The influence of Mr. Vassar so completely overcame the man that he yielded, and gave his heart to
Christ.

Dear reader, are you using the tongue God gave you in
speaking words of comfort to weary sin-sick souls ?

Oh, how oft do we hear Christians say, " I can't talk to
sinners." My friend, you can excuse yourself with men,
but " can'ts " do not count with God. He says, " I will
be thy mouth." Go, then, in the name of Christ, and the
words you shall speak will be as " good seed, sown in
good ground," bearing a precious harvest of fruit. Mr.
Vassar took God at his word, and his influence with sinners was wonderful. Can you find an excuse why your
life should not be such a living monument to the love of
Christ ? If not, then cast in thy sickle for the Lord.

*" And they that be wise shall shine as the brightness of
the firmament ; and they that turn many to righteousness,
as the stars for ever and ever."* — DAN. xii. 3.

" He that winneth souls is wise." — PROV. xi. 30.

" He that is wise winneth souls." — REV. VER.

There is a story of a despondent Christian who thought
his work a failure. One night, it is said, he had a dream ;
he dreamed that he was dead, and that angels came and
wafted him over the dark river to the city of God. There
he met an old friend ; and as they walked along the crystal

pavements together, he noticed every one turn suddenly, and look in the same direction. They saw, as the golden chariot rolled up, the blessed Jesus. When opposite them, he beckoned the friend to get into the chariot while he took the dreamer aside, and pointing afar off he asked him what he saw. The dreamer replied that his eyes rested upon what looked like the world from which he came. "And what else?" asked the Saviour. "I see further on, a great pit." "And what else?" asked his Lord. "I see great multitudes of men rushing hither and thither as if blindfolded. Many are falling into the awful pit, others are on the very brink." — "Well," said the Christ, "would you stay here in this haven of bliss, and see countless thousands fall headlong into that gaping abyss, and you not turn a hand to stop their mad career?"

The dreamer begged to be sent to warn them of their doom, and to make amends for his life of neglect.

Reader, such is a true picture, that is about you to-day. A gaping abyss, and countless thousands falling headlong into it.

What is your duty? Is it to sit with folded hands, or is it to throw the seeds of life in their pathway, and hinder all you can, their rapid progress? You cannot save all of them, but you may be the means of rescuing one, — yea two, — possibly many. "He that winneth souls is wise."

"*Go home to thy friends, and tell them how great things the Lord hath done for thee, and hath had compassion on thee.*" — MARK v. 19.

A gentleman of great wealth and social position, residing in one of the suburbs of London, was suddenly stricken down with a dangerous disease. The elegant and happy home was transformed into one of anxiety and mourning. The devoted wife, fearing the result of her idolized companion's illness, begged that a clergyman be summoned; but the husband rather abruptly replied, "No, send for our coachman." Anxious to gratify every wish, the coachman was hastily summoned, and soon stood at the bedside of his sick master. "John," said the sick man, "not long since I heard you, standing in a wagon, preach to a crowd of poor people. You did not see me, for I stood behind you, and heard every word you said. You told them how Christ had saved you, and that he was able and willing to save every one. I have sent for you, that you may prove out of the Bible the truth of your sermon." The coachman opened his Bible, and began to read of the great love of God in giving his Son to save mankind. He proved to his master what he had on a former occasion preached, and convinced him that we are not saved by doing, but by believing in the Lord Jesus Christ. The gentleman took God at his word, gave himself entirely into his hands, and ere many days was recovered, and began active service in leading souls to Christ. He went to an intimate friend, who yielded to the call, and gave his life to preaching the Word to dying souls.

Thus the coachman's testimony bore rich fruit. Then too, he started a wave of influence that has rolled on and on, and scores of souls found eternal life by his telling what great things the Lord had done for him. Oh! my Christian reader, are you telling the world what preciousness you have enjoyed by having your sins blotted out? Would to God we were more awakened to this important duty. Would to God, our hearts were more ablaze with the fire of his love, that we would tell those around us " what great things he hath done for us."

"Your labor is not in vain in the Lord."
1 Cor. xv. 58.

A gentleman, passing along the streets of one of our magnificent cities some years ago, held in his hand a small religious tract. His eye fell on a promising young man, standing beside the passageway, and as he passed by him, he handed him the tract, with the request he would carefully read it. The young man, for curiosity's sake, accepted the paper, and promised to do so. He sat down and read and re-read it, saw in himself a great sinner, and a heart as black as the blackest darkness. He resolved in his heart to seek Christ with all his soul. Peace soon dawned upon him, he rejoiced, and was glad, he forsook his old street-loafing habits, and devoted his life to preaching Christ to sinners. To-day he stands among the ablest and most earnest men in our country.

Christian brother, sister, let us never weary in our efforts in sowing the seeds of eternal life. We may never see the result of our labors until we reach heaven, and find this one, and that one pointing us out, and saying, He led me to Christ. Oh, what honor! as I stand in the sight and presence of the living God, to have some saved soul take me by the hand and say, You turned my feet from the ways of hell to heaven. But that is not all. Christ says, " Your labor shall be rewarded."

" Therefore, my beloved brethren, be ye steadfast, unmovable, always abounding in the work of the Lord, forasmuch as ye know that your labor is not in vain in the Lord." — 1 Cor. xv. 58.

The writer of these lines was standing on the street corner one evening about eight o'clock. It was a bitter cold night, the thermometer registered near 30° below zero. The bright, electric light, shining on the snow-covered surroundings made a picture not within the power of the artist to portray. As he stood there handing each passer-by a printed invitation to attend gospel services, held in the vicinity, a middle-aged man came rushing along, as if in search of something. As he reached forth his hand to take the paper handed him, he halted to read it, then asked where the room was in which the services convened. As the writer walked down the street with him, he said he had for some time past felt the need of a Saviour. His soul had been ill at ease. He longed for some servant of God to speak to him, but none came. He added, "At times I thought how careless Christians must be; then again I would think that the hereafter must be a myth; but my conscience said, 'No, it is real.'" He was lead to Christ, and to-day is a living witness to his saving grace.

Christian friend, we that profess Christ are too careless. We do not know the thoughts of those around us. May this illustration teach us to "watch" and to speak often to those with whom we come in contact, and to pay more attention to sowing the seeds of life eternal, and less to the results of the harvest.

"*I will speak of the glorious honor of thy majesty, and of thy wondrous works.*" — Ps. clxv. 5.

In a New England town, a gracious revival was in progress, and in order to invite many who did not attend the services, the Christians called a meeting to divide the town into districts, and assign each member a certain portion of the town, to personally invite every one to attend the services at the church. Among those that were appointed to "go out into the highways and hedges," was a poor, ignorant man, who felt he could not perform the task assigned him.

In his district lived a man noted for his wickedness and hatred of all religious objects. The missionary called at the home of this man and, to his great relief, found that he had gone to the field near by to attend to some work. He left, feeling greatly relieved, and congratulated himself that he had so easily escaped the taunts and abusive language of the man. But before he had gone far, his conscience smote him for his thoughts, and he turned to search for the man. Just then, he saw him coming toward him. He exchanged greetings, and in simple, earnest words, told him that he had come to extend to him a personal invitation to attend the meetings at the church, that many blessings had been bestowed upon them, and that they felt a deep interest in him, and that earnest prayers had ascended to the throne of grace in his behalf. As the man continued his simple, earnest pleadings, he noticed the reviler turn his face from him that his emotions might be hid; turning suddenly, he said, "I have wondered why some of you Christians did not come to see me. I have hoped and expected you; I am so glad you have come, I will go immediately and attend the meeting." He did go, and became a living witness to the saving power of Christ. My dear Christian reader, from this simple narrative may we not take new courage and let no opportunity pass, of speaking to some unsaved soul. God says, "I will not let my word return unto me void." Some of us say, "The way does not seem clear, I can't do it." My dear friend, God will gladly open the way for us if we make a start, but he never removes the obstruction until we come to it. The Red Sea was not opened until the Israelites came to its banks. God never leaves capital lying idle. If we poorly invest the few talents left us, he will withhold his treasury from us, but if we use what we have, he will abundantly supply us with all the capital that we can use. Let us then cease not to speak of "the glorious honor of his majesty," the unsearchable riches of his love, and the wondrous working of the Spirit in the heart.

"Let your light so shine before men, that they may see your good works, and glorify your Father which is in heaven." — MATT. v. 16.

While Mr. Moody was conducting revival services in London, several years ago, a well-known sporting character was led to Christ and became an earnest worker in saving souls. The converted man had two sons, whom he was educating in his wicked ways — their father's example led them to accept Christ, also a companion, who had been their bosom friend. The three young men gave themselves to the cause of Christ, and are to-day successful missionaries. The light of God shining through the father led the sons to devote their lives to glorifying God. Reader, how many have seen your godly life and are to-day rejoicing in Christ, while another bright star has been placed in your heavenly crown?

" The Lord seeth not as man seeth; for man looketh on the outward appearance, but the Lord looketh on the heart." — 1 SAM. xvi. 7.

A little shepherd boy was keeping his sheep one Sabbath morning. The church bells were pealing forth their summons to the house of worship. The lad saw people wending their way thither. The beauty of the sight overcame him, and, for the first time in his life, he felt it his duty to worship his Maker. But what could he say?

he had never learned any prayers; he had never knelt at a mother's knee. He knelt down on the green grass, and began repeating the alphabet from A to Z. A gentleman passing along the road was attracted by the boy's voice, and halted to listen. He heard the lad repeat over and over the alphabet. "What are you doing, my little man?" he asked. The boy looked up in surprise, and, in his childlike simplicity, said, "Please, sir, I was praying. I felt that I would like to pray, and I did not know anything to pray, so I prayed the A B C." How many professing Christians refuse to pray in public because they are afraid their words will not be so beautiful as their neighbors. Friend, take this text with you, and meditate upon it.

"*My word . . . shall not return unto me void.*"

Isa. lv. 11.

A Christian missionary was canvassing a sparsely settled district in one of our now prominent States. In a small receptacle he carried some little tracts with pointed texts printed thereon.

He called one day at a cabin by the roadside, but found its occupants absent. He drew from his pouch a tract, and passed it under the door. The family soon returned home, and the father stopped as he passed in, and picked up the tract. As a verse of Scripture met his eye, he became very wroth, and stamped and swore and raved like a madman. A little girl of the household begged him to let her have the paper, and that night she requested her father to read it to them, the others being unable to read. At first he refused, but, as it was a request from his favorite child, he finally complied with her wishes. When the family were gathered around the great log fire, the father read aloud of the love of God in giving his Son to suffer and die for us that we might be saved. The teachings of earlier days came to him: his thoughts ran back to the long ago; when, around his father's hearthstone, he had so often heard the very same story. The Spirit touched the poor father's heart, and Christ's mercy came as a flash of light, and settled on him. The next evening he read again the tract, and re-read it to his family, explaining in his plain, simple way. Then they knelt around the new altar, and he poured out his soul to God. Before many days he saw his entire household rejoicing in Christ, and living to honor God. We should never weary in telling souls of Christ's love. At times the outlook may seem dark, but God's word cannot return bearing no fruit. Let us sow daily some seed, and in the Master's own good time the harvest will ripen unto the salvation of some lost soul, and unto his own name, honor and glory.

"*Go thou and preach the kingdom of God.*"
LUKE ix. 60.

There is an old story of an Arab poet who was converted to Christianity. The missionary requested him to compose for him a poem on the duties of a Christian missionary. He wrote the following, which, when translated, reads, —

"Go on, go on, go on, go on,
Go on, go on, go on,
Go on, go on, go on, go on,
Go on, go on, go on."

It should be the motto of every Christian. As we see the thousands on our right and on our left fast going to destruction, it surely is time for us to "go on, go on," and "preach the kingdom of God."

CHAPTER IX.

PRAYER.

"PRAY WITHOUT CEASING."
1 THES. v. 17.

PRAYER.

"*Yea, I will sing aloud of thy mercy in the morning.*"
Ps. lix. 16.

It is said of King Alfred the Great that before he took up the daily cares of his kingdom, he spent some time alone in singing praises to God, and imploring divine guidance upon his daily life.

How much lighter would be the cares of every child of God if they would, as they rise in the morning, implore divine guidance, and seek the sleepless eye of God to follow them through the duties and busy scenes of life. How many crooked paths would never be made, if we only besought the guidance of him that never errs.

"*Pray that ye enter not into temptation.*"
LUKE. xxii. 40.

There is a custom among the Breton sailors, when launching their boats, to offer this prayer, "Keep me, my God; my boat is so small, and thy ocean is so wide."

The life of a Christian may be likened unto a frail bark cast upon the mighty ocean, which unless rightly steered may run into some contrary current that will toss it about and turn its course. In this great ocean of ungodliness, it is necessary to pray that the current of sin does not turn us from our course. "Pray that ye enter not into temptation," and if ye do, "call upon me in the day of trouble, and I will deliver thee," saith the Lord.

"*Pray without ceasing.*" — 1 Thes. v. 17.

Among the Japanese people there is a certain sect whose religion compels them, on rising each morning, to make some ejaculatory prayer, lifting up the fingers of the right hand. They imagine by this devout precaution they frustrate the wicked devices of the devil, and insure the guidance of their gods.

How appropriate at the early dawn to assemble, before our minds are engrossed with the cares of the day, and seek divine guidance of him whose eye is ever upon us; and plead for strength to frustrate Satan's devices. " Pray that ye enter not into temptation," Implore the light of Christ's presence to go before you each day and hour.

"*I had rather speak five words with my understanding, that by my voice I might teach others also, than ten thousand words in an unknown tongue.*" — 1 Cor. xiv. 19.

" It is related of the Buddhists that they write their prayers upon long, narrow slips of paper, and wind this around a cylinder. Each revolution of the cylinder counts for the repetition of all these prayers, so it is only necessary to occasionally give the machine a turn, and thereby secure the benefit of yards of prayers.

"Some, it is said, go so far as to apply to these prayer cylinders, water power, or other mechanical contrivances, and while they are busy with worldly matters, their devotional exercises are still going on."

How often are we led to doubt God when we do not see an immediate answer to our mechanical prayer. How very foolish would some of our prayers seem even to us could we read them as they have been repeated by us, in our half-earnest way. Christ says, " When thou prayest, enter into thy closet, and when thou hast shut the door (to exclude every worldly care and thought), pray to thy Father," etc.

"*The effectual fervent prayer of a righteous man availeth much.*" — JAS. v. 16.

We are told that Mary, Queen of Scotland, who desired to establish papacy in that country, once said, "I fear the prayers of John Knox more than an army of ten thousand men."

How carefully doth the Lord God guard his people. What mighty defences lie in righteousness and the favor of Jehovah; what sweet comfort in the thought that the selfsame God that closed the mouth of the lions and delivered Daniel — that hushed the flames and brought forth the Hebrew children — is *our* God. We may safely trust him at all times, and in all places.

"The effectual, fervent prayer of a righteous man availeth much. It penetrates the very heart of Jesus Christ, and moves his sympathetic hand to our aid.

"*The effectual fervent prayer of a righteous man availeth much.*" — JAS. v. 16.

Some years ago a minister was invited to hold revival services in a frontier neighborhood. On his arrival at the little cabin called a church, he met a company of Christian men and women praying for the outpouring of the Holy Spirit. The revival continued many days, and scores were brought to the fold of Christ. In the vicinity lived a young man, whose praying mother had daily begged him to attend the meeting, only to be ridiculed for her foolish entreaties. In order to escape the influence of the Christian community, he left the neighborhood, saying that he had to attend to some business in another village. Many were the earnest prayers offered for him. In a very short time he returned home to tell of his miserable condition of soul and body. The spirit had been striving with him, and he found no peace; he arranged to start the next day in an opposite direction, on the pretence of attending to some other business; in a day or two he again returned, even more miserable than before. He could no longer carry the burden of his guilt, and he resolved to find Christ and lay his load upon his strong shoulders; he attended the revival service, and asked the way of life. The glorious peace of a penitent's pardon came to him, and he became an earnest and an active worker in the master's cause. The prayers of the mother were answered even to a greater degree than she had anticipated.

How many pangs of heart over our children and loved ones would we be spared if we could but learn to go to God with our troubles, and pour out our souls in effectual fervent prayer for our loved ones. "The effectual fervent prayer of a righteous man availeth much."

"*Whatsoever ye shall ask the Father in my name, he will give it you.*" — Jno. xvi. 23.

Two little brothers in a western State, who had heard wonderful stories of Santa Claus, conceived the idea of making their wants known in a way as impressive as it is novel. Their mother had taught them that God was always ready to answer prayer. One afternoon, just before Christmas, their mother missed them from the sitting-room, and began to search for them. Before she had searched far, she was attracted by their voices to an adjoining room; silently opening the door, she paused to listen, only to be dumbfounded by seeing them on their knees, earnestly praying to their Heavenly Father to put it into the heart of Santa Claus to bring them each a new sled, a pair of skates, and some candy. When they awoke next morning, they sprang out of bed, to find the very toys they had prayed for.

When Christians learn to exercise this childlike faith in God, the answers to their prayers will be more marked and direct than they now are.

"*Evening and morning and at noon will I pray.*"
Ps. lv. 17.

It is said of Scipio Africanus, that each morning at the break of day he went into his chamber, and there remained a great while, advising with his gods concerning the duties of the day.

What a happy frame of mind must he possess who has learned to daily go to Christ, and there sweetly commune and ask his presence through the busy scenes of daily life.

"Cast your care upon him, for he careth for you."

"Lord, in the morning thou shalt hear
My voice ascending high,
To thee will I direct my prayer,
To thee lift up mine eye."

"*But thou, when thou prayest, enter into thy closet, and when thou hast shut thy door, pray.*" — MATT. vi. 6.

It is related of one of the lord treasurers of England, that when he undressed at night he would throw off his official robe and say, " Lie there, lord treasurer." As though he were bidding adieu to the pressing cares of his official station, that he might the more sweetly repose on his couch of rest. So with the Christian. To rightly worship God we should come before him with no thought of worldly cares, but rather enter into our closets and shut the door, thus barring out every thought of worldliness.

Oh! how many of us approach his majesty with one eye running over the scenes of this life while the other is looking upward. And how many of us go away empty-handed!

CHAPTER X.

CHARITY.

"THE GREATEST OF THESE IS CHARITY."

CHARITY.

"*I was sick and ye visited me, I was in prison and ye came unto me.*" — MATT. xxv. 36.

A gentleman on board a steamer saw late one evening an officer of the vessel go stealthily to a state-room and deposit something, and close the door. He suspected it a case of some dread disease. He went to the officers and pressed them for a true statement; at last they admitted that a priest on board had the yellow fever. The gentleman insisted on being shown to his room, where he found the poor man in great agony, and suffering for want of attention; he was tenderly cared for and recovered. Imagine the surprise of the gentleman when he found it to be a very dear friend of his boyhood days. Oh the glad surprise awaiting those to whom Jesus will say, "I was sick and ye visited me, I was in prison and ye came unto me." "Inasmuch as ye have done it unto one of these, my brethren, ye have done it unto me."

"*Do good to them that hate you.*" — MATT. v. 44.

Calvin said, when Luther had wronged and spoken evil of him, "Let Luther hate me, and call me evil names, yet will I love him and acknowledge him a precious servant of God."

Oh! that such a spirit would possess the hearts of

God's children to-day, and make our loyalty to Christ turn our enemies to shame.

How oft do we find the cause of Christ dishonored by the foolish words and acts of his professed followers toward one another.

Such things are Satan's seeds sown in our hearts, and if not choked out will ripen into our destruction.

"*The tongue is a fire, a world of iniquity.*"

Jas. iii. 6.

A poor, ignorant man came one day to a gentleman, noted for his learning, with the request that he would teach him a Psalm. The learned man turned to the thirty-ninth Psalm, and read, "I said I will take heed to my ways, that I sin not with my tongue."—"Hold!" cried the ignorant man, "that will do. I will first go and learn that."

After the lapse of several months, his teacher inquired when he would be ready to proceed with the reading. He answered, "I have not yet learned my old lesson."

Forty-nine years after, some one asked him the same question, and was answered as before.

"The tongue is a fire, a world of iniquity." A small member, yet no man can bridle it.

"*Let us not be desirous of vainglory, provoking one another, envying one another.*" — Gal. v. 26.

There is a Persian fable about a gourd which wound itself around a lofty palm, and in a very short time climbed to its very top.

"How old mayest thou be?" asked the vine of the palm. "About a hundred years," answered the palm. "A hundred years, and no taller? Only look! I have grown as tall as you in less than a hundred days." — "That may be very true," replied the lovely palm. " Every summer of my life a gourd has climbed around my body, as proud as thou art, and as short lived as thou wilt be." A very natural result of a proud, vainglorious spirit, short-lived and disastrously ended; but the humble are not so, for God protects them from the storms of temptation, and gives them grace to battle against the withering blasts of the evil one, while the proud wither, and droop under the pressure,

> Oh, Lord, the pride in me remove,
> My selfish will displace;
> Fill thou the vacancy with thy love
> Uphold me by thy grace.

"*Judge not, that ye be not judged.*" — MATT. vii. 1.

On board one of the east-bound trains out of Chicago was a young man dressed in the height of style, and supporting a very fine cane. He carefully brushed the dust from the seat he was to occupy, which chanced to be next to that occupied by a gentleman who at once concluded the young man possessed better clothes than brains. Just opposite to them sat a sad-faced and tired-looking woman holding in her arms a sick baby. The benevolent looking gentleman settled in his seat, and began reading his paper, while his young, well-dressed neighbor leaning over the aisle, said to the lady, "Madam, you look so tired, please let me care for your baby while you take a nap." The lady very kindly thanked him, and allowed him to take the babe from her arms. She told him her story. She had been to the far West to see her sick husband who died ere she reached him, and she was on her way home, without sufficient money to secure a berth in the sleeper. The young man insisted that she take a nap, which she did, and awoke feeling much better. The young man then went through the train telling the sad story of the lady, which touched the hearts of the passengers, who contributed quite liberally, and the lady was given a berth in the sleeper for the remainder of her journey, and was made quite comfortable. As the young man was leaving the train, the benevolent-looking old gentleman quoted the words, "Judge not, lest ye be judged."

Man looketh on the outward appearance, but God looketh at the heart.

"*Be not forgetful to entertain strangers: for thereby some have entertained angels unawares.*" — HEB. xiii. 2.

It is told of Bernard that when he saw a man dressed in fine apparel, he would say, "Maybe, this man, under his delicate clothes, has a better soul than I have."

Or when he met a man, in mean apparel, he would say, "It may be true that this unfortunate man in his mean attire has a soul more pure than I," showing what great charity the man had for his fellow-man.

"*He that will love life and see good days, let him refrain his tongue from evil, and his lips that they speak no guile.*" — 1 PET. iii. 10.

"A young Mohammedan was accustomed to wake at certain intervals during the night to say his prayers. He took great pride in letting others know how devoted he was to his religion. On one occasion he called his father's attention to his religious life, and referred to his brothers and sisters sound asleep. 'My son,' said the father, "you had far better be asleep than to lay awake to find fault with others.'"

An excellent rule, and one by which we each can profit: its application is this, to refrain from speaking at all of a person unless we have something good to say of him. How frequently do careless words fall from our lips that cause our fellow-man much hurt.

"*Be ye all of one mind, having compassion one of another: Love as brethren, be pitiful, be courteous.*"

1 PET. iii. 8.

Years ago a young lady took a drive in a beautiful park. On her way something occurred that irritated her. She left the carriage, and sat down by the river bank, hoping no one would appear to disturb her. Presently a man stood before her; his clothes were of fine material, though badly worn and very ragged. His manner at once told that he was not a common tramp; he asked the young lady if she could give him any work to do that he might earn a little money to buy some food. "What work could I have for you," she said. The man turned and walked away. When the young lady arose and walked to her carriage, she again met the man, who said, "I am very wretched; if you would use your influence, you could get me some work." The young lady made no reply, but entered her carriage, and was driven home. Next morning, as she glanced over the paper, her eyes fell on the account of a man being found in the river; his struggle with ill health and poverty unmanned him, and he sought relief in death. He had appealed the day before to every person he met for work. "Alas, and his last appeal was to me," said the young lady. "And I refused to aid him." Fifty years later, the face of that man came to the now old woman, as she lay on her bed, and seemed to condemn her for her lack of charity. "Inasmuch as ye did it not to one of the least of these, my brethren, ye did it not to me."

"*There is no fear in love.*" — 1 Jno. iv. 18.

I remember when I was a very little boy, my elder brother told me, in a simple, childlike way, about heaven and hell. The impression made on my childish heart can never be blotted out.

He told me, in his boyish manner, the final abode of the good and the bad. I resolved I would escape the awful doom of the wicked.

When I grew to the estate of manhood, and more fully understood the great love of God, this awful fear partially left me, and now I try to serve Christ not because hell's torments haunt me, but because I love him for making the escape from those torments so easy. "Perfect love casteth out fear." Reader, why are you striving to live for Christ?

"*Follow peace with all men, and holiness, without which no man shall see the Lord.*" — Heb. xii. 14.

Mr. R. W. Dale says, "God has no ultimate use for a man that is not holy. A rose-tree that does not blossom is of no use in a garden. A vine that bears no grapes is of no use in a vineyard. A criminal has no place in the State. In that everlasting kingdom in which the glory of God and the perfection of man will be at last revealed, there can be no place for those that have not an intense passion for holiness, and who do not themselves illustrate its dignity and beauty."

How blest the man whose love for God enables his

steps to tread the path of righteousness, and whose heart constantly yearns for the fulness of Christ, and whose soul delights in the holiness of his Saviour; and whose constant walk is in the footsteps of Christ our Lord.

"*Let us not be desirous of vainglory, provoking one another, envying one another.*" — GAL. v. 26.

There is in Grecian literature a story of a man who through envy took his own life.

His countrymen had reared a magnificent monument to the victor in the public games. So strong was this rival's envy that he went forth in the stillness of the midnight hour to destroy the monument. He succeeded in moving it from its pedestal, but alas! in its fall, it crushed him to death. How vividly this incident illustrates the effects of envy in the human heart; while seeking to drag others down, our sins fall on us, and crush our own souls.

"*Naked and ye clothed me.*" — MATT. xxv. 36.

St. Martin one day met a poor, ill-clad beggar by the roadside, shivering with cold. He took off his long, heavy cloak, and threw it over the shoulders of the unfortunate sufferer. That night he dreamed that the adorable Lord stood beside his couch, wearing his cloak that he had given the poor man. "As oft as ye did it unto the least of these, my brethren, ye did it unto me."

How many of us can profit by this lesson on charity. One duty the Christian world may improve in, and that is charity toward our fellow-man; — charity for those less fortunate than ourselves; — charity for the unsaved, with whom we come in daily contact. Christ's rule was to win by love. Love should be our motto. How many poor unfortunate souls in distress we could win to Christ by showing them that we love their souls. Oh, my soul, beget within thee a deeper love and a more charitable spirit.

> I need, O Lord! more of thy love,
> For souls that are lost in sin;
> Come, Holy Spirit, from above,
> Open my heart and enter in.

"*Be kindly affectioned one to another.*" — Rom. xii. 10.

Jerome relates of John that when he became old he used to go among the churches and assemblies, and every where repeat the words, "Little children love one another." His disciples, wearied at the constant repetition, asked him why he always said this. "Because," he replied, "it is the Lord's commandment; and if it only be fulfilled, it is enough."

Oh what a sweeping power the army of Christians would have if they would only exercise more love, more charity, for the fallen that are around them.

Let us remember if we win a lost soul, it must be by our love operating with the boundless love of God which melts their hearts.

"*Who is like unto thee, O Lord, among the Gods? who is like unto thee, glorious in holiness, fearful in praises, doing wonders.*" — Exod. xv. 11.

So great was the love and respect of the heathen Egyptians toward their gods, that they often resorted to the most extreme measures rather than cast the least dishonor upon one of them.

During an extreme famine it is said that they ate one another rather than eat such animals as they held to be sacred. Diodorus Siculus relates, as an eyewitness, an incident in which a Roman soldier at Alexandria killed a cat, — an unpardonable offence, punishable with death, — the populace surrounded his house, took him, and subjected him to the most terrible torture, and only released him when death ended his pain. Such was the admiration of the heathen for his dumb god.

But, "Who is like unto Thee, O Lord, among the gods." Certainly this story of the Egyptian heathen can teach us a lesson. We, who ofttimes shun our duty ; — we, who by nature abhor the holiness, purity, and love of our true and everlasting Creator and God, and admire not his ways and precepts ; — we, who are ignorant of the glory of His holiness, and the wonder of his power, — can learn from this simple illustration a more complete sense of the holiness, and a more devout reverence for the God of Gods.

"*But if ye do not forgive, neither will your Father which is in heaven forgive your trespasses.*"—MARK xi. 26.

An old woman was going along the streets of New York one day, carrying a basket of apples. A rough sailor ran against her, and caused the basket to upset, and scatter the apples on the ground. The sailor then turned, expecting to hear the old woman scold and swear at him ; but she picked up her apples, and turning to the sailor said, "God forgive you, my son, as I do." The words pierced the sailor's heart, and he insisted on the old woman taking pay for his mean trick, promising never again to do such a mean act.

Sometimes it is hard to overcome our human nature, and forgive our enemies, but it is not an impossibility.

If Christ is the sole ruler of the heart, we cannot harbor any such feelings toward our fellow-man. We are also commanded to " pray for them that despitefully use us," and whenever we are living in this spirit we have evidence that we are not far from a precious nearness to Christ.

" I shall be satisfied when I awake with thy likeness."
Ps. xvii. 15.

One cold New Year's morning, a Christian lady took a little street waif to her house, and cared for, clothed, and fed her; as the lady was busily engaged, in attending the wants of many other unfortunate ones, she noticed this little girl intently watching her every movement. After the good lady had made her little guests comfortable, she asked each one of the company to tell her what they most desired above everything else.

One wished for this, one for that, one for certain toys, one for wealth, one for a nice home. When this little girl's time came to express her wish, she looked up in the sweet face of her benefactor, and in her childlike earnestness, said, " Of all things I most wish that I was just like this kind lady who has taken us, and been so kind to us as to give up her own pleasure to-day, in order to make us happy."

What an inspiring thought it is to know that some day we shall awake in the likeness of Christ, and be clothed with his righteousness.

CHAPTER XI.

THE CHRISTIAN'S REWARD.

"THY WORK SHALL BE REWARDED."
JERE. xxi. 16.

THE CHRISTIAN'S REWARD.

"In my Father's house are many mansions."
JNO. xiv. 2.

A gentleman erected an elegant dwelling, and moved from his old one to the new.

As he was showing his little son through the magnificent apartments, the little fellow would exclaim, as he passed from one room to another, "Is this our's?" and "Is this our's?" The contrast made a lasting impression on his little mind.

So will it be when we get to heaven. As our Saviour acquaints us with the exquisite grandeur of our eternal home, and points out the riches of God's love in giving us so happy an abode, what a contrast, too grand for our uneducated eyes to behold, too sublime for the highest conception of our minds to comprehend. Yet, reader, such is the abode of the blood-washed soul; such is the everlasting habitation of the soul, made pure in the cleansing fount of Christ's blood. Will it surprise you if you should cry out in your amazement, "Is it ours? Is it ours?" To this end our adorable Lord has now gone to prepare a place for you and me, that where he is, we may be also.

In anticipation of this grand and eternal haven of rest, and whilst we await the coming of the angelic messengers to summon us to that peaceful repose, is it not our duty to set the feet of some fellow-traveller in the same path? Is it not our privilege to turn our efforts toward those around us, and lead them also to such an inheritance?

"*Thy work shall be rewarded.*" — Jer. xxxi. 16.

A few years ago, a gentleman was stopping for a few days at a fashionable watering-place. Early one morning, as he was strolling along the beach, he heard a cry of distress, followed quickly by calls for help. He hastily turned in the direction of the call, and saw a young lady being carried by the tide into deep water; he rushed in to her rescue, and reached her just as she was sinking for the last time, and bore her safely to shore. Some years later he received a letter with a draft for five thousand dollars, and stating that the lady whom he had rescued had died, leaving him that amount. So it is with God's servants; we have his unerring word that our "labors shall not be in vain," and we know that at some time — it may not be this side of eternity, but some time — we shall receive our reward. Whether our lives have been good or bad, God has in store for us a reward.

"*Woe unto them that call evil good, and good evil; that put darkness for light, and light for darkness; that put bitter for sweet, and sweet for bitter!*"

"*Woe unto them that are wise in their own eyes, and prudent in their own sight!*" — Isa. v. 20, 21.

"Some years ago there was shown to us a sheet of blank paper, the centre of which was perforated by a maze of pin pricks, apparently without order or design. But when the paper was held up against the light, there appeared, outlined on the opposite wall, the head of

Christ encircled by the crown of thorns. There are certain scientific critics to-day who try to make the Old Testament only a very ill-arranged collection of tradition and prophecy, with here and there a historical fact thrown in. Yet, held up against the light of the cross, this same Old Testament reveals the gradual unfolding of God's plan of salvation, and distinctly foreshadows the Saviour."

"*There remaineth therefore a rest to the people of God.*"
Heb. iv. 9.

There is a pass in Scotland, called Glencoe, which supplies a beautiful illustration of what heaven will be to the man who comes to Christ. The road through Glencoe takes the traveller up a long and steep ascent, with many a wind and turn in its course. But when the top of the pass is reached, a stone is seen by the wayside, with these simple words engraved upon it, " Rest and be thankful." — Ryle.

Rest! rest! what a wonderful word. How it should cheer our poor, aching, weary, careworn, longing, bleeding, sorrowful, tempted, doubting, bereaved hearts, and stir up our very souls within us as we realize that "There remaineth, therefore, *A REST* to the people of God." A rest where the weary and heavy-laden may lay aside his cares and sit down in the joys of his Lord. A rest in which the whole renovated creation shall share. An eternal sabbath of sweet repose, where the Triune God shall rejoice in the work of his hand. A rest where the redeemed of Christ shall, and in one grand concert, sing a new song to " Him that sitteth on the throne, and unto the Lamb that was slain, and has redeemed us to God by his blood."

Oh! cast-down soul, is not the anticipation of this enough to cause thee to beget new courage, and patiently run the race "set before thee, looking unto Jesus, the author and finisher of thy faith," and the giver of this unending period of felicity? Oh, cold and slothful soul, is not the expectation of this rest sufficient to stir within thee a desire to take up thy cross and closely follow him who died for thee, and hast gone to prepare a rest to him that overcometh? Oh, sorrowing and bereaved heart, is not thy burden too great for thee to longer bear? Lay it on him who bids you enter into the rest prepared for them that love God. Oh, unsaved soul, is not the load of thy sins becoming too heavy? Then cast thy burden on Jesus Christ, who bids you come unto him, and he will give you rest.

CHAPTER XII.

THE BIBLE.

"FOR THE WORD OF GOD IS QUICK AND POWERFUL."
HEB. iv. 12

THE BIBLE.

"I rejoice at thy word, as one that findeth great spoil."
Ps. cxix. 162.

A certain prince became affianced to a lovely princess to whom he sent a very magnificent gift, as a token of his affection. The messenger arrived with the present, which proved to be an iron egg. The princess became very angry, and cast it upon the floor. Upon a second thought she took it, and began to more closely examine it, when, by accident, she touched a spring which caused the outer casing to part, revealing an egg of brass. She touched the spring to this, and it fell to the floor, leaving in her hand an egg of silver, which when opened, disclosed an egg of gold that soon swung open, and a magnificent diamond of rare beauty and value fell in her lap. Each time she looked at it, pleasant memories of the donor came to her, and each time she examined the at first uninteresting gift, she found hid within, a rarer gem. And so it is with the word of God, the world picks it up, and glances at it with the natural eye, and again casts it aside as dry and uninteresting.

When the Holy Spirit touches the heart, the outer casing falls away, and the convicted soul finds his own life pictured in a manner too unmistakably plain to doubt, and when the scenes drive the soul to the Fount for sin, then the silvery lining appears, and when Christ lifts the great load from the heart then the golden jewels sparkle on every page until earthly scenes are no more, and the rare pearls of the precious promises bear on wings of triumph the trusting spirit to the presence of Him who is the Father of all spirits. Therefore, " I rejoice at thy word, as one that findeth great spoil."

"*For the word of God is quick and powerful.*"
HEB. iv. 12.

A gentleman passing along the street halted in front of an Italian woman's fruit stand, whom he found busily engaged in reading a book, —

"What are you reading there, my good woman, that so interests you?" inquired the man. — "The word of God," replied the woman. — "The word of God? Who told you that?" said the man. — "God told me himself." she answered. — "God told you? How did He do that? Have you ever talked with God? How did He tell you that was His word?"

Not accustomed to discuss questions of theology, the woman was a little confused. Recovering herself, she said, "Sir, can you prove to me that there is a sun up there in heaven?" — "Prove it," said the man, "Why do you ask me to prove it, it proves itself. It warms me, and I see its light. What better proof can any one want?" The woman smiled, and said, "Just so, you are right; and that is just the way God tells this book is His word. I read it, and it warms me, and gives me light. I see Him in it, and what it says is light and warmth which none but God can give; and so he tells me it is His word. What more proof do I need?" — *Dr. Jos. A. Seiss.*

The Scriptures have two sides. A side that the world may read and profit thereby, and a side that none but the trusting, praying child of God can realize.

Oh the sweet consolation afforded the child of God as the Holy Spirit unfolds the riches of the promises and the beauties of precepts of which the world cannot know.

"*Now ye are clean through the word which I have spoken unto you.*" — JNO. XV. 3.

Bishop Hopkins said, "I have somewhere read a story of one who complained to an aged holy man, that he was much discouraged from reading the Scriptures because he could fasten nothing in his memory that he had read. The old man bade him take an earthen pitcher, and fill it with water; when he had done so, he bade him empty it again, and wipe it clean, that nothing should remain in it; which, when the other had done, and wondered to what this tended. "Now," said he, "though there be nothing of the water remaining in it, yet the pitcher is cleaner than it was before." — "For the word of God is sharper, and more powerful than any two-edged sword, opening the eyes of the spiritually blind, and unstopping the ears of the spiritually deaf, making wise the simple, and strengthening the weak, and is the power of God unto salvation." For "the words of the Lord are pure words." "Given by inspiration of God, and profitable for doctrine, for reproof, for correction, for instruction in righteousness." Therefore, dear reader, " Let the word of Christ dwell in you richly in all wisdom; teaching and admonishing one another in psalms and hymns and spiritual songs, singing with grace in your hearts to the Lord." "Finally, my brethren, be strong in the Lord, and in the power of his might. Put on the whole armor of God, that ye may be able to stand against the wiles of the devil, and take the helmet of salvation, and the sword of the spirit, which is the word of God."

"*Therefore, shall ye lay up these my words in your heart and in your soul . . . . and ye shall teach them your children, speaking of them when thou sittest in thine house, and when thou walkest by the way, when thou liest down, and when thou risest up.*" — DEUT. xi. 18, 19.

Says one, "We ought not to measure, censure, and understand the Scriptures according to our own natural sense and reason, but we ought diligently by prayer to meditate therein."

The devil is a skilful interpreter of Scripture. He has multitudes to-day under his tutorship, and leading them gradually down, down, under the hellish guise of morality, liberalism, etc. My friend, the Holy Ghost should be our master, our guide, and our interpreter.

"*Search the Scriptures, for in them ye think ye have eternal life.*" — JNO. v. 39.

God always through his word instructeth the heart, to the end that it may come to the serious acknowledgment of itself, and to know how wicked it is, and spoiled; yea, that it is at enmity with God. Afterwards God leadeth a man so far, that he cometh also to the knowledge of God, and how he may be freed from sin, and after this miserable, vanquishing world, how he may obtain a life that is everlasting. On the contrary, human sense and reason are, with all their wisdom, only able to bring it no farther than to instruct and direct people how to live a civil kind of life. But how they should learn to know God and his dear son Jesus Christ, and to be saved, the same teacheth the Holy Ghost only, through God's word; for philosophy understandeth nothing of divine matters. — *Martin Luther.*

"*Take the helmet of salvation, and the sword of the spirit, which is the word of God.*" — EPH. vi. 17.

A gentleman who has made the fowl tribe a study tells us that the crane, whose body is light, is unable to resist the storms at sea, and that when it intends taking a journey over the salty waves, it first goes and fills itself with sand and small pebbles until its body has weight sufficient to enable it to keep its course in the raging storm.

So should it be with the young Christian. Before he attempts to walk alone, he should fill himself with the "sincere milk of the word," which gives him weight and strength to "withstand the wiles of the devil," who can make no inroads upon those who resist him with the "sword of the spirit, which is the word of God."

"*For the word of God is quick and powerful, and sharper than any two-edged sword, piercing even to the dividing assunder of soul and spirit, etc.*"
HEB. iv. 12.

A Romanist promised a Christian missionary to read the Bible to his wife one hour each evening. Before many evenings he turned to his companion and said, "Wife, if this book is true, we are wrong." A few evenings later he again turned to his wife, and said, "Wife, if this book is true, we are lost." A little later he, for the third time, addressed his wife, and said, "Wife, if this book is true, we may be saved." After the lapse of several evenings, he turned the fourth time to his anxious wife and said, "Wife, if this book is true, and, thank God, it is, we are saved." And both found new joy, such as they had never known, in Christ. How many families in our very midst that have no Bibles, and how many might be led to Christ if we would awaken to our duty, and supply such a need.

"*I will be with thy mouth, and teach thee what thou shalt say.*" — Ex. iv. 12

A man went to an attorney to secure his services in defending him at the bar of justice for some misdemeanor charged against him. The attorney bade him state his case just as it was, to confide in him, and give the details of the case.

The man did so. "And now," said the attorney, handing his client a piece of paper closely written, "take this and carefully memorize it so thoroughly that any amount of cross-questioning will not make you forget it. When you come to trial, don't you try to make your own defence, but answer just as I have written on that paper."

How easily could we silence the argument of unbelievers if we only rightfully studied God's word. If we only would answer as it is written. Take no care what we shall say, but speak in the spirit of God.

"*We are journeying unto the place of which the Lord said, I will give it you; come thou with us, and we will do thee good.*" — Num. x. 29.

A gentleman, becoming desirous of changing his place of residence in the east for a western home, wrote to a number of prominent men at the place to which he had decided to emigrate, for full particulars as to the climate, soil, cost of living, the amount of wages, school, church, and social privileges. In reply to his numerous questions, he received a large number of printed pamphlets, telling all about the country. The gentleman read them eagerly, and studied every detail, for, said he, "This is a matter of great importance to me. I am going to make it my home, and before I fully decide, I want to know to what sort of a place I am going." Beloved friend, you are soon to leave this world and take up your abode in another, why plunge along in your blindness? The Bible minutely describes the country to which you are going. Oh, that each of us would take new hold upon the blessed Book, and seek to gain an insight to its precious truths.

"*For the word of God is quick and powerful, and sharper than any two-edged sword, piercing even to the dividing asunder of soul and spirit.*" — HEB. iv. 12.

In the office of an eminent lawyer sat a young student absorbed in the study of law, by which he hoped some day to gain a great reputation. As he sat poring over some knotty point, his eye rested upon a Bible that lay on the table. He paused; a still, small voice whispered to him, "What if that Book is the word of God? It may not be, but suppose it is, what then?" He took that book from its resting-place, and began to read it. The more he read, the more he became interested, until the duty of asking God for the illumination of the Holy Spirit came to him for the first time in his life; he went to his closet and communed with Christ. The love of God was revealed to him; he consecrated his life to the service of his master, and became a shining light by simply reading the Bible. The sharp edges of the precious gems therein, severed the ties of worldliness, and freed him from the bondage of satanic ambition, filling him with the love of his Saviour, instilling into his heart a desire to tell others of the "pearl of great price" that he had found. Oh! that we each more fully realized the importance of a knowledge of the word of God. Oh! that we were better acquainted with the promises, the warnings, the invitations, and the commands therein given.

"*Search the Scriptures.*" — John v. 39.

Luther said of the blessed Word of God that "the holy Scripture is the best and purest book — truly of God, full of comfort in all manner of trials and temptations; for it teacheth of faith, hope, and love far otherwise than by human reason and understanding can be comprehended. And in times of trouble and vexations it teacheth how these virtues should light and shine; it teacheth also that after this poor miserable life, there is another which is eternal and everlasting."

The books of the heathen teach nothing of faith, hope, and love; neither knew they anything of the same. Their books aim only at the present, while of trust in God and hope in Christ nothing is written there of him.

PART II.

CHAPTER XIII.

GOD'S LOVE TO MAN.

"FOR GOD SO LOVED THE WORLD THAT HE GAVE HIS ONLY BEGOTTEN SON, THAT WHOSOEVER BELIEVETH IN HIM SHOULD NOT PERISH BUT HAVE EVERLASTING LIFE."
JOHN iii. 16.

GOD'S LOVE TO MAN.

"*For God so loved the world that he gave his only begotten son, that whosoever believeth in him should not perish, but have everlasting life.*" — JNO. iii. 16.

Mr. Moody says as he was passing along the street in Brooklyn one day he met a young man without any arms. A friend pointed him out, and told his history. When the war broke out he enlisted in the army; he was engaged to be married to a very estimable lady; while absent, letters frequently passed between them. After a great battle, the usual letters failed to reach the lady. A painful silence followed. One day a letter came, addressed in a strange handwriting. The young man said he had been badly wounded in the battle, and that he would never be able to gain a support for her whom he loved more dearly than ever, but he released her of her promise to him, not caring to have her share the lifelong misery in store for him. The next train that left the town the young lady was aboard, bound for the hospital where her lover lay wounded; gaining permission, she hurried down the long aisles, amid suffering and distress, to where her lover's couch was; throwing her arms about his neck, she declared she would never forsake him." Her love was so strong and so true, she could not forsake him, and his pitiable condition even made that love more tender. Such an act of love touches a cord in our own hearts, and causes us to almost love her too. But, friends, this is only a shadow of the love God has toward the vilest sinner; he gave up his only son to suffer the most shameful as well as painful death because his love for you and I was so strong that he could not see us rush headlong into eternal death. He so tenderly loved you and I, that he gave his only begotten son to save us, saying, "believe," — "believe." Do you believe?

"*On him they laid the cross.*" — LUKE xxiii. 26.

It is said that when the Scottish chieftains wished to raise an army, they would take a wooden cross and set fire to it and carry it through the mountains, where thousands of brave men would flock to the standard, ready to die for their country.

When God in his infinite love wanted to redeem a fallen world, He gave his only begotten Son, on whom wicked hands laid the cross, and who was nailed thereon that the human family might flock to the standard of redemption, and escape the hurling darts of the enemy.

It is this cross, my gentle reader, that I bring before you to-day. It is this cross that every true child of God carries through the world, ablaze with the love of God. May you be led to it, and to the saving power of him whose life went out thereon.

"*Greater love hath no man than this, that a man lay down his life for his friends.*" — JNO. xv. 13.

Napoleon, in exile at St. Helena, said to Montholon, "Alexander, Cæsar, Charlemagne, and myself founded great empires, but upon force; Jesus Christ alone founded his empire upon *love*, and to-day millions would die for him; none else is like him."

The motive that prompted Napoleon, Alexander, Cæsar,

and others to found great empires was the love of fame, notoriety, and selfishness. The motive that prompted Christ to leave his heavenly throne, and suffer self-abasement was *true unselfish love* toward a lost and fallen world.

It was love that enabled him to bear the taunts and sneers of sinful men; — it was love that made him take on himself human pains and woes; — it was love that made him the actor in the scenes of Gethsemane and Calvary; — it was true, unbounded, unselfish love that prompted his sojourn for thirty-three years in a world of sin, sorrow, and pain, in order that sinful man might be delivered from the eternal condemnation of his fallen state, and elevated to sonship, and made heir with himself of God's kingdom.

Friendly reader, for you he underwent all this; — for you he died, arose, and ascended to the Father, where he now pleads your cause. To you he sends the invitation to come unto him, and be saved, —

" Come without money and without price, and whosoever will, let him come."

"*Herein is love.*" — 1 Jno. iv. 10.

After Joan of Arc had won the great victory at Orleans, and made clear the way for Charles the Seventh to be crowned king, she was taken prisoner, and subjected to the most brutal treatment at the hands of her enemies; still her ungrateful king refused to make a single move to liberate the one who had freed his subjects, and made him heir and king.

My unsaved friend, you are doing the same thing. As you read the simple narrative, you doubtless will say, " King Charles was ungrateful, and deserved punishment." Yet Jesus Christ left his heavenly home, came down to earth, suffered, and died that you might be crowned the "child of a king," and you refuse to even acknowledge him. Should the anger of God consume you, could you say aught in your defence?

"God so loved the world that he gave his only begotten son, that whosoever believeth should not perish but have everlasting life."

"*Who gave himself for us, that he might redeem us.*"
TITUS ii. 14.

On board a great vessel, loaded with passengers, was a mother and little son; when well out to sea, and during what promised to be a pleasant voyage, a sudden cry of "fire" was heard. The captain remembered that he had on board a quantity of gunpowder, and at once ordered the lifeboats lowered, and began to clear the burning vessel of her precious cargo. The last boat was being filled; it became evident that there was not room for all. As it moved slowly away, a lady, with her little boy, came running to the side of the ship, and imploring them to take herself and boy. Her entreaties finally moved the inmates of the boat, and they decided to go back to the burning ship and take them; when they began rearranging the passengers, it was found that, at most, the boat would carry but one more. Without hesitation, the weeping mother pressed her child to her bosom, and planted on his cheek a farewell kiss, lowered him into the lifeboat, and sank back to meet her fate. She died to give life to one she loved. Reader, Christ has died that you might have a place in the boat of eternal life. Though it cost him sorrow and shame, suffering and death, yet shrunk he not. Does reason teach you that it is your duty to keep on in sin, and continue in the broad road to destruction? Or do you see it your duty to give your heart to him who gave himself for us, that he might redeem us to God and life eternal. God asks nothing unreasonable of you. He only requires you to give to him your puny, weak, and sin-stained heart, and he even returns that, after he has washed and purified it.

"God so loved the world that he gave his only begotten son, that whosoever believeth in him should not perish, but have everlasting life."

"*Herein is love.*" — 1 Jno. iv. 10.

Not long ago Thomas Canfield, a lad of seventeen, was crossing Broadway Bridge, Boston, when he saw a boy, younger than himself, fall into the water. Without halting to see if he would be rescued, the brave lad sprung from the bridge into the water, forty feet below, and, at the imminent risk of his own life, saved the drowning boy. The question may be asked what prompted him to run this great risk to rescue a boy whom he did not know, or probably had never seen before? I answer by saying it was *unselfish love*. And so it was with God, who so loved the world that he gave his only begotten son, that poor, lost, suffering humanity might be rescued from the mad waves of sin, and restored to the favor of Jehovah. We wonder and applaud the unselfish love of brave Thomas Canfield, but what a love it was that prompted Christ to leave his kingly throne in heaven and come to a world full of sin, sorrow, and pain, to rescue a race who were his avowed enemies. How vain are the attempts of human speech to describe this love! What can I say more than to say to *you*, my reader, that this love was for *you*. Can you, with a clear conscience, go on in your sinful course?

Can you, in view of this great fact, afford to longer trample this love under foot? I simply leave you here to answer the question before your God.

"*Come now, and let us reason together, saith the Lord.*"
Isa. i. 18.

"An aged minister, now at rest, related the following incident, that came to his notice while laboring in the State of New York. One of his church members, a farmer, in comfortable financial circumstances, had three sons, the younger of whom he was very proud, and upon whom he had expended various sums to satisfy his boyish whims.

"This son soon showed a desire to rid himself of parental restraint, and to do as best pleased himself. One day the aged father called him into his room, and, after recalling the very many instances in which he had bestowed upon him especial favors, requested that he change his course, and fulfil the long-cherished expectations of his anxious parents. To this very just and reasonable request, the ungrateful son refused to listen, and declared he would be compelled to no longer follow his parent's desires, reasonable as he knew them to be. At this the tottering father walked to the door; opening it wide, he said, 'My son, here is the door, and before you is the wide world. Go and forget the father whom you have so illy treated, and I, if I can, will forget my ungrateful son.' The son instantly saw he was not compelled to remain at home. A change came over him, and he rushed into the open arms of his father, and implored forgiveness."

So God does not compel us to accept the conditions of salvation. True, he longs to see us come to him, but, my friend, if your soul and mine is lost, heaven will be as real as ever; our absence from the angelic throng will not lessen the glory of that throng. We are not compelled to go to heaven, and if we miss it, it is our own fault. God is under no obligation to make any especial effort to save us. Let us cease to think he cannot get along without us; such ideas are misleading. But let us come to Christ, and give him our hearts, because he so loved us as to give himself for us.

"*Greater love hath no man than this.*" — Jno. xv. 13.

"In a small village lived a blacksmith. One bright morning the people had assembled at the house of worship, and in the midst of the services the cry of 'mad dog! mad dog!' was raised. Women and children began to scream and climb over one another in seeking a place of safety. Men stood in fear as the great shaggy animal walked down the aisle, frothing at the mouth, and snapping right and left at imaginary objects. The great, stout blacksmith bade all be quiet, and seizing the mad animal held him with an iron-like grasp, at the same time telling his friends to disperse while he held the object of their dread. When they had gotten outside the church, men came to his assistance, and killed the dog; not however, until he had terribly lacerated the arms of the poor smith. When the excitement had subsided he went to his shop, and made a great iron chain, and riveted it around his arms and limbs; having first securely fastened the other end to the floor of his shop, and requested his friends to bring him food until the dread disease manifested itself, and when he was dead to bury his remains."

Wondrous love, yet a mere shadow of the love of God manifested toward you, kind reader.

What a blessed thing to so love Christ as to be willing

to take up our cross and live for him under any and all circumstances. What a glorious thing to come to Christ and have our hearts renewed in the cleansing fount of his sacrifice for us. What a precious thought to know that he so loved us that he voluntarily laid down his life to rescue us from the awful consequences of our natural depravity. What wondrous forethought to make the foundation of this salvation so broad and so free that all the world might partake of it. What an unsearchable love to you, and to me, dear friend, is that shown by our adorable Saviour.

"*He that loveth father or mother more than me is not worthy of me.*" — MATT. x. 37.

"Mamma," said a little boy, "I cannot love God and you both, so I'll choose *you*." "Why, my child," replied the mother, "what do you mean by saying you cannot love both?" "'Cause that's what my Sunday-school lessons says, I must love God with all my heart, and there isn't but one *all* to it, so if I love him with all, there won't be one bit left for you."

The mother smiled, and asked her child to go to the cellar with her and help her to fill a large basket with potatoes. "There," said he, piling on the last one, "it's full." "Full, yet there is room." and she took a bag of beans and began filling the crevices between the potatoes. When she had done this, she said, "Neither is it full yet," and she poured a shovelful of sand over it. "Not full yet," she again said, and began pouring water on the heap. "My child," she said, "you now see how anything can be full and hold more; so your heart may be full of the love of God, and still have plenty of room for papa and mamma, and brothers and sisters, and toys and books."

"*Greater love hath no man than this.*" — JNO. xv. 13.

A missionary of the South Sea islands was once reading from Jno. iii. 16, to a native who asked that it might be read to him again. As he listened to it, he burst into tears, retired to meditate on it, and was completely overcome, and converted to God by thinking of his wondrous love.

How wonderful when we stop to think of it. A love so strong for such as you and I as to give his only begotten Son to pay the penalty. Yet amid all this, some, it may be you, are trampling this love under foot, and fast going to destruction. Dear soul, salvation is before you. If you are lost, the free path to eternal life will remain the same. The wondrous love of Christ will not be changed. If you are lost, it is your own free choosing, and not God's will. Don't once think God must save you, and that heaven will be incomplete without you, but remember your future depends on your own personal decision.

"*And ye are not your own, for ye are bought with a price: therefore glorify God in your body, and in your spirit, which are God's.*" — 1 COR. vi. 19, 20.

A gentleman, one day, was travelling with a friend. As they took their seat in the railway train, two other gentlemen entered; one took his seat, and the other reached out his hand to bid him farewell. A thought came to him, and he said, "By the by, have you an insurance ticket?" — "Oh, yes," he replied, "I am insured." One of the gentlemen sitting just in front of him turned, and said very quietly, "Are you insured forever?" The gentleman looked up, and said, "I only insure for one year at a time." — "But I," said the gentleman, "am insured forever." Still misunderstanding, the gentleman replied, "Yes, I know you can insure that way, but it costs so much." — "Yes," replied the other man, "mine was done by one payment, and it cost a great deal too. It cost me nothing, but it cost God his Son."

Free insurance, free because "God so loved the world that he gave his only begotten Son, that whosoever believeth on him should not perish but have everlasting life." Free because Christ paid the premium, and insured our souls against loss by sin, and all its woes; insured us against the attacks of old Satan; insured us in the company of eternal life.

Oh, soul thou art not thine own, but art "bought with a price," and your redemption is recorded in heaven's records. Why will you longer roam the bleak pathways of sin, and follow your downward course? Consult your soul's eternal interests, and make Christ your insurance against Satan, and your assurance of everlasting life.

"Herein is love." — 1 Jno. iv. 10.

During the civil wars of Rome, a detachment of soldiers came to the residence of a certain man of high repute, with orders to arrest and hang him. A trusted servant of the man put on his master's official robe, and came out to meet the soldiers, delivering himself into their hands, as the one for whom they were searching. He was taken into custody, and executed without discovering the mistake. What can be more noble than the servant giving his life to save his master? Unless it be the master giving his life to save the servant; and not only a servant, but a degraded, wicked, rebellious, sinful, debauched, servant. Oh! the boundless love in such an act; a voluntary, free-will act that prompted God to give up his Son to die for a lost and perverse race of sinners. "Herein is love." Love as boundless as eternity. Friend, if God so loved your soul, is it asking too much of you to demand your love and service? If the love that God bears your soul prompted him to give up his only begotten Son to save you, I ask is it trampling on your liberty and personal rights to ask you to give your heart to him, and your efforts to his cause? I do not here design to argue the question, but to simply state it to you, and let you answer it, and settle it with your God. You understand the case, and are familiar with the consequences. I therefore leave it with you, and urge a decision **TO-DAY.**

CHAPTER XIV.

CHRIST THE ONLY WAY.

"FOR THERE IS NONE OTHER NAME UNDER HEAVEN GIVEN AMONG MEN WHEREBY WE MUST BE SAVED."

Acts iv. 12.

CHRIST THE ONLY WAY.

" I am the light of the world, he that followeth me shall not walk in darkness, but shall have the light of life."
Jno. viii. 12.

Very soon after Mary Stuart was crowned Queen of Scotland, she noticed what a powerful influence over her people John Knox commanded, and seeing the advisability of gaining the good will of such a man, she succeeded in attracting him to her palace. Knox appeared in his Calvanistic dress, a short cloak thrown over his shoulder, the Bible under his arm. The Queen, anxious to gain his favor, covered him with her flatteries. Expecting she would soon ask of him the favor of which her winning talk foretold, he said. " Madam, words are more barren than the rocks; Satan cannot prevail against a man whose left hand bears a light to illuminate his right." Oh, what a glorious provision Christ has made to help his children to walk in the narrow path. Victory over temptation, victory over sin, victory over Satan, and victory over everlasting death, he has given those that come to God by him. Christ is the sum and substance of all Scripture, and he that carries in his heart the teachings of God's word, need not and shall not walk in darkness, but shall have the blessed light of life, Christ Jesus the Righteous, to guide him. " I will guide thee with mine eye," is the cheering word of our Redeemer, and may be applicable to you, dear reader. And if you have that unerring Light, what more do you need? If Jesus be for you, what harm can befall you.

> "Come to that light,
> 'Tis shining for thee;
> The light of the world is Jesus."

"Not every one that saith unto me, Lord, Lord, shall enter into the kingdom of heaven; but he that doeth the will of my Father which is in heaven."
MATT. vii. 21.

It is told of Frederick of Prussia that one day as he was examining a class in the public school, he took out his watch, and asked the class to what kingdom of nature it belonged. "To the mineral kingdom," was the reply. Next he held up his cane, and asked, "To what kingdom does this belong?" "To the vegetable kingdom," came the quick response. Then he stood before them, and again asked, "To what kingdom do I belong?" A silence followed; presently a little girl held up her hand, indicating that she had a solution to the problem; the great Frederick bade her give her answer, which she did by saying, "To the heavenly kingdom."

Frederick was so overcome that he wept, and said, "Would to God that every one of my subjects belonged to the kingdom of God." Reader, did you ever think what it is to belong to the kingdom of Him whose intense love broke down the barriers that kept you out of the kingdom of heaven? Do you now know the sweet assurance of an abode in the everlasting kingdom of God?

Can you look forward with joy to the coming of your Lord, who has gone to prepare a place for you, that where he is, there you may be also? Can you with Paul say that you know "that if your earthly house of this tabernacle be dissolved, you have a building of God, a house not made with hands, eternal in the heavens"? All these and more belong to the child of God, who gives his heart to Christ.

All these and more are within your easy reach.

All that is required of you is to give to Christ your heart, and rest on his unchanging love.

"*And I say unto you, ask, and it shall be given you; seek, and ye shall find; knock, and it shall be opened unto you.*" — LUKE xi. 9.

"Some years ago there lived in a village in Western England a young man, not considered very intelligent, and known as 'Foolish Dick.' One day he was going to the well for a pitcher of water, when a good old man met him, and said, 'So, Dick, you are going to the well?' — 'Yes,' was the answer. 'Well, Dick, the woman of Samaria found Jesus at the well.' — 'Did she,' replied Dick. 'Yes,' said the Christian man. Dick passed on with the words riveted on his mind. The Holy Spirit touched his heart, and he said to himself, 'Why should I not find Jesus, too, at the well.'

"He sought him, and found him then and there; he left his pitcher, and went to his friends and told them of his find, at the same time proving his faith by seeking to lead others to the saving power of Christ."

Take courage, unsaved one, and know that wherever you are, and whatever your life may be, Christ can be found if you seek him. Knock, and the door of Jesus's love will swing open unto you, and admit you to the saving power of the adorable Christ Jesus who waits to save you in all your sin.

"*And I, if I be lifted up from the earth, will draw all men unto me.*" — Jno. xii. 32.

It is told of Mr. Alfred Cookman that as he lay dying, a sweet smile rested on his face, and he said, "Jesus is drawing me closer and closer to his great heart of infinite love." And such has been the testimony of thousands of other trusting, faithful servants. Oh! how sweet, when the shades of death are falling upon us, to feel the great, strong arm of a loving Saviour gently drawing us closer, and illuminating the dark valley of death with the glorious light of his presence.

Then, too, what a wonderful thought it is that this promise extends as wide as the world, and as high as the heavens, and takes in the entire human family. Every race and kindred that will believe, every nation and tongue that will confess and trust, may be made partakers of this drawing power of Christ our Lord, and be drawn from sin and sorrow, anguish and pain; may be drawn from disappointments and bereavements, reverses and dangers; may be drawn from temptations and allurements, from Satan and his allied forces; may be drawn from death unto life, from the power of Satan unto God; may be drawn from a degraded plane to a blest abode, and eternal life in the sweet haven of unending felicity.

Oh! Christian, seek for a closer walk with him! Oh, sinner, seek for an escape from your doom in him who was lifted up, and who "ever liveth to make intercession for you."

"*I am the light of the world.*" — Jno. ix. 5.

The statue of Liberty enlightening the World, which stands on Bedloe's Island, in the harbor of New York, stands out the most artistic conception of modern times. "The torch of the goddess lights the nations of earth to peace, prosperity, and progress, through liberty." My friend "liberty" is an empty word to the thousands of sin-bound mortals whose taskmaster is an hundredfold more tyrannical than any king of ancient history.

If dark forebodings come to you, if across the horizon of the future comes dark clouds, if your present course threatens to overwhelm you in despair, let me point you to the Cross of Calvary, and there read these memorable words of our Saviour, "I am the light of the world." Shedding the rays far and wide for every one to "guide you into all truth," and land you in immortal glory.

"*Fear thou not ; for I am with thee : be not dismayed ; for I am thy God.*" — IsA. xli. 10.

I read once from the *Christian Standard* a very impressive little illustration of this text.

"A lady had a favorite text which she frequently repeated, and which was included in a collection she used for daily help. 'Fear thou not, for I am with thee; be not dismayed, for I am thy God ; I will strengthen thee ; yea I will uphold thee by the right hand of my righteousness.' On the morning of the day she died, it was repeated by her bedside, with the remark that it was the text for the day. When she looked up amid her pain, and said, 'Is that the text for to-day?' And on being informed that it was, she replied, 'Oh, then, I will just go home on that.'"

Dear reader, there will come a time when you and I will need something that this world cannot give. There will come to you and to me an hour when we will need some strong arm to support us. I leave you this one question to decide for yourself. Is there in this world anything that will support you in that trying hour? If you have found it, you have made a discovery that thousands have in past ages, searched for. If you cannot find it, let me point you to the Lamb of God that taketh away the fear of death, and enables you to possess this assurance, "Though I walk through the valley of the shadow of death I will fear no evil, for thy rod and thy staff they comfort me." This is the song of the redeemed of God as they leave this world, and enter into the joys of their Lord. May this, dear friend, be made your song.

"*Commit thy way unto the Lord.*" — Ps. xxxvii. 5.

No matter how low down you are, no matter what your disposition has been, you may be vile in your thoughts, words, and actions; you may be selfish; your heart may be overflowing with wickedness and corruption; yet Jesus will have compassion upon you, he will speak comforting words to you: not treat you coldly, or spurn you as perhaps those of earth would, but speak tender words, — words of love and affection and kindness." — *Moody.*

"A friend that sticketh closer than a brother" awaits to walk with you along the journey of life, and to aid you in the vexing difficulties that will come to you. Dear soul, "commit thy way unto the Lord," confess thyself unable to battle against the wiles of Satan. He will come to thy rescue, relieve thee of thy burden, and make you free indeed. Will you commit your way unto him?

"*A broken and a contrite heart, O God, thou wilt not despise.*" — Ps. li. 17.

Martin Luther went one day to see a lad who lay dying. Among the questions asked him was this:

"What will you take with you to God?" — "Everything that is good," was the reply. "How can you, a poor sinner, take anything to God?" asked the great man. "I will take to God in heaven an humble and a contrite heart, sprinkled with the blood of Christ," was the reply of the dying boy. "Go then, dear son, you will be a welcome guest with God," responded Luther.

Blessed thought! "A broken and a contrite heart, O God, thou wilt not despise." But with tender, loving hands reach forth, and take unto thy bosom. Oh, soul! herein is a sufficiency; herein is a balm for all thy ills; herein is a cloak for all thy shortcomings; herein is a refuge in time of storm; herein is a harbor for thy frail craft; herein is a promise that will bear thee up as thou walkest through the dark valley. "Oh, praise the Lord for his goodness."

"Lay not up for yourselves treasures upon earth, where moth and rust doth corrupt, and where thieves break through and steal: but lay up for yourselves treasures in heaven, where neither moth nor rust doth corrupt, and where thieves do not break through nor steal."

MATT. vi. 19, 20.

A young lady had been to church, and listened to the earnest plea of the preacher calling on the unsaved to accept Christ. She went home in deep thought, feeling a need of something she had not. She felt that she could hardly give up her worldly pleasures; yet her soul was not at ease. After dinner was over, she took her Bible, as was her custom to do on Sunday afternoons, and went to a shady spot in the garden to read. Near her was a flower-bed, and her attention was called to the buzzing of a bee. She turned and watched the little creature as it extracted the sweet from the bloom; presently the bee had accumulated all it could well carry, and took its flight to the hive to deposit its load, where it would be preserved for its sustenance during the long winter months. As she watched its course, the thought came to her, "That little creature is doing exactly what I am; he is laying by a store. The moth will come and rob it of all its hard earnings, and leave it to suffer and perish in midwinter, when all the flowers are withered and dead, and nothing left to sustain it. I will here and now turn my course." On opening her Bible to look for some words to guide her, her eyes met those of our text, and she turned her course, determined to build upon the solid foundation, even Jesus Christ, and place her treasures in his keeping, against the great day when we all "shall stand before the judgment seat of Christ."

Oh! how foolish to build the foundation of our hopes upon the sandy soil of worldliness, and when the waves of time shall beat against it, it gives away, and we find ourselves in the hour of great need, a wreck. Friendly reader, where are *you* placing your treasures?

"*Casting all your care upon him, for he careth for you.*" — 1 Pet. v. 7.

Two gentlemen were one day walking past a very beautiful mansion, and met a miserable-looking, ragged beggar, who asked them for a small sum with which to buy something to eat.

Each of the gentlemen placed a piece of money in his hand, and in their conversation one of them asked him, who owned this beautiful mansion. "Why," said the beggar, "that was the residence of Mr. B——." "What a happy lot must be his," said one of the gentlemen.

"Nay, friend," said the beggar, "he was the most miserable man on earth. His misery became at last unbearable, and he put an end to his existence by taking his own life. He trusted everything to riches; he amassed great wealth, and lived in the grandest style; disease overtook him, pain racked his frame, he lost his family, sorrow came upon him, he had no one on whom to lay his burden. He knew not Christ, and in order to escape his misery, he ended his own life." Not so with the soul that trusts in God. Though reverses come to him, and bereavements almost crush his heart, though sore trials and divers temptations fall on him, though sorrows and afflictions befall him, still he finds comfort in his God. When earthly sympathy forsakes him, and friends cast him off, yet he finds a refuge in the God of his salvation. Reader, have you learned to cast on Christ the burden of your heart? He careth for you. His great heart melts in sympathy as he beholds you. His great arm of love delights to reach out to you, and bear your burdens, and in words of tenderness says to you, "Come unto *me*. I will give you rest." "Cast all your care upon him, for he careth for you."

"*The son of man is come to seek and to save that which was lost.*" — LUKE xix. 10.

Almost a century ago a collier, living in the vicinity of a great coal mine, was awakened one night by loud cries from the direction of the mines. He arose and went to the door, to more exactly locate the cry; presently he heard a voice, crying, *Lost! lost! lost!* He hastily dressed himself, and, seizing his lantern, set out on his errand of mercy. He had gone only a short distance when he came to where the lost man stood. He found him standing on the brink of a very deep shaft, with only one step between him and death.

Would to God that you, my unsaved reader, might see your great danger, and cry out, *lost! lost!* that the great light of Christ might shine around you and guide you from the pit of eternal death to the port of life everlasting. For you He left his heavenly home, and came to earth "to seek and to save." You are now on the brink of the bottomless pit. Oh, that you could realize that you are lost.

"*I am the light of the world; he that followeth me shall not walk in darkness, but shall have the light of life.*" — JNO. viii. 12.

Mr. Peloubet says, "Once when half sick, full of doubts, unable to realize God or heaven, or feel the full assurance of hope, I was sailing across the Bay of Fundy in a thick fog in the night — a symbol of my spiritual condition. During the night I was awakened by the sharp whistles, the stopping and starting of the engine, and went on deck. For half an hour I watched the captain, with whom I was acquainted. I saw the precautions he took, how he sounded with the plummet, and listened for the fog bell; how carefully he sailed his steamer. I returned to my room and slept, saying, 'I can trust such a captain as that.' Then I said to myself, 'How much more can I trust my Heavenly Father and my Saviour, even in the darkest and dreariest night.'"

How sweet to the doubting soul is the assurance found by returning to Christ, and pleading his sufficiency to give to our hungry souls the Bread of Life, — and to show us the light of his countenance.

"*If the Son therefore shall make you free, ye shall be free indeed.*" — JNO viii. 36

I remember reading a very beautiful allegory in which the dreamer saw the world as an inn by the seaside, where no one could live longer than one day, and from which the majority were taken before noon. On account of the behavior of the occupants, the inn was in very bad repair. The king, to whom the inn belonged, greatly loved the people, and sent his only son, whom he dearly loved, to provide a means of escape for the people from their present and future perils. Strange to relate, they treated him in a most shocking and cruel manner, and finally drove him out at the gate through which each one must pass sooner or later, and which they very much dreaded. Those who persisted in their acts of rebellion against the king, were ruthlessly dragged away in chains and cast into slavery, where they were treated in a very ill manner. Those who accepted the terms of reconciliation provided by the prince were transferred to a land a very great way off, where they were allowed to serve the king, and were presented faultless before him, and were given free access to his palace.

The visit of the king's son to the inn was the one great event in its history. The usual garments worn by the occupants were declared utterly unfit for the voyage that all must take, and altogether out of keeping with the occasion of the prince's visit. So the prince provided a great wardrobe in which were robes of exquisite beauty and richness, pure and white as the driven snow, and for each occupant of the inn. The coin in circulation at the inn was pronounced counterfeit, and of no value whatever at the court of the king. So he established a great treasury for them, filling it with his own riches, and then sent forth an edict, saying that every one that made personal application should be made rich, and none that applied should be turned away empty-handed.

The gate of departure was so narrow, and presented an appearance so very gloomy and desolate, that it held in constant dread all the dwellers at the inn. When the prince was driven through the gate, he tarried long enough to let the unseen hands shoot all their arrows into his own body, that those that followed him should be relieved of the terrible dread of having their bodies pierced with the poisonous darts.

Those that followed the prince through the dark pathway could sing as they passed through "O! death, where is thy sting? O! grave, where is thy victory?" As the prince passed through this dark scene, his hands and feet were terribly lacerated, his body was pierced, water and blood flowed from his wounds, in his anguish he cried out aloud, "It is finished," and returned to his father. Dear friend, do you detect anything in this narrative that is familiar to you? Does it not sound somewhat like the story of the only begotten Son of God who left his throne in heaven and came to earth to suffer and die for you and I, that we might escape the piercing darts of sin and condemnation, and be relieved of our depraved nature? "God so loved the world that he gave his only begotten Son, that whosoever believeth in him should not perish, but have everlasting life." Do you believe?

"*Lay up for yourselves treasures in heaven.*"
MATT. vi. 20.

"When the Emperor Licinius (A. D. 300) ordered forty Christians to be martyred, his chief governor tried all manner of ways to draw them from Christ. As a last resort, he offered each a goodly sum of money to confess their error and forsake Jesus. It is said they spurned his offer and cried out with one consent, "Eternity! Eternity! gives money that will supply every desire, and glory that far surpasses that of your emperor, who will soon lay aside his flimsy honor and be imprisoned in woe." Oh! what rich treasures await such love as this, Oh, what glory awaits him who has laid up in heaven his treasures. Gentle friend, has it been your lot to seek the perishable treasures of earth? has it been your desire to live for the present? let me invite, yea urge you to turn, turn to Christ with all your heart and lay up for yourself riches that will fade not away, and glory and honor, peace, and joy through all eternity.

"*Set your affections on things above, not on things on the earth.*" — COL. iii. 2.

When a certain king lay on his death bed, and felt the cold hand of death laid heavily upon him, he turned to his weeping wife and said: "Love not this vain world; as one who stands on the brink of eternity, I warn you to make not the follies of this world your god. I have let Satan ruin my soul by weaving around me the pleasures and follies of this life, I now leave it all without one hope in the future." When he had thus spoken, he sank back lifeless.

Friendly sinner, how is it with thee? has the god of this world entangled you? have the petty follies of this life laid fast hold upon you? You too may be called upon to leave it all, and pass away without one hope in the future. Set not your affections on things on the earth! As dry chaff the wrath of God consumes them and takes away everything that supports you. In the twinkling of an eye the fierce anger of Jehovah will consume them and leave you unsupported when support is so much needed. Set, therefore, "your affections on things above," upon things whose foundation rests on the Solid Rock — even Christ Jesus. Set your affections upon that which, when the storms of life beat, and the tempest rages, and the fierce winds roar, and the mad waves roll high, you will find security, peace, and safety, because you have builded upon a solid foundation, of which Jesus Christ is the head and chief corner-stone. The placing of the affections thus will make the dark valley of death aglow with light, and the dying couch only a bed of sweet repose, whereon the eyes close in sleep, and the immortal soul awakes in eternal glory.

"*He only is my rock and my salvation.*" — Ps. lxii. 6.

A few years ago a heavily laden passenger train on one of the Eastern railroads was rounding a sharp curve when the engineer saw two children playing on the track; he pulled the reverse lever, and blew the whistle, but the children seemed not to hear it, or to see their great danger. As the great train came almost upon them, the sister seized her little brother, and snugly tucked him away in the niche of an immense rock; and as the train passed by, he clapped his little hands until it was out of sight, as if defying it to harm him.

So is he that makes Christ his rock, and his salvation. The hosts of hell may come nigh unto him, the innumerable temptations and devices of Satan may press hard upon him, but he can clap his hands, and defy them to harm him, because he is hid in *The Rock*. Dear troubled soul, are the marshalled hosts of Satan at thy heels? Are the combined devices of hell's train constantly in thy pathway ? Is the army of worldly temptations surrounding thee ? Get thyself to the Rock of thy salvation, and thou shalt find refuge in the " Rock of Ages," where thou mayest go in and out in peace, and find rest unto your troubled soul. And be

"Safe in the arms of Jesus,
Safe on his gentle breast,
There by his love o'ershadowed,
Sweetly your soul shall rest."

"*And before him shall be gathered all nations, and he shall separate them one from another.*" MATT. xxv. 32.

In the early history of gold mining, the miners would put the ore into a pan of quicksilver with a copper bottom ; the chemical action amalgamated the gold with the copper and separated it from the foreign substances which were thrown away. So it will be at the last great day, Christ will come and separate the good, leaving the bad to be cast away. Reader, which will be your portion ? As you read these lines, your decision may determine this great question.

Oh ! that I might help you to decide it. Will you deliberately choose that which will forever shut you out of heaven, or will you choose Christ " The Only Way," and thus find rest unto your waiting soul ?

"*And I, if I be lifted up from the earth, will draw all men unto me.*" — JNO. xii. 32.

As a heathen ruler lay on his death bed, with the assurance that he would soon stand before his God, he commanded his attendants to make a cross, and lay him on it that he might breathe his last thereon. As the breath was leaving his body, he realized what Christ had done for him, and turning his eyes heavenward, exclaimed, "It lifts me! it lifts me! it lifts me!" and passed to his eternal abode trusting in his Saviour. Wonderful truth, as broad as the ocean, and as high as the heavens. It lifts the lost sinner from the lowest dregs of sin, and fits him to stand before the heavenly Tribunal in spotless purity. It lifts the wayward feet from the miry clay of selfish appetite, and places them upon the Solid Rock. It lifts the sin-sick soul from the pit of despair, and establishes his goings under the all-seeing eye of God. It lifts the heart bowed down by bereavement, and makes it to rejoice in the undying love of God Almighty. It lifts the soul overflowed with trouble and vexations, and surplants it in the sweet peace that passeth all understanding.

It lifts the penitent, seeking soul out of the snares of old Satan, and binds up the wound with the balm of eternal life in Christ. It lifts the feet of the faithful servant from this weary life, and gently lands him into the eternal joys of the realities of heaven above. It lifts the tempted out of the path of temptation, and bids hell and all its forces to come thus far, and no farther.

Kind reader, it will lift your feet out of the broad road to everlasting destruction, and place you in the path leading to immortal glory, where at last you will mingle your voice with that of the redeemed of heaven, in a world without end. May you prostrate yourself at the foot of the cross, and be lifted up to him who said, "I, if I be lifted up, will draw all men unto me."

"*I am the light of the world ; he that followeth me shall not walk in darkness.*"—Jno. viii. 12.

"During our late war, a prisoner one night escaped from prison, and succeeded in getting beyond the picket lines. When he had gotten away from the light of the camp fire, he found it so dark that he could not tell north from south, and for fear of moving toward the enemy's ranks he gave up in despair, and sat down to meditate what course to pursue. Presently he saw a fire-bug flying near him; he reached out his hand and caught it; holding it near his pocket-compass he was able to locate the point of the needle, and safely made his escape."

Jesus Christ is the light of the world. He that followeth him shall not walk in darkness, for "I will guide thee with mine eye." Oh! cast-down soul are you despairing of escape from the darkness of this world? do the chains of Satan hold you fast? does the darkness gather thick about thee? do the waves of despair nearly overflow thee? "Come to that light, it is shining for thee." You need not grope in darkness when the penetrating rays of the Light of the World are about thee.

> While the enemy is nigh
> Quickly to thy Saviour fly;
> To this glorious shining light
> Sinner flee with all thy might.

Then this light not only guides you out of despair and groping darkness, but it guides you to walk in the path along which lighthouses stand to guide you, and save you from the rocks and reefs, and at last lights you through the "valley of the shadow of death," and lands you in immortal glory with the redeemed of God and the Lamb.

"*Broad is the way that leadeth to destruction.*"
MATT. vii. 13.

During the earlier history of our western country, it was sometimes the custom of the railroad companies to run their trains from the east on the wide gauge roads, and then to take out the trucks and put under narrow gauged trucks, and send the train over the western roads.

Gentle reader, if you and I ever get to heaven, it will be on the narrow gauge way. We will have to go to Christ, and have the wide gauge foundation removed from under us, and have it replaced with trucks that fit the narrow way: for " broad is the way that leadeth to destruction." If you and I ever get to heaven, it will be by being reconstructed and made to fit the track which Jesus Christ has laid, and " other foundation can no man lay." The foundation upon which you stand is broad, and its terminus is destruction. Will you allow Satan to register you as one of the many that gather there, or will you have God's grace to fit you for everlasting life?

" *To him that knocketh, it shall be opened.*"
MATT. vii. 8.

A lad who had been blind from infancy was restored to sight. The oculist, after having operated upon him, put a heavy bandage over his eyes, and after a few weeks had gone by, the bandage was removed; when the light met his eyes, and he realized that he could see, he turned to his mother, and said, "Oh! mamma, is this heaven?"

So is the soul born into the blessed light of Christ's love. As the scales fall from his eyes, well may he exclaim, " Is this heaven?" Then, too, this is a free gift. Our Saviour said, " To him (every one) that knocketh it shall be opened." Nothing on our part but simply ask, and Christ bestows on us the spiritual sight that will serve to guide us into the eternal joys of God's presence. Reader, will you come to him?

"*Whom having not seen, ye love.*" — 1 Pet. i. 8.

The feasibility of loving one whom we have never seen is beautifully illustrated by the following incident.

An elder brother of a large family of children crossed the plains during the gold excitement of 1849 and 1850. He remained absent many years. Soon after his departure a sister was born, and as the years rolled by she grew to womanhood. She had never seen her elder brother, yet through his letters she had ofttimes heard of him, and had learned to love him quite as dearly as either of the brothers or sisters.

Our Saviour says, " Blessed are they that have not seen, and *yet* have believed."

Satan sometimes makes us believe that the record of Jesus is too frail for our philosophic minds to rest upon, and in our search for a foundation, he leads us farther and farther from Christ, and at last we land at hell's door, where our religion of philosophy and science perish with us. Oh! doubting minds, let us take Christ as he is, and not let Satan mix up his poisonous unbelief into our religion.

"*Be thou my strong rock, for an house of defence to save me.*" — Ps. xxxi. 2.

Rev. Edwin M. Long relates the following incident. He says, " One morning a village on the Pacific coast was thrown into consternation by tidings that fragments of a wrecked vessel were floating about the harbor. A passenger vessel was due that day, and steamers were at once despatched to make search; it soon became evident that a terrible wreck had taken place, and probably all on board had perished. The excitement in the little city was intense. The remains of a number of the passengers were picked up along the coast. On the following day, word came that a human voice had been heard high up among the rocks. Search was at once instituted, and men were let down, by ropes, among the rocks. At last one poor fellow was found in the cleft of a rock, and safely rescued. From his statement, it appeared the ship had drifted helplessly against the rocks, and was dashed to pieces, and all on board perished save himself, who was carried by a wave to the cleft in the rock." Safe is he who makes Christ his rock of defence and house of refuge. Though the fierce waves of temptation assail him, they can never overflow him. Though the storms of Satan's allied forces seek to draw him down, the Rock in which he hides is unmovable.

Happy is he who sings, "On Christ the solid rock I stand, all other ground is sinking sand." Wise is he who builds the hope of his immortal glory upon the "Rock of Ages." Reader, let me ask you a candid question. When the storm of death comes to your door, and you find the fierce waves carrying your frail bark toward that awful abyss of darkness, what can you find to anchor to?

You now have an opportunity of anchoring to the Solid Rock, Christ Jesus, who alone can hold you amid the storms that come to you in this life, and who alone can support you in that trying hour of death. What will you do with this great question?

"When he had found one pearl of great price, went and sold all that he had and bought it." — MATT. xiii. 46.

A few years ago there was on exhibition in the show window of a jeweller, a large and magnificent diamond. The jeweller had placed it there as an advertisement.

One evening three men drove up to the store, quickly

alighted, and with a large stick smashed the great plate-glass window, and seizing the diamond drove swiftly away. Detectives were put on their track, and after a long and fruitless search they abandoned the case. The thieves had risked all they possessed to gain this pearl; their liberty, their reputation, the honest toil of their hands, — all were at stake.

So, my friend, if the pearl of eternal life requires it, we should willingly sacrifice every other object to gain it. It will be capital placed at an enormous rate of interest. But thanks be to God for giving his Son to open up and make a way so clear, so easy, and so inviting that "whosoever believeth shall not perish, but have everlasting life." *And whosoever means you.*

"*He was wounded for our transgressions, he was bruised for our iniquities.*" — Isa. liii. 5.

A wicked king rode out one day to view his army, as it was his custom to do at certain intervals. He rode down one line, and up another until it became monotonous, and he bethought of a novel plan to amuse himself, by riding at full speed through the ranks to see the soldiers scamper away from danger. Suddenly his steed became frightened, and dashed away, trying at every leap to throw his rider. The king was powerless to check his gait, and cried loudly for help. A man sprang in front of the animal, and with an iron-like grasp seized the bridle, and checked him — not, however, until he had been dragged some distance and bruised and mangled almost beyond recognition. The king dismounted, and found his rescuer dead at his feet; wounded for the king's transgression of the laws of brotherhood, and bruised for his heart's iniquity.

My gentle reader, you have treated in a far more shock

ing manner the dear Son of God, who gave his life to rescue you from an eternal death.

Your actions say "away with him, I will not have him rule over me," I am able to care for my own self. But, my friend, when your grasp on this world is released by death's cold hand, and your support all gone, let me ask you this question: On what will you depend for support? Jesus Christ ceases then to plead for you, but sits to pronounce sentence upon you, "Depart from me." What, friend, will support you through this trying ordeal? the world you have left behind? the Saviour of mankind you have rejected? — who will deliver you from the body of that awful death awaiting the lost soul?

"*Behold, I have set before thee an open door.*"
Rev. iii. 8.

Dr. Newton tells of a man who dreamed that he was in the midst of a large field, hedged in on all sides with thunderings, lightnings, and hailstorms. The dreamer thought he saw houses in the distance, and making toward one of them he craved admittance, till the storm was over. "Who art thou?" asked the master. The dreamer replied, "I am Mr. ———." — "And I," said the master of the house, "am called Justice; from me you must not look for comfort."

The dreamer set out to reach another house in hopes of finding shelter. His knock on the door was responded to by Truth — one that he had never loved, so therefore must expect to find no shelter there. He looked around, and saw not a great way off, another house. Summing up what courage he had left, he pleaded for admission. This was the home of Peace, whom he did not know. In despair he resolved to try once more at the next door; here he was admitted. This was the house of Mercy, and the dreamer was taken in, and made welcome. So it is with the poor sinner when the habitations of Justice, Truth, and Peace are closed against him, the door of Christ's Mercy stands wide open to admit all who will enter. When once admitted through this door, the apartments of Joy, Peace, Truth, and Justice will also welcome you too. "No man cometh to the Father but by me."

Friend, art thou looking for Peace, Joy, and Rest of soul? These all stand wide open to you, but in order to be admitted you must first enter the door of Christ's Mercy, or you can never bask in the pleasures and beauty of the others. Christ this very moment stands calling to you, "I am the door, by me if any man enter, he *shall* find rest unto his soul."

"*Your adversary, the devil, as a roaring lion, walketh about, seeking whom he may devour.*" — 1 Pet. v. 8.

On the morning of July 30, 1864, near Petersburg, Va., a terrific explosion was heard. A moment later, as the dense smoke cleared away, the eye could see the immense heap of ruins of the once strongly fortified fort of the Southern forces. For days the enemy had been secretly at work digging an underground passage, which, when completed, enabled them to place under the fort a great amount of powder, which blew it to atoms.

All this time, while the enemy was at work undermining them, they felt secure, but all at once they were hurled into death. The unsaved often go the same way by letting their sins undermine them; and in a moment they are hurled into eternity without time in which to make the least preparation to meet their God.

How often, too, do we find persons who feel their great need of something more than this world. Yet who refuse to let go some secret sin, which is continually undermining them, and destroying their immortal souls. Like the young man who came to Christ, and went away sorrowful, preferring to trust in his morality than to give up his pet sin. Reader, are you trusting to the letting go of almost all your sins for salvation? Let me tell you that unless you forsake all, and come to Christ, you cannot be his disciple. One thing thou lackest; it is Jesus Christ in your heart; it is the application of his cleansing blood to your soul. Unless you have this, you might just as well go into eternity with a million sins as a hundred. I say to you, "One thing thou lackest"; that is *Christ.*

"*A refuge from the storm, a shadow from the heat.*"
ISA. xxv. 4.

Not long since, a gentleman was passing through one of the Middle States, and saw from the car window a room cut in a huge rock. Upon inquiry he learned that it was a place of refuge from the terrible cyclones that pass over certain portions of the country. The citizens living in that vicinity had made this a place of refuge to shield them from the raging tempest. But, friend, there is a Refuge from the storm of God's fierce wrath, and a Shadow from the scorching heat of Jehovah's anger, even Jesus Christ the righteous.

"Fear not them which kill the body, but are not able to kill the soul: but rather fear him which is able to destroy both soul and body in hell (MATT. x. 28). Happy the man who seeks refuge in the "Rock of Ages," where the storms of hell shall not prevail against him, and whereunto the devices of Satan shall not reach. Blessed is the man who makes God his refuge, and who stands upon the solid Rock, Christ Jesus; he shall be likened unto a man who built his house on a rock, and when the winds come and the fierce waves of Satan lash against it, it shall firmly stand, because "greater is he that is for us than he that is against us." Reader, do waves of worldliness beat fierce upon thy frail bark? Fly for refuge to a compassionate Saviour. Do the storms of gross sins almost sink thy drifting sail? Fly for refuge to the Rock of Ages. Do the winds of despair almost upset thy feeble ship? Fly to him who spake to the sea and it obeyed his voice. Do the evil forbodings of an endless future haunt thy course? Seek that Port where storms never come. Does the life beyond rise like a great mountain of darkness and despair? Fly to that haven of rest and peace found in Jesus Christ, the solid Rock and everlasting Refuge.

"Come unto me all ye that labor and are heavy laden, and I will give you rest."

"I am the way, the truth, and the life." — Jno. xiv. 6.

A gentleman was travelling over a mountain in Montana, before that country was settled. He was on the top of a very high peak, when night overtook him, and the blinding snowstorm and intense cold made his condition one not to be envied; he was cold and hungry, and decided to stop and wait until morning. He rode a little out of the way to find a place to tie his horse, when his eye caught the rays of a candle light. His heart leaped with joy, and he turned his steps toward it. He soon found himself at the door of a little cabin, and knocked for admittance. The owner welcomed him in, and treated him kindly.

Happy is he that seeks a light to guide him from the path of sin to faith in Christ. To such an one Jesus says, "I am the way, the truth, and the life. He that followeth me shall not walk in darkness."

CHAPTER XV.

CHRIST'S WILLINGNESS TO SAVE.

"MIGHTY TO SAVE."
Isa. lxiii. 1.

CHRIST'S WILLINGNESS TO SAVE.

"*Return unto me, and I will return unto you.*"
MAL. iii. 7.

A certain king was presented with a magnificent, richly jewelled crown by one of his subjects who was living in open rebellion against him. The king sent the crown back to the giver with these words, "return first to your allegiance, and then I will accept the crown as a token of your loyalty." Just so with a multitude of self-righteous men who expect to gain the favor of God by occasionally giving certain sums to advance his cause while at the same time living the very reverse of his requirements. Satan-devised delusion! Oh, man! your acts of service will never reach heaven's records. You must first return to God with your heart ere your service will find favor with Him, and in returning to God, He will meet you, and accept you. On the other hand, all the morality in the world cannot save you, unless you first accept Christ, who is the foundation of salvation.

"*God was in Christ, reconciling the world unto himself.*" — 2 COR. v. 19.

"A certain stubborn, reckless youth had a violent quarrel with his kind father, and after stealing money from his drawer, ran away. A year or two afterward the father learned that the scapegrace was in London, living fast, and drinking hard.

He employed a detective to ascertain his son's whereabouts; and at length the officer found him, shattered and sick, in a house of infamy. The father hastened to the spot, and the words, 'That youth is my son,' were the passport to the room. As the father aroused the wretched youth, who turned his bloated face and bloodshot eyes toward him, his first words were, 'My poor boy, I have come after you; will you come home?' In a flood of tears the subdued rebel sobbed out, 'Father, can you forgive me? Then I will go home with you.'" — *T. L. Cuyler.*

So it is when the penitent sinner comes to Christ. His past sins rise up before him, and haunt his memory, and the first thing he wants to do is to see them washed away. Thanks be to God that Christ is ever ready and willing to wash them away, and present the believer before his Father in spotless purity.

Oh! unsaved soul, do you want your sins washed away? do you want to be reconciled to God? do you want Christ's presence with you in life? do you want to give your life to Christ because he gave his life for you? do you want his strong arm in the hour of death? do you want life eternal, and an abode with the blest? if you do, then come to Christ, and take him for your personal Saviour. Come, as if you were the only person in the world, and make him your refuge, and he will receive you and be your God, and you shall be his son.

"*He that . . . hateth his brother is in darkness.*"
1 Jno. ii. 9.

Mr. Moody relates the following story of a young lady that attended one of his revival services. After he had finished his sermon, and was walking down the aisle, he spoke to a young lady, and asked her if she was a Christian. She said, no; she could never be a Christian as long as that lady, pointing to a member of the congregation, was recognized as such. She did not think her case more hopeless than that one, and many others. Oh! what a hell-devised pit is this which Satan thrusts before thousands of poor creatures to drag them down to woe. Oh! that the very finger of God would move across the heavens, and write, "Every man shall answer for *his* sins."

Reader, are you thus deluded? Remember, you must personally appear before "the great white throne" to answer for what you have done. You will not, as Satan may tell you, be called upon to answer for any other than your own sin; but bear in mind if you meet God with only your own sin, you will be condemned and rejected. All the sins of earth would not any more condemn you. God cannot tolerate the least sin, and unless Christ interpose, and take your sin on himself, you are lost. But he says "Come unto me, though your sins be as scarlet they shall be as snow." He will willingly pardon and save you. For this he came to earth, for this he left his heavenly glory, — now he says, "Come, for all things are now ready."

"*Forgetting those things which are behind, and reaching forth unto those things which are before.*"
PHIL. iii. 13.

When Archimedes made a very important scientific discovery, he was about stepping into a bath. Forgetting his clothes, he ran through the street, crying, "I have found it! I have found it!" But the discoveries of all ages are nothing to compare with that of a single soul who finds Jesus Christ. How his heart goes out in love as he seeks to draw others unto the cleansing fount of Christ Jesus, and while the heavens resound with the glad songs of angels, he desires to tell what great things the Lord hath done for him.

"But I will punish you according to the fruit of your doings, saith the Lord." — JER. xxi. 14.

"In Ethiopia there is found a stone which has two opposite and peculiar qualities; while one side attracts the iron toward it, the other side repels it.

So God has two hands; the one of mercy, the other of judgment; the one of love, the other of wrath. While with one he has opened a fountain where we may wash away our sins, with the other he casts the rebellious spirit into eternal torment. While he holds one outstretched to receive the penitent sinner, with the other he forever casts off the evil doer."

Reader on which side are *you?*

"If we confess our sins, he (Christ) is faithful and just to forgive us our sins, and to cleanse us from all unrighteousness." — 1 JNO. i. 9.

A merchant of London, eminent for his wealth and commercial position, had an only son upon whom he had bestowed every luxury that money could buy, and upon whom the hopes of the father centred. The favored son grew to manhood with every prospect of becoming the successor to his father's vast riches.

But he fell into bad company, and went from bad to worse, regardless of the earnest expostulations of his father, until he sank to such a depth of degradation, that his father refused to have more to do with him, and cast him off; he erased his name from the family record, and disinherited him.

Years went by, and the father lost all trace of his once brilliant son. One day, a gentleman drove hurriedly up the beautiful driveway to the elegant mansion of the father; he was met at the door by a servant, the gentleman asked to see without delay the great merchant. He was shown to the library, where he met an aged, haughty-looking man, surrounded by every luxury money could procure.

The gentleman without introducing himself asked, "Have you a son named Joseph"?

"No, sir, I have no such son," replied the haughty man, "I had at one time a bright, lovely boy by that name; but he is no longer my son. I long since disinherited him, he rebelled against me, and left my roof by his own folly."

"But, sir, I just came from your son, who now lies at the point of death, and desires that you will come and forgive him, ere he crosses the dark river." The father quickly arose, and followed the messenger, who took him to a miserable side street tenement row, and up an uninviting stairway, into a dingy attic, there to find his own son in poverty and filth, such as he had never seen before. As the eye of the dying son met the tear-dimmed gaze of his father, he said in a weak and trembling voice, "Father, I shall not recall the scenes of my past life, I want to ask you, before I go to my long home, to forgive me for the pain and dishonor I have brought on you."

The father fell beside the dying son, and said, "Let the past be forgotten, I would have forgiven all, long, long ago, had you but asked it. I willingly forgive all, you must come home at once."

Oh! Satan-deluded soul. The mighty arms of Jesus Christ stand outstretched to forgive your past life, and welcome you to the joys of his Father's abode.

Why will you longer live in the rags and filth of sin, when such a happy lot is yours. "The master is come, and calleth for thee." Arise, and unload thy burden of guilt, and put on the robe of righteousness, that he so willingly gives to those that come to him.

"*Whatsoever a man soweth, that shall he also reap.*"

GAL. vi. 7.

One night at the close of an earnest appeal to sinners by one of our Y. M. C. A. workers, an invitation was given to any who felt any anxiety as to their soul's welfare, to remain a moment after the audience was dismissed.

Among the number that had remained, was a poor, uncouth woodman, who had long enjoyed the camp life in the great pineries of the north.

As the man of God took him by the hand, he asked him how it was with his soul, and why he desired to "flee from the wrath to come"? He began by telling his past history, he said he had lived the most wicked life imaginable, that he had spent for liquor and carousing what should have been given to the support of a lovely family. That he had murdered the best of wives by his ill-treatment and neglect in providing the necessaries of life. That he was in the habit of subjecting his wife to the most inhuman treatment, and "Now, sir," said he, "that wife lies cold in death. My once lovely children are gone, and I am reaping the fruits of my own sowing. I am an outcast, I am a most miserable wreck, and worse still, I am forever doomed to hell's torments."

The Christian gentleman listened with interest to his

story, and then pointed out the saving power of Christ, which the sin-sick soul eagerly grasped, and he became an earnest Christian worker.

Dear reader, I give this illustration to show you the glories of my Saviour in reaching down to the lowest depth of iniquity, and rescuing a penitent soul.

It matters not how low you may have sunken in sin. His long arm can reach you. It matters not how degraded and deep in the slime of ungodliness you may have fallen, for just such, Christ came to seek and to save. Then, my friend, take new courage, and come with a true penitent heart, and his precious promises will be verified. " Come unto me, *all* ye that labor, and are heavy laden, and I will give you rest." " Him that cometh, I will in nowise cast out."

" How hardly shall they that have riches enter into the kingdom of God." — MARK X. 23.

Among the legends of Hindostan is one that illustrates these words of our Saviour.

One Rawana, a Brahmin, was offered by his god anything that he might name. Rawana prayed his god to bestow upon him the government of the world. His god immediately granted his wish. Then he prayed for ten heads, with which to see and rule the world. After Rawana had well fortified himself, and was surrounded by riches, honors, and praise, he forgot his god, Ixora, and bade all the people worship him, — an act which greatly angered the god Ixora, and he destroyed Rawana.

How true to human nature was the course of Rawana! and how many we find to-day that have forgotten the God that gave them all they possess! Right here come in the words of our Saviour: "How hard for them that trust in riches to enter the kingdom of heaven"; because the cares of this world spring up, and choke the seed of the Spirit. Beloved reader, I am going to ask you a plain, solemn question, and leave you to answer it in your own heart, before God. Have you any right to usurp the time that belongs to your soul, and apply it to something else? This is what you are doing, while Christ awaits to give you an immortal inheritance in the blissful abode, which he has gone to prepare for you.

"*Naked, and ye clothed me.*" — MATT. xxv. 36.

A soldier was placed on duty, one bitter cold night, between one sentry box and another. A poor workingman chanced to pass along, as he was walking his beat, and, moved with pity for the poor fellow, took off his coat, and gave it to the soldier to keep him warm, adding that he should very soon reach home, while the soldier would be exposed to the cold all night. The cold was so intense, the soldier was found frozen at his post. Some time after, the man lay on his deathbed, and, in a dream, he imagined he saw an angel appear to him "You have got my coat on," said the man. "Yes, this is the coat you lent me that cold, bitter night, when I was on duty, and you passed by. 'I was naked and ye clothed me.'"

So Christ took off the cloak of his glory, and endured all manner of persecution, suffered shame, that he might clothe us with his cloak of righteousness, and win us back to God. Though he died in the attempt, yet he succeeded, and again took up his own glory.

"*It is a fearful thing to fall into the hands of the living God.*" — HEB. x. 31.

"When I lived," says Borgia, "I prepared for everything but death. Now, I must die, and am unprepared."

What a true picture of the life of millions of our fellow-men to-day! Rushing along life's pathway, busy attending everything for the present, finally there comes the summons, "Come hither"; then, like Borgia, they will say, "I must die, and am unprepared." Then they will realize the force of this text.

> "When this mortal life is fled,
> When the death shades o'er thee spread,
> When is finished thy career,
> Sinner, where wilt thou appear?
>
> "While the Holy Ghost is nigh,
> Quickly to thy Saviour fly.
> Waiting, patiently, he receives.
> Every penitent that believes."

" God is light and in him is no darkness at all."
1 Jno. i. 5.

When Charles Kingsley was dying, he said, "It is not darkness I am going to, for God is light. It is not lonely, for Christ is with me. It is not like taking a journey to a strange country, for the guiding hand of Jesus my Saviour is outstretched to lead me." O child of God! how comforting is the assurance Christ Jesus gives in this dark hour to those that trust him! Oh, the grandeur in the thought that the loving hand of Jesus is outstretched to bear our immortal souls to his Father's house, where joy "reigns unspeakable and full of glory!" My friend, such scenes must come to each of us. I ask you, therefore, this one question, do you want Christ to support you in the hour of death, when all earthly aid will be powerless to help you? Upon what will you then lean? Give your heart an honest answer to this question, while your Saviour patiently waits at the door of your heart to come in. Oh, grieve him not away!

"*Mighty to save.*" — Isa. lxiii. 1.

Two ministers were travelling through a thinly settled district, on their way to a public gathering of their church. As they came to a small clearing in the dense wood, they saw not far away a cabin on fire. They urged on their horses, and soon reached the house, to find the roof all ablaze. They quickly dismounted, and ran to the burning building. In one corner of the little room lay a poor old man, crippled and utterly helpless. He begged them for mercy's sake to save him from the awful death. They soon succeeded in arresting the flames, and assured him danger was past. The old man, with tearful eyes and trembling voice, thanked them for saving him. They told him to give the praise to God, who had brought them just at that time to rescue him.

"Wonderful mercy!" as his eyes dropped to the floor, and he confessed that he had never believed in a God. "Now I believe there is a God, and that he has sent you here to rescue me." He then inquired who the strangers were. On being told, he added, "how strange! I never allowed a minister to cross my threshold, and now God has sent two of them to rescue such a worthless old cripple as I am from an awful death." He briefly recalled his past life, and said, "Now, I feel the guilt of my waywardness." He then fell at the foot of the cross, and plead for mercy, and wondering how such a hardened sinner could be saved from the death he so richly deserved.

Oh! my unsaved friend, take courage, lay your case

before the adorable Lord, for he is "mighty to save," and "able to save to the uttermost all that come unto God by him."

"Come with thy sins, confessing,
Thou shalt receive a blessing."

"*If we confess our sins, he is faithful and just to forgive us our sins and to cleanse us from all unrighteousness.*" — 1 Jno. i. 9.

During the trial of Joan of Arc, the judges and the priests privately besought her to confess that she had erred in defending her country and in aiding to crown Charles the Seventh as king.

She promptly refused all their offers, tempting as they were. They offered her liberty, offered to make her a distinguished personage at the king's court, still she never relaxed in her persistent refusal. They well knew that a confession from her would forever dishonor the crown she had been the means of placing upon the head of Charles the Seventh. When she was led forth to the stake, and saw the great pile of fagots awaiting the torch, she was again urged to confess her error, which she refused to do. As the flames reached her body, they stood near her to hear any confession she might make; but she died rather than accede to their demands. So it is with the sinner. Christ stands waiting to clothe him with his own righteousness upon a confession of faith in him, and bestow upon him his guiding care, shield him from the temptations of life, provide him grace to walk the narrow way, instil in his soul the assurance of immortal glory and a crown that fadeth not away. One says, "Time enough"; another, "Wait awhile"; another, "I am afraid I can't hold out"; another, "Want of feeling"; another, "Do not feel as others do"; another, "Too many hypocrites"; another, "I must prepare myself"; another, "Too great a sinner"; another, "Can't understand the new birth"; another, "Do not know how"; another, "Am not such a great sinner"; another, "Don't care to give up all yet"; and another, "Cannot believe."

My dear unsaved friend, these are hell's trusted bulwarks: they are the rocks upon which thousands of souls have been wrecked. They are Satan's most trusted weapons. You can overcome them all by humbly throwing yourself on Christ Jesus, and *confessing* your sins, confessing your inability to do anything; confessing that unless Christ rescues you, you are lost; confessing that you are weary of your burden of sin, and that you desire him to relieve you; confessing that you have formed a determination to serve him to the end. These are the paths to victory and an everlasting habitation with the redeemed of God in heaven.

"Come with thy sins, confessing,
Thou shalt receive a blessing."

"*He came unto his own and his own received him not.*"
Jno. i. 11.

I had in my youth, a friend about my own age. He was the only son of his parents, and a boy of no ordinary promise. He was the idol of his parents' hearts. Of him they could talk by the hour. As the years rolled by, and he grew to manhood, he suddenly became a raving maniac, and it was found necessary to place him in an insane asylum, where he is to-day confined. His poor, sorrowing mother made frequent visits to the institution to see him. On one occasion, as the attendant unlocked the door of his apartment, he met the eye of his weeping mother, who had so long suffered and endured hardships for him. No sooner had he glared at her, when he cried out, "Take her away, take her away: she is a witch, come to torment me." The attendant tried to explain to the poor boy that it was his loving mother, the best friend he had on earth; but he persisted, and refused to allow her to come in, and minister to him. The attendant locked the door, and led the heart-broken mother away.

So it is with the sinner. Dear friend, you have a Saviour who suffered and died for you, who paid the price of your going astray, and redeemed you from everlasting doom, and who now seeks and claims you; but your actions cry out, louder than words, "Away with him! away with him! I will not have this man to rule over me." There will come a time, Christ says, that "when ye call, I will not hear." But to-day he invites you, and bids you "*come.*"

"*Who his own self bare our sins in his own body on the tree, that we, being dead to sins, should live unto righteousness.*" — 1 PET. ii. 24.

During a fierce war which raged in India between Tippoo Sahib, and the English, a number of the latter were captured, and thrown in prison. Among them was an officer named Baird, and who was then suffering from a severe wound. One day the natives brought in fetters to be put on each prisoner. An aged English officer turned to the guards, and asked them if they intended putting the irons on the wounded and suffering Baird.

"There are just as many fetters as there are prisoners, and each pair must be worn," was the reply. "Then," said the aged officer, "put two pairs on me. I will wear his, as well as my own." His request was granted, and he wore the two pairs, while his wounded friend soon recovered, and gained his liberty. But the generous brother officer was cast into a dungeon, where he soon died.

So the blessed Christ took on himself the fetters of our sins, and bore them in his own body on the cross that we might recover, and gain our liberty, and be redeemed to God by his blood, and made us sons of God and heirs of the kingdom which he hath prepared for those that love him.

And now he bids us come and partake of this redemption, and find rest unto our souls.

"The Lord hath laid on him the iniquity of us all."
Isa. liii. 6.

"One day a minister had occasion to move his library to a room upstairs; his little son came into the room, and the father requested him to aid in the transfer of books. Presently, he met his little boy about half way up the stairs with the largest book in the library. He could go no farther; the book was too heavy for him, and he sat down on the stair, and began to cry as if his heart would break. The father placed his arm about him, and carried him, book, and all, up the stairs." — *Moody.*

Beloved is thy burden too heavy? do troubles and cares weigh hard upon thy heart?

Your heavenly Father bids you lay all upon his strong arm. Jesus Christ says, "Come unto me," I will relieve you, and give you rest. "Cast thy care upon him, for he careth for you." Is this not easier than to mourn over your case? Just come as you are, and Jesus will help you.

CHRIST'S WILLINGNESS TO SAVE. 235

" Whosoever will, let him take the water of life freely."
REV. xxii. 17.

Travellers in the East tell us that certain seasons in the year, carriers may be seen going along the streets of the villages with water to sell, and crying out, "Who'll buy, who'll buy the gift of God."

Jesus Christ comes to every heart, and says, "*I* will *give* you the water of life, whosoever WILL let him partake freely; he that drinketh of the water that I shall give shall never thirst." Kind friend have you accepted the great invitation?

"Oh precious is the flow
That makes us white as snow,
No other fount I know,
Nothing but the blood of Jesus."

"Peace I leave with you, my peace I give unto you: not as the world giveth, give I unto you." — JNO. xiv. 27.

A physician was summoned to the bedside of a dying man.

As he noticed the sweet composure and loving faith, — such as only a firm trust in Christ can give — of the dying man, he said, "Oh! if I only had that sweet trust and assurance, how happy I would be." The scene led him to meditation, and he gave to Christ his heart.

Not long after, the messenger of death came to him. With an unwavering faith he welcomed the call, and passed beyond to an inheritance incorruptible, and full of glory.

Oh! troubled soul, do the realities of the future haunt thee? doth thy inability to escape the judgments of a just God weigh down thy heart? do the evil forebodings of death make thy life unhappy?

Take courage, there is a remedy for such ills, Jesus Christ is waiting to heal such maladies. Come just as you are, and tell him you are so weary, and his great hands will gently unload your burden, and take it unto his own self.

He came to *seek* and to *save* just such as you, and the sweet peace which he gives, this world knoweth not.

The assurance he bestows not only cheers and strengthens you in this life, but as you pass through the valley of the shadow of death, and when all earthly help is gone, he gently takes you by the hand, and leads you to an eternal inheritance prepared for those that love him.

To believe, repent, receive, is your part: to cleanse, purify, guide, bless, love, and save, is Christ's part.

"*He is able also to save them to the uttermost that come unto God by him, seeing he ever liveth to make intercession for them.*" — Heb. vii. 25.

The story goes that Mr. William Dawson of London, at the close of one of his earnest appeals to sinners to accept Christ, said "there was not a man, woman, or child in all London that Christ could not save."

The next day as he sat in his study, the sharp ringing of the door-bell interrupted him; the servant opened the door, and a neatly dressed young lady asked to see Mr. Dawson. She was shown into his study, and said, "In your sermon yesterday you said that there was not a man, woman, or child in all London that Christ could not save." Mr. Dawson replied, "I admit I did say so, and moreover, I will say further that you may apply the assertion to the whole world."

The young lady continued. "I have been talking with a poor, miserable dying man to-day, and told him what you said; but he declares Christ cannot save such a wreck as he. I did all I could, and feel sure if you will go to see the poor man, you can so present Christ that he will accept him, and yet be saved." Mr. Dawson readily consented to visit the sick man. On a narrow street up a rickety stairway they found, upon a bed of straw, a wasted form, showing a life of dissipation. The godly man bent over him, and said, " Friend." The sick man quickly looked up into his face, and said, " Sir, you must be mistaken, I have no friends. My own family cast me off. I am a wretched, poor outcast, friendless and dying." — "Yet, sir," replied Mr. Dawson, "you have a friend that sticketh closer than a brother. Christ is the sinner's friend." At first the words had very little effect, but ere long the peace of God dawned upon the dying man, and he eagerly grasped the great and precious promises that were read to him. His face brightened, and amid all the misery and filth of his surroundings he crossed his hands in death, trusting in Jesus. Oh! unfortunate friend, the same loving arms that rescued this poor man from the very brink of hell is ready and willing to lift you out of the mire and filth that sin has brought upon you, and set your feet upon solid ground. He is able to the uttermost to save you; regardless of the depth of your degradation his arm can reach you, and bring you back to eternal life. Come then,

"Just as you are without one plea,
But that his blood was shed for thee."

CHAPTER XVI.

CHRIST INVITES ALL MEN TO SALVATION.

"COME UNTO ME, ALL YE." — MATT. xi. 28.
"HE THAT COMETH I WILL IN NO WISE CAST OUT."
JNO. vi. 37

CHRIST INVITES ALL MEN TO SALVATION.

"*Ho every one that thirsteth, come ye to the waters, and he that hath no money; come ye, buy and eat: yea, come, buy wine and milk without money and without price.*"
Isa. lv. 1.

One cold day, a poor, ill-clad woman halted before the window of a king's conservatory, looking at a cluster of grapes, which she longed to have for her little daughter, who was ill.

She went home, and by extra exertion earned a florin, and came and offered it for the cluster of grapes. The gardener ordered her off the premises.

She returned home, took the blanket from her bed, and pawned it, and went and asked the gardener to sell her the grapes, offering him five shillings. He became furious, and bade her leave the place at once. The princess heard the rough language, and asked what was wrong. When the story was told her she said, "My dear woman, you are mistaken in the place. My father is not a merchant, but a king. His business is not to sell, but to give." So saying, she plucked the cluster of grapes, and dropped them into the woman's apron, and she went away happy.

So Christ came, not to sell and make merchandise of the joys of heaven, but to *give* us a passport to its eternal bliss. He came to "*give* life and to *give* it more abundantly." And he bids you, dear reader, to "*come* and buy without price, and he that hath no money to come and buy, "Ho *every one* that thirsteth, come." Oh, what a benevolent God to give *free* that which cost him so much. Reader, will you come?

"*He is also able to save them to the uttermost that come unto God by him, seeing he ever liveth to make intercession for them.*" — HEB. vii. 25.

A Christian gentleman was one bright Sabbath morning invited to hold religious services in a prison. He earnestly pictured the scene on Calvary to the army of unfortunates. After the services, he was granted permission to pass along the corridors and speak with the men in their cells. Some he found reclining on their beds reading, some playing cards, some writing letters. For each he had a cheerful word; when he came to the last row, he halted in front of the cell of a poor convict who sat with his face buried in his hands, a true picture of despair. He spoke gently to him, and asked what his trouble was; the man told him that he was the most miserable of men, the memory of the crimes of his long life of iniquity came up and haunted him by day, while the gaping jaws of hell made the quiet hours of night unbearable. The gentleman spoke words of comfort, and told him that he knew an effective remedy for such ills, and pointed him to the blessed Saviour. "My dear sir," said the man, "do you for one moment suppose such a man as I could find pardon there?" The gentleman read the broad invitations of Christ to the poor man. "Can that include me?" asked the convict. The godly man assured him it did, when the troubled soul cried out, "Oh, show me how to find him." They knelt down, and the convict reached his hand through the iron bars and grasped the Christian as he prayed for the spirit to light up the despairing man's heart. The gracious light did come, and illuminated the dark recess of his heart, until his eyes and countenance told that he was enjoying peace through the cross of Christ.

"Able to save to the uttermost," that includes me; that includes you, dear reader; it matters not how sinful, it includes you, but to avail ourselves of its reality we must *come*, show a desire, believe, and be saved.

"*And Jesus, moved with compassion, put forth his hand, and touched him, and saith unto him, I will: be thou clean.*" — MARK i. 41.

A Chinese convert relates the following: "A man had fallen into a deep, dark pit, and lay in its miry bottom, groaning, and unable to move. Confucius walked by; nearing the edge of the pit, he said to the poor, unfortunate man, 'Poor fellow, I am exceedingly sorry for you. Why were you such a fool as to get into this awful place? Now, take the advice of a friend, and when you get out, don't go near such a place again.' Next came a Buddhist priest, and said, 'Poor fellow, indeed I am sorry for you. I think if you could scramble up part of the way, I could help you out.' But the man could do nothing to help himself. Next, came the adorable Jesus, and, hearing loud cries, went to the pit, stretched down his long arm, and rescued the prisoner, saying, 'Go, and sin no more.'" Such is the love and compassion of the beloved Son of God, and for such a cause came he into the world, to rescue those that were deep sunken into the pit of sin and iniquity, and it matters not how deep the pit may be, he is able, and his great arm is long enough to reach to the bottom. All the sinner has to do is to ask to be raised, and Jesus is moved with compassion, and lifts him up, and sets his feet on the solid rock, and cleanses him from all sin. Could you, dear reader, could I, could lost humanity ask more?

"*Whosoever will, let him take the water of life freely.*"
Rev. xxii. 17.

In Oriental countries, during the dry season, it is looked upon as a grateful act of kindness to give to a thirsty traveller one cup of water. In Christ we have a fount as free as it is boundless, and as boundless as eternity. A fount that sends forth the water of life unto life everlasting. A fount that sends forth living water, and whosoever drinketh thereof shall never thirst. A fount which flows for all mankind, and *whosoever will* let him take of the water *freely*. A fount where the soul laden with iniquity may wash and be made whiter than snow. A fount where the penitent may drink, and go his way rejoicing in free pardon and full salvation. A fount where the hungering and thirsting after righteousness may be filled. A fount where the weak may drink, and be made strong in the Lord, and in the power of his might. A fount where the tempted and tried may drink and find strength to resist the evil one. A fount where the servant of the Most High God may find strength to labor in the heat of the day. A fount where the suffering and the bereaved may find consolation. because "he was tempted in all points as we are," and because "he was a man of sorrows and acquainted with grief." A fount where the aged may drink, and the hoary locks will be transformed into the bloom of youth, and in an eternity never grow old. A fount that gives joy, peace, and glory in a world of endless bliss.

Such, my dear reader, is the fount of living water, even Jesus Christ. *Have you been made a partaker thereof?* You alone must decide whether or not you will come and take this water.

"*If we confess our sins, he is faithful and just to forgive us our sins, and to cleanse us from all unrighteousness.*" — 1 Jno. i. 9.

A minister was holding services in a little English town. Among his congregation was a miserable-looking ragged man, whose very appearance showed him to be a profligate and prodigal. The minister went to him at the close of service, and heard his story, and found his bad habits had caused him to be driven from a good home, and loving parents. He advised him to write at once, and tell them of his determination to reform, and win back the esteem of all his friends.

"Oh, no, sir!" said the poor fellow, "I have led such a life, they would shut the door against me; I cannot hope to gain their forgiveness." — "You certainly do not know the love of parents. I am sure they will take you back," said the minister. The young man wrote the letter, and very soon he came to the minister with the reply full of love and tender words from his father, and urging the son to come without delay.

Even so, unsaved friend, Christ sends you the invitation to come to him. Come, in all your sin and pollution; — come, however black your heart may be; — come, with all the guilt of your past life; — come, in all your rags and filthiness of a life of crime; — come, just as you are, without one plea; — "come, all ye that labor, and are heavy laden" with sin;—come, confessing your sins to him who is "faithful and just to forgive us our sins, and to cleanse us from all unrighteousness";—come, though your sins be as scarlet, they shall be white as snow;—come, for the sake of him who died on Calvary's cross, and poured out his life for you;—come, for your soul's eternal sake, and secure a part in that inheritance prepared for those that love God.

"*Silver and gold have I none; but such as I have, give I thee.*"—ACTS iii. 6.

Socrates once had a trusted servant, who, seeing others giving presents to his master, came to him one day, and said, "Because I have nothing else to give thee, master, I here give thee myself." Socrates saw the earnestness of the servant, and said, "Do so." After bestowing upon him gifts, and advancing him to the head of his servants, he called him one day, and said, "I now give thee back to thyself better than when I received thee."

Just such a spirit as this is what Christ requires of us; and when we come to him with such a trusting love, he takes us out of our sins, and through his own blood cleanseth us, and maketh us heirs of the kingdom of God. Dear unsaved friends, though you may be poor, wretched, and miserable, it matters not what or who you are, Jesus bids you come. And when you come, he will make you "free indeed." Come as you are;—come, saying "Just as I am," and he will in nowise cast you out.

"*I will arise and go to my father.*"—LUKE xv. 18.

There lived in one of the New England States a well-to-do merchant, with an interesting and happy family.

The merchant's home was known far and wide as the happiest in the town. Suddenly, reverses in business came to him. As he saw his once-prosperous business gone, his health failed, disease settled in his system, and death laid his cold hand upon him. Unscrupulous creditors came and took the home, leaving the heart-broken widow without any means of support, save the efforts of a fifteen-year-old son.

They struggled along for some time, until the son, led away by reading stories of dime novel adventures, left his mother to seek his fortune in a distant state. After he had been gone some years, during which no tidings of the lost boy came to cheer the widowed heart, though letters were sent to many places in the hopes that they might reach him, only to be returned to the writer as unclaimed, — one day, as the poor mother sat alone, a sharp knock was heard at the door, the now aged parent responded, to find before her a gentleman with long, flowing beard. She at first failed to recognize him; presently she saw great tears trickling down his cheeks, and she exclaimed, "My lost boy! my long-loved, lost son!" The happy mother entreated her son to come into the house, but he declined. "No mother," said he, "I can never cross that threshold until you forgive me for what I have done in treating you so shamefully, and causing you so much pain." The mother threw her arms about him, and forgave all.

My friend, the adorable Christ stands at your heart's door, knocking for admission, and with outstretched arms he is saying, "Come unto me, all ye that labor and are heavy laden, and I will give you rest." "Knock, and it shall be opened unto you; seek, and ye shall find." He is willing to forgive your past treatment of him, and **remember** it no more against you forever.

"For thou wast slain, and hast redeemed us to God by thy blood." — Rev. v. 9.

A very ancient Assyrian legend, found among the writings of Berosus, gives the account of man's creation in this wise, "Bel, one of the three great gods, gave his blood to be mixed with the clay out of which man was formed, thereby endowing him with reason, and instilling into his soul the essence of divine nature."

The effect of this legend upon the hearts of those dark ages we are not told; but it very forcibly illustrates the scene of Calvary, when the blood of the blessed Christ, mixed with the agony of that hour, opened up the way of eternal life to a fallen world, and endowed them with the peace of soul that "passeth all understanding," and posted sentinels the world over to cry, "Whosoever will may come, I am the way, the truth, the life." Reader, have you been washed in the blood of him who was slain, and has redeemed you to God by his blood?

"God so loved the world that he gave his only begotten Son, that whosoever believeth in him should not perish, but have everlasting life." — Jno. iii. 16.

An aged man, noted for his wickedness, was taken violently ill, and for many days suffered intense agony of body and soul. He yearned for that sweet peace found in believing in Christ. He longed to know the assurance of heaven's eternal bliss. One day he called his little son to his bedside, and said, "Johnny, can you read to me?" The little boy readily assented, promising to skip the hard words. He took down the Bible, and it opened at John, third chapter, and Johnny read as best he could, until he came to the sixteenth verse: "God so

loved the world that he gave his only begotten Son that "
— here he halted; he spelt and respelt the word, and
could not make it out, so he said, " I'll just skip that, and
go on." So he began at the first, and read, " God so loved
the world that he gave his only begotten Son, that . . .
believeth should not perish, but have everlasting life."
The father looked at the lad eagerly, and said, " I do so
much wish you could make out that word: it is just what
I want to know, and what I need." So eager was he to
know, that he arose from his bed, and called to a gentleman passing the street, and asked him to tell him what
it was.

The man took the book, and said, "That is *whosoever*."
— " Whosoever, why, what does it mean ? " said the sick
man. " It means *anybody*," said the man, as he turned
and walked away.

The old man at once saw that he was included in the
" whosoever," and laid hold on the Saviour, and rejoiced
in saving faith.

That very word includes you, my reader, whoever you
are; you have a share in that wonderful love. Christ
sends it to you, and bids you to come and drink of the
water of life, freely. Rest assured, if you come, he will
not cast you out.

" *Whosoever will, let him take the water of life freely.*"
REV. xxii. 17.

A few years ago a benevolent gentleman gave a New
Year dinner to the poor people of the city, and published an invitation that all who wanted to, could come
and partake of the meal, free of charge.

The poor, the lame, the halt, the blind, flocked to the
feast in great numbers, and enjoyed the bountiful repast

set before them, and were loud in their praises of the donor for his remembrance of their class.

The blessed Son of God has prepared for us, dear friend, a feast, and sent heralds throughout the earth, proclaiming the invitation, "Whosoever will, let him come." There is room enough for all. "Come without money, and buy;— come and partake of the water of life freely."

Oh, how our hearts should send forth the grateful praise for a free salvation!

"*In returning and rest shall ye be saved.*"

ISA. xxx. 15.

During the reign of one of the European kings a certain class of his subjects formed a society whose main object was to rebel against certain restrictions laid upon them by their king.

The king, not caring to put them to death, issued an edict, informing them that if they would return unto him, and show that they sought to live under his flag, that he would forgive their spirit of rebellion and protect them. Some of the rebels came back to their king, and he forgave all; while others would not, and fell by the sword of the king's army.

My dear, unsaved readers, you are living in open rebellion against the King of Heaven. You know not "what a day may bring forth." To-morrow you may be called to stand before the King. In the still hours of night, the dread messenger may call for you. To-day, I bring unto you this edict from the King of Heaven: "Return unto me, and I will return unto you. He that cometh, I will in no wise cast out. Come unto me, *all* ye that labor and are heavy laden." "In returning and rest shall ye be saved."

"*He that believeth on me hath everlasting life.*"
JNO. vi. 47.

There is a little incident in the life of Napoleon which gives us a beautiful illustration.

It is said that he rode out one day to view his army. His prancing steed became frightened, and ran away. As he passed swiftly down the line a soldier, at great risk of his own life, sprung in front of the flying steed, and grasped the rein, checking him. When the great general saw the bravery, he took off his hat, and said, "From this time on, I make you captain of my guards."

The captain ordered the man to again take his place in the ranks, but he refused.

"And why not?" asked the captain. "Because I am captain of the guards," he replied. "The great Napoleon has thus appointed me."

The captain believed that such was the case, and pressed his orders no further.

My friend, Christ says, "Come and you *shall* be saved." Can you not take him at his word?

"*The poor among men shall rejoice in the Holy One of Israel.*" — ISA. xxix. 19.

A Christian physician, in order to make his services more useful in relieving the ills of mankind, established himself in one of our large cities. He ordered a sign painted, giving the hours that he could be found at his office. In large letters at the bottom were these words, "The poor treated free of charge." He soon had a large practice, and won the confidence of both rich and poor. Not only did he prescribe for the ills of the body, but he also told of another Physician who could cure the ills of the soul. In the midst of his career of usefulness death sought him out, and laid his cold hand upon him. Many were the sad hearts as they gathered around their benefactor's coffin to take a last look at the lifeless form. As the long procession of mourners followed the remains to the grave, hot tears trickled down many a furrowed cheek, as the thought of their irreparable loss came to them.

O my poor friends, poverty may come to us, property may take wings and fly away, friends may forsake us, loved ones may be called to yonder shore, the future may seem dark, our pathway may be studded with dark clouds, — yet, amid all these, we have a friend that "sticketh closer than a brother." Jesus Christ still sends you this message. "Come unto me, *all* ye that labor and are heavy laden, and I will give you rest." He is the friend of the poor. He knows how to sympathize with us, for himself "had not where to lay his head." He himself was tempted like as we are. He knew want and sorrow. He is thoroughly acquainted with our hearts, and sympathizes with us. He is always ready to stretch forth his mighty arm, and bear our burden for us.

Therefore, "Cast thy care upon him, for he careth for you."

"*Come ; for all things are now ready.*"
LUKE xiv. 17.

It was the custom in the earlier ages to issue invitations to a feast several weeks before the event, and when the day arrived, and all preparations were completed, a runner was sent out to inform those bidden, that all the details were arranged, and the master says "Come."

So the blessed Christ came, announcing the kingdom of heaven as at hand, and when the last pang upon the cross went out, he said, "It is finished." "Let every one that thirsteth come." "All things are now ready." The avenues of eternal salvation are opened, an offended God is reconciled, all arrangements are now complete. Come."

This invitation is personal to you, kind friend. Will you take it, and come to Jesus?

"*Return unto me, and I will return unto you.*"

MAL. iii. 7.

I remember a few years ago of reading the story of a prominent business man in one of our large cities who had a lovely daughter, highly educated, refined, and beautiful, — the pride of the father's heart. For some time the young lady had been secretly meeting a young man that she well knew her father would not permit to cross his threshold. These secret meetings terminated one day in the elopement and marriage of the young lady to her lover, who was far below her in rank and social standing. The father was heart broken to think his accomplished daughter would thus throw herself away. He sought the aid of detectives to find her whereabouts. Weeks and months passed without finding any trace of her. One day the detective walked into his office, and informed him that the lost one was found. The father was overcome with joy. He sent for his son, and told him to go to the place, and tell his daughter to return home, and all would be forgiven. The son went, and induced her to come back to her father who was waiting with outstretched arms to meet her and welcome her home.

Reader, are you unsaved? The blessed son of God says, "*Come to* ME. The past will be forever blotted out; no difference how black the record may be, it will be wiped away, and a hearty welcome sung by the holy angels in the presence of God."

He sends you this invitation: "Return unto me, and I will return unto you, with open arms, and will receive you, and care for you, protect you, and save you."

"*By grace are ye saved, through faith; and that not of yourselves; it is the gift of God.*" — Eph. ii. 8.

A very ignorant man who had long been noted for his great wickedness and opposition to the cause of Christ, sent a request to a minister to call on him. The godly man was surprised when the man requested the privilege of coming to the house of God, and publicly confessing Christ. His request was granted, and among the questions asked him was this: "Can you explain the work of salvation and the way you came to Christ?" — Oh! yes," he replied, "I did a part, and Christ did a part." — "What part did you do?" was asked. — "I opposed him all I could, and Christ did the rest." Oh what activity the powers of hell show when a soul decides to shake off the shackles and turn to God; but what an inspiring thought to know that "He that is for us is *greater* than he that is against us."

Take courage then, oh reader, and come as you are to a full and free salvation, by grace, through faith in Christ.

"*As many as received him, to them gave he power to become the sons of God, even to them that believe on his name.*" — Jno. i. 12.

A gentleman residing in the fashionable part of London, and thoroughly carried away with the follies of society life, was walking down the street one day with a Christian lady. He asked her this question: "How is it that you religious people are always trying to rob us of our pleasure? I enjoy life, and I can't see why you should be forever trying to rob me of what pleasure this short life affords." — "You are greatly mistaken, sir," replied the lady. "We do not want you to give up anything, but to *receive.*" The gentleman kept thinking of the word *receive.* The word refused to leave him. Not long after he called on the lady, and told her his life was miserable, and inquired what to do to receive that which would render him peace of soul, and joy of heart. She led him to the Saviour, and he found pardon and comfort in his blessed invitations and promises. Oh what a strong emphasis Satan puts on this very point, that of giving up our earthly joy and worldly pleasure. Dear reader, is such an excuse keeping you away from Christ? Let me say to you that Christ stands ready to bestow upon your immortal soul, life eternal, and all you will be required to do is to *receive.*

Then, too, let me say that when you do receive the sweetness of Christ's love in your heart it will cut away the desire of worldliness, and you will a thousand times feel like praising him for opening your eyes, and rescuing you from the power of Satan, and drawing you unto God.

"*Him that cometh to me, I will in no wise cast out.*"

Jno. vi. 37.

A minister was invited one day to dine with a gentleman, who had a lovely daughter just blooming into womanhood.

After dinner the minister and young lady were alone in the parlor. They conversed about the topics of the day, and after a while the subject of religion was introduced. The minister asked her if she had no serious thoughts about the welfare of her soul. She replied that that was a matter of which she preferred not to speak, and entirely her own private affair. The godly man, in a moment, saw that his words had given offence, and quickly turned the subject of conversation. That night, as she lay on her couch, her thoughts ran back to the events of the day, and she began to meditate upon the words of the minister. The more she thought, the more serious became her case, until finally the Spirit drew aside the veil and showed her, her own heart; alarmed at such a sight, she shrank back and looked about for means of escape. The next day she laid her troubles before the minister, who gave her words of comfort, and told her to lay the burden of her heart on Jesus. "But how can such a sinner as I come to Christ?" she replied. She was told to come just as she was, and Christ would receive her. The peace that passeth all understanding flowed like a river into her soul, and she went rejoicing with exceeding joy. This was none other than Charlotte Elliott, whose name has become famous, and who has left us a witness of her change of heart in this beautiful hymn, which she composed on the day of her conversion, —

"Just as I am, without one plea,
But that thy blood was shed for me,
And that thou bidd'st me come to thee;
 Oh, Lamb of God, I come."

Dear unsaved friend, there is hope for you yet. Why wait to grow better? "Come, just as you are, without one plea," and cast yourself on the merits of Jesus Christ, who is "able to save to the uttermost," and who says, "I will not cast out any that come."

"*Whosoever drinketh of this water shall thirst again. But whosoever drinketh of the water that I shall give him shall never thirst: but the water that I shall give him shall be in him a well of water springing up into everlasting life.*" — JNO. iv. 13, 14.

"In the hill country of India is a very touching myth about a queen, greatly beloved by her people, and whose life was devoted to their interests. In olden times, the people of Chambra suffered grievous distress for want of water. The queen, taking the sorrows of her subjects greatly to heart, consulted the will of the gods, how the constant curse of drought might be removed. The reply was, 'If the ruler of Chambra die for her people, abundant water will be given.' 'Here am I,' said the generous queen. Bravely standing on the lofty position designated by the gods, the devoted queen was buried alive for the sake of her people. Thereupon, a fountain of pure cold water flowed from the spot, descending to quench the thirst of the people of Chambra, visiting each hut, and bearing to each the life-giving blessing."

While the above is only a myth, it bears a striking resemblance to the story of the King who left his heavenly throne and descended to earth to remove the curse of sin from a fallen race, and to open up a fountain of eternal life, and he that partaketh thereof shall *never thirst*. So great was this love he bore for his people that he laid down his life, amid shame and sorrow, that those whom he loved might be relieved of the terrible curse of everlasting condemnation, and won back to God and life eternal. Gentle reader, this same king extends to you a pressing invitation to come and take of the "water of life freely," and "he that drinketh of this water shall never thirst." "*Ho, every one, come.*" The rich, the poor, the lame, the blind, the halt, the sick,— *yea, every one.* "He that cometh, I will in no wise cast out." There is an eternal unchanging fount open, wherein sinners may plunge and lose all their guilty stains. Will you, reader, take Christ at his word, and come *now* and lose all your guilt, and lay the foundation of an everlasting inheritance in the home above? You must decide this yourself.

"*Who his own self bare our sins in his own body on the tree, that we, being dead to sins, should live unto righteousness.*" — 1 Pet. ii. 24.

The following old and touching illustration is probably familiar to us all, yet for the illustration, it will never wear threadbare. A stranger was seen one day planting a flower over a grave in the cemetery at Nashville, Tenn. A gentleman passing by asked him, "Is your son buried there?" "No." "A brother?" "No." "A relative?" "No." After a moment's pause, the stranger said, "I will tell you. When the war broke out, I lived in Illinois. I had a large family dependent upon my daily labor for support. I was drafted. Having no means to pay for a substitute, I prepared to go to the war. In the neighborhood was a young man who had heard of my circumstances. On the day I was to start, he came to me and said, 'You have a large family to care for; I will go in your place.' He did go, was killed, and here in this grave rest his remains." On a board at the head of the grave were written these words, "He died for me." The stranger, with tears of gratitude trickling down his cheeks, told of his long journey to see this grave, and delighted to recall the fact that "He died for me."

My friend, the beloved son of God bore your sins on Calvary's cross to give you life. He suffered in your stead, and in mine. He relieved you from the awful consequences of an eternal lost and ruined state, and set before you a plain road to everlasting life. Prompted by a boundless love, he took on himself your shame and disobedience, and purchased, at the cost of his own life, the eternal redemption of your soul. He now says, "Come unto me and be saved." Will you heed his call?

"*If the son therefore shall make you free, ye shall be free indeed.*" — JNO. viii. 36.

It is told of Mr. Amos Lawrence, the millionaire, that he purchased all the forged paper of a certain forger. In order to influence the man for good, he offered him the paper on the condition that he confess himself bankrupt, and put all his affairs into the hands of his benefactor, an offer of which he gladly availed himself, and was allowed to go free. My unsaved friend, this is exactly what Jesus Christ has done for you, he bids you come to him in your bankrupt, sinful state, and confess your inability to pay the debt charged against you, and he will pay all, and allow you to walk free through all eternity. Will you open the door of your heart, and allow him to enter?" Bear in mind, between you and God is a vast gulf; Christ says to you he will bridge that over, and reconcile an offended God.

Come believing, come trusting.

"*But that ye may know that the Son of Man hath power on earth to forgive sins.*" — MATT. ix. 6.

There appeared in print not long since a beautiful legend, which ran somewhat as follows: There once stood in an old baronial castle a musical instrument upon which nobody could play, owing to its complicated mechanism, and during years of disuse, the dust had gathered and clogged it, while dampness and variations of temperature had robbed the strings of their harmony. Various experts had tried to repair it, but without success, and when the hand of a player swept over the chords, it awoke only harsh discords and unlovely sounds. But there came one day to the castle a man of another sort. He was the maker of the instrument, and saw at a glance what was lacking.

With skill he cleared the dust from the chords, and brought each string into place, and then it filled the hall with the most exquisite strains of music.

So with our souls, human efforts may be employed to bring them into harmony, but not until God, the Maker, repairs and adjusts them can they ever be brought into harmony of praise and adoration to their Maker. Why be discouraged oh, cast-down soul, Christ is waiting to bring our souls into direct harmony with God.

Patiently he stands, calling, entreating, and pleading. "Come unto me, come unto me, I will give rest unto your soul."

"*Come unto me, all ye that labor and are heavy laden, and I will give you rest.*" — MATT. xi. 28.

Two small boys were on their way to school one morning, and met an old woman bearing a very heavy load.

The lads insisted that she let them relieve her, and took the great basket, and bore it for her.

So to you, friend, Christ comes upon the highway of destruction, and insists that you let him bear your burden for you, and allow you to go free." "Come unto *me*, all ye that labor and are **heavy laden**, and *I* will give you rest." "He that cometh, I will in nowise cast out." For just such as you, these promises go out; — for just such as you, these promises were made; — for just such as you, Christ came to "seek and to save." May the cry go to heaven to-day from your lips, "Oh, Lamb of God, I come, I come!"

"*Come unto me, all ye that labor and are heavy laden, and I will give you rest.*" — MATT. xi. 28.

In a church in the Isle of Wight stands a monument whose history beautifully illustrates the comfort of having accepted the great invitation in this text. Princess Elizabeth, daughter of Charles the First, during the wars of the Commonwealth, languished in the Castle of Carisbrook, separated from her loved ones, and everything on earth that she held as dear to her. One morning her attendant went to her apartment, and found her with her head resting upon the open Bible, her marble-white finger pointing to these words, "Come unto me, all ye that labor and are heavy laden, and I will give you rest." The weary soul had taken its flight, resting on the promises of its Lord. The tired heart, worn and harassed with persecutions, had found comfort in the promises of its compassionate Saviour. The longing spirit hailed with gladness the summons to "Come up higher," and as it took its flight, carried with it the promises of its Maker, and made them the password through the heavenly portals.

Reader, this same broad invitation is for you, this same support in the trials and cares of life is within your easy grasp; this same peace and joy in that trying hour of death is yours, for the asking.

Will you come, saying, "Lord Jesus, my **Saviour**, I come, I come," "help thou mine unbelief."

CHAPTER XVII.

ONLY BELIEVE.

"HE THAT BELIEVETH ON THE SON HATH EVERLASTING LIFE."
JOHN iii. 36.

ONLY BELIEVE.

"How that Christ died for our sins." — 1 COR. xv. 3.

During the late war, a company of men were arrested, tried, and convicted of desertion, and sentenced to be shot. Among the number was a man who had loved ones at home, and from whom he had received a letter, stating that they were sorely afflicted, and urging him to come at once. The poor fellow, failing in his application for a permit to visit them, deserted the army, and decided, at the great risk of his life, to go to his family. The strict military rules would not excuse him on such a defence, and he was, with the other deserters, marched out to be shot. As he took his place in line, a young man, knowing the circumstance, stepped forward, and offered to take his place, and die in his stead. Dear reader, as you read this simple narrative, methinks I hear you say "Brave fellow!" Let me tell you that you stand to-day condemned by heaven's court. Jesus Christ saw your condition, and placed himself in your stead, died, and redeemed you to God, leaving you to do nothing but believe on him. Will you do it?

"He was wounded for our transgressions, he was bruised for our iniquities: the chastisement of our peace was upon him." — ISA. liii. 5.

In the State of New York, some years ago, on adjoining farms lived two thrifty farmers. One was the father of two charming daughters; the other had two sons of unusual promise, who bore a very striking resemblance to each other. The sons were in the habit of making frequent calls at the home of the daughters, and everything went well, until the father of the girls had left to him, by a wealthy relation, a large amount of money. One night a robber gained access to his room, and, after beating him into a senseless condition, took the money, and made his escape. While descending the stairway, the robber met one of the daughters, who, being attracted by an unusual noise, was on her way to her father's room. As the burglar passed her, she raised his mask, and recognized him as her lover, and the son of the adjoining farmer. The alarm was given, the robber was arrested, tried, and sentenced to a long term in state's prison. The other son remained at home for a number of years; finally, he was stricken down by disease. He saw that it was useless to entertain a hope of recovery, and requested that the neighbor and father of the two daughters be sent for. His request was granted, and the neighbor hastily summoned. As he took his seat beside the couch of the dying man, the latter, in a trembling voice, confessed that it was he, and not his brother, who had robbed and so cruelly beaten him, and that his brother had suffered all these long years in his stead, simply to shield the one he loved. Immediate steps were taken to secure the brother's release. When he was given his freedom, he said he knew of the guilt of his brother, but, rather than have him convicted, he took on himself the penalty, and suffered in his stead. So the blessed Christ saw that we were in an eternal prison of sin; to release us, he suffered shame and imprisonment in our place, and freed us from its consequences. Only believe, and thou shalt be saved.

"*So, then, every one of us shall give an account of himself to God.*" — Rom. xiv. 12.

When Daniel Webster was Secretary of State, during President Fillmore's administration, he was one day invited to dine at the Astor House, New York, with a select party of eminent statesmen.

Mr. Webster seemed weary with his journey, and, speaking but little, if at all, sank into a sort of revery, quite out of keeping with the occasion.

After several unsuccessful attempts to draw him into conversation, a member of the party put this question to him: "Mr. Webster, will you kindly tell me what was the most important thought that ever occupied your mind?"

The venerable Webster slowly passed his hand over his forehead, and, in a low, soft tone, said, "The most important thought that ever occupied my mind was *my individual responsibility to God.*"

And the same is the most important thought that ever entered the conception of any human mind, because "every one of us shall give an account of himself to God."

An account of the deeds which we have done, and the deeds which we have left undone. And, in view of this great fact, it behooves us to prepare to meet our God. And while our God is a God of justice, he also is a God of mercy, and has provided a way by which we may escape that which unfits us for his presence. Love and mercy led him to give his only begotten Son, upon whom he laid the guilt of our evil deeds, and who paid their penalty on the Cross. And now he comes to you and to me, and says, "He that believeth on the Son *shall* be made a partaker of his righteousness, and shall have his evil deeds blotted out forever."

"*Open thou mine eyes.*" — Ps. cxix. 18.

There is an old legend, dating back to the seventh century, of St. Modabert who had such sympathy for his blind mother that he one day rushed forward, and kissed her eyes, and her sight came immediately to her, and she rejoiced in the beauties of nature as they shone about her.

Whether the legend contains any truth, it matters not; but it certainly gives us a very striking illustration of the kiss of Christ's love as it opens the eyes of the penitent believer, and reveals to him the riches and beauty of the pardon of all sin, and makes him a dweller in the kingdom of our God. The sweet kiss of a sympathizing Saviour which relieves us of the haunting memories of our past life, and fits us for the joys of the presence of God.

He will open your eyes, if you only believe.

"*So Christ was once offered to bear the sins of many.*"
Heb. ix. 28.

A minister relates the following, which occurred at one of his meetings among the Indians. He was preaching from the text, "Christ and him crucified." He drew a powerful picture of the scene at Gethsemane. The congregation was much moved. One tall Indian arose, and walked toward the pulpit with tears trickling down his red cheeks. "Did Jesus die for me — a poor Indian? Me have no lands to give Jesus; but me give Jesus my gun and my dog and my blankets." The minister told him that Christ could not accept such gifts. The Indian then hung his head in silent meditation, and presently said, "Will Jesus take poor Indian? If so, here is poor Indian who gives himself to Jesus."

ONLY BELIEVE. 269

Nothing so pleases the adorable Lord as to have the penitent, sin-sick seeker cast himself, soul and body, on him.

Oh, what a lovely spirit, that which prompts us to fall at his feet, and cry, "Here, Lord, I give myself away: 'tis all that I can do." And, my dear reader, all Christ requires us to do is to come and lay ourselves, sins and all, at his feet, and believe.

"So Christ was once offered to bear the sins of many." Ample sacrifice, free salvation, life everlasting, complete pardon, perfect reconciliation, all branch out of that sentence, like so many streams from the spring as it gushes forth out of the hillside rocks; and they each act as sentinels along the path from Calvary's cross to heaven's courts.

"*He that believeth on the Son hath everlasting life.*"
JNO. iii. 36.

The Emperor of Russia, some years ago, decided to liberate the forty millions of serfs of that country. He laid his plans before his councillors, but they did not approve of them. One morning the tramp of soldiers was heard in St. Petersburg, and there went forth a proclamation that every serf in Russia was forever *free*. All the serfs had to do was to believe; they did believe, and were free. My friend, eighteen centuries ago there went forth a proclamation to all the earth, of every nation and clime, of every tongue and language, that the slaves of sin, the slaves of Satan, were *forever free*, and all that was necessary on the part of the slave was to *believe*, and he would be lifted from the degradation of slavery and raised to the exalted position of the glory and honor of being made a son of the most high God. That proclamation has been opposed by the combined forces of hell for all these long centuries, but to-day it stands out a more self-evident fact than ever before. It stands on the solid rock, Christ Jesus, and offers pardon, peace, and rest to every one.

Oh! soul, will you *believe* and be pardoned of sin and its attendant woes; be relieved of the degrading name of servant, and assured of an everlasting habitation in that blest abode which the Son of God has gone to prepare for those that believe on him. "He that hath the Son hath life." "He that believeth shall be saved," and "He that hath *not* the son shall not see life, but the wrath of God abideth on him, and he that believeth not shall be damned."

"*What must I do to be saved?*" — Acts xvi. 30.

There is a very touching incident told of a minister, who had a son — a deaf mute. In the vicinity of their home, a gracious revival was in progress. The anxious father saw that his son was striving with the Spirit, but he could not communicate with him sufficiently to explain the way of salvation. The son wrote, in a scrawling hand, upon his slate, "*Father, what must I do to be saved?*" The father answered back, "My son, you must repent of your sins, and believe on the Lord Jesus Christ." — "But how must I do this?" the son wrote. The father explained it as best he could, but the unfortunate lad could not understand it. The distress of the parents became intense; finally, they sent for the teacher at the asylum which the boy had attended; but this failed to bring the desired result. All this time the anxious parents were pouring out their souls to God, that his spirit might come and enlighten their son. Suddenly, one day the spirit lifted the veil, and sweet peace filled the soul of the mute. His joy was wonderful; he became an earnest minister among his own class, and told many the way of life. His difficulty was, he could not conceive the simplicity of salvation.

It was so simple he could not see how it could save him. "Believe on the Lord Jesus Christ, and thou *shalt* be saved." Friend, this is all there is to it — only believe. This simplicity leaves you without one excuse; without the remotest shadow of being justified by any defence you may bring to relieve yourself of the awful sentence awaiting the unsaved. "He that believeth shall be saved, but he that believeth not shall be damned."

"*For we shall all stand before the judgment seat of Christ.*" — Rom. xiv. 10.

During our late war, a pressing call was made for volunteers to enlist in the defence of the Union. Men came flocking to the standard from all directions. Some whose appearance indicated a life of toil, some wearing the garb of humble citizens, some dressed in fine apparel, and whose life had been one of ease and luxury. They were all marched into line, and as they passed a certain point each one was required to place his name upon an immense register, and to exchange his clothes for the army uniform. The tattered garments of the hod-carrier, and the elegant dress of the gentleman, were each laid aside for uniforms of the same material. Whatever might have been the line of social separation in the past was now to be known no more. So it will be in that great day when all earth shall assemble before Christ the Judge. The poor, the rich, the small, the great, will all be assembled, unmindful of position, and be judged in common by the blessed Jesus. Those that have believed on him and have taken him as their Saviour will meet him with joy and gladness. Those that have refused his mercy and pardon will be rejected by him. Dear friend, which will ye choose? The decision may be made *now*, and the same shall regulate all time to come. Christ is able and willing to save you; waiting at the door of your heart to save you *now*.

You may ask, " But how can I be saved ? " I answer, " Believe on the Lord Jesus Christ, and thou shalt be saved. Simple as anything can be, 'only believe.'"

" For the son of man is come to seek and to save that which was lost." — LUKE xix. 10.

Several years ago a young man left his widowed mother's home in England to seek his fortune in a far-off land. Hardly had he established himself in his new home, when he fell into bad company, and gave himself up to utter worldliness, regardless of the prayers and parting words of his aged mother. During a business trip to another city, he was passing the door of a church one evening, when a lady handed him a gospel tract with the request that he read it carefully. He went to his room a little later, and to pass away the hour, began to read the tract. Its perusal led him to see how very inconsistent his course of life was. He left his room, and went to the nearest bookstore, purchased a Bible, and began reading it. The truths, the warnings, the invitations, the promises, found therein fastened deep the arrow of conviction on his soul; for several days he carried his awful load of sin; finally he came to the words, " For the son of man came to seek and to save that which was lost." He gave himself wholly into the hands of his Saviour, and new light shone around him, and he was led to rejoice in Christian faith.

For you, dear friend, Christ came to seek and to save. All that lies between you and eternal life is your will.

If you want to be saved, all you have to do is to give up your will, and your all into the hands of Christ, and thou *shalt* be saved.

"*Some men's sins are open beforehand, going before to judgment; and some men they follow after.*"

1 TIM. v. 24.

A condemned criminal one night lay dreaming in his cell. He dreamed that he was led forth to the scaffold, the rope carefully placed about his neck, and just as he felt the trap give way, the victim of his crime appeared, and seizing him by the legs gave him a sharp jerk; he thought his body was placed in a rude box, and taken to the grave. The murdered man followed him, and as he was being lowered in the grave, he exclaimed, "Oh, the wretch!" The blood was oozing out of his side, and the dreamer begged him to let him alone, but he would not. He tried to extricate himself, but his victim held firmly to him, and hissed in his ear, "You think you are going to heaven, but not so; you will go to hell, and there I will be to torment you." And so it is, some men's sins go before them to judgment, and condemn them, while others remain hidden until they stand before the throne of God. But in either case the consequences are appalling. Whether or not they rise up and precede you to judgment the eternal purposes of God cannot be altered, and one jot or tittle of his law cannot be changed. You stand, therefore, condemned, unsaved reader, and no power can remove or stay your sentence save Jesus

Christ the righteous. Simply believe on him, and trust the balance to him; simply plead his merits and broad promises, and he will remit your sentence, and give you that liberty of which the world cannot know.

"*For without are dogs, and sorcerers, and whoremongers, and murderers, and idolators, and whosoever loveth and maketh a lie.*" — Rev. xxii. 15.

A few years ago in the city of St. Louis resided a lawyer of reputation, but who was an infidel. One Sabbath afternoon he started to go to a drug store for some medicine for a member of the family. On his way he saw an immense crowd of people listening to a minister speaking of the love of Jesus. He halted a moment, but could not hear a word the speaker said. Near by, mounted on a wagon, stood a man who was pouring forth a volume of blasphemy, and cursing the Bible and Christianity.

The lawyer noticed he had quite a group of sympathizers around him, who laughed at his coarse jests, and loudly applauded his vile sentiments. He noticed also that this group of listeners was made up of the very dregs and scum of society. Thieves, burglars, prostitutes, and drunkards, constituted the admiring audience. The lawyer hung his head, and passed on, reflecting that he was thoroughly identified with these vile scoffers. He walked along chagrined and mortified, and without attending one of the revival services, without hearing a sermon, he renounced infidelity, and became a Christian, and to-day is an able minister of the Gospel.

"For without are dogs, and sorcerers, and whoremongers, and murderers, and idolators, and whosoever loveth and maketh a lie."

How many of us shun these classes in this life, but in

the end will be found without the wedding garment, and will be consigned to the same abode. Oh! friend, would you escape such associates? Let me tell you there is but one way: "Believe on the Lord Jesus Christ, and thou shalt be saved." Saved from the eternal torment of hell and its associates, saved from remorse and shame, saved from banishment, and saved from the company of evil doers. Will you come and be saved? The question is with you, and for you to decide.

CHAPTER XVIII.

NOW.

"NOW IS THE ACCEPTED TIME."
2 Cor. vii. 2.

NOW.

"Thou art my hiding-place and my shield."
Psa. cxix. 114.

There is a story of an infidel, who, having a large amount of money with him, had occasion to pass through the wild mountainous region of Kentucky. One evening he perceived that he had lost his way, and to add to his solicitude, night was upon him. He rode along some distance, and as the shades of evening closed around him, he saw near by a little cabin; he rode up to the door, and asked if he could stop until morning. The lady informed him that her husband was out hunting, but would shortly return, and no doubt grant his request. While they were talking, a great, stout man, dressed in deerskin from head to foot, and carrying on his shoulder a rifle, while by his side hung a large hunting knife, walked up. The traveller's heart almost failed him at the sight of such a fierce-looking man. He was given permission to remain through the night. When the hour to retire came, the hunter told him that he would conduct him to his room when he was ready to retire. Fearing his life, the traveller concluded to sit up all night, and guard his treasure. Finally, the hunter said, "Well, stranger, if you will not go to bed, you must attend family prayers. I never lie down without first reading a chapter in the Bible, and thanking God for his mercies." He then took down the old family Bible, and after reading a chapter, knelt and asked God to bless also the "stranger within his gates." The infidel retired in perfect confidence, and rebuked himself because the Christianity that he had always so vigorously rejected could, in the hour of trial and danger, bring him a sense of such absolute security.

So my friend, though you reject the Spirit's offers of mercy now, yet when danger o'erwhelms thee, methinks I see you fleeing to God with your plaintive cry, seeking shelter. To insure his unchanging grace, I entreat you to heed the entreaties of God's spirit, and come *now* and accept Christ, and it will be well with thy soul.

"*I have called, and ye refused.*" — Prov. i. 24.

A Christian gentleman went into a remote settlement to do some missionary work. Among the first calls he made was one at the home of a lady, about thirty years old. He asked her if she was a Christian, she replied "No." He then asked her if she felt no concern about the welfare of her soul. "Yes," she said, "I think few have been more anxious than I once was. About fifteen years ago, I felt that I was a great sinner, living in open rebellion to God; my distress ofttimes drove sleep from my eyes. I felt the calls of the Holy Spirit. I also knew that I ought to yield to His pressing entreaties." — "Why did you not yield"? asked the missionary. — "Because I did not want to cut off my pleasures in the bloom of youth. I tried hard to shut my heart against all thoughts of eternity, but they would return to me. I tried novel reading, and as a last resort, I went to the ballroom to drown such thoughts; there I succeeded, and since that time have had little or no such trouble." — "Do you not fear you have grieved away the Spirit of God?" said the missionary. — "I have not the least doubt of it, and that I am totally lost. Nothing that you or any human power can do or say will move my stony heart to repentance and faith in Christ. It is too late now. The die is cast, my doom is sealed."

Oh! my lost reader, are you rejecting the Blessed Spirit's calls? Are you drowning his entreaties in the folly of worldly pleasure? God sends to you these words, "My spirit shall not always strive with man." There may come in your case a time when such gracious calls will be withheld, and leave your soul to its final abode in the torments of hell.

"*Behold, I stand at the door and knock.*" — Rev. iii. 20.

A gentleman who had spent much of his life in the gold mines of Australia, where he accumulated large wealth, decided to return to America, and visit the home of his boyhood. A great change had taken place since his departure; the loving parents had long since gone to their reward, and an only brother lived at the old homestead. He arrived at the station late one night, and decided to walk to where his brother lived, thinking the exercise would benefit him after his long voyage; he soon arrived at the scene of his happy boyhood, and walked to the door he had so often entered, only to find it securely barred; he rapped, and a call came from within, " Who is there ? " — " A friend," was the reply. " Well, what friend " ? — " A brother," responded the weary traveller. — " No one is admitted into this house at such an untimely hour as this, neither would any one with good intentions be prowling around at such an hour of the night; begone at once, or I will help you," said the disturbed brother. The brother, not caring to disclose his identity, quietly left the premises. At the breakfast table next morning, the different members of the family were each offering a solution of the mystery, when a knock was heard at the door, and in stepped the long-absent brother. The scene can better be imagined than written. Suffice it to say, the brother at home was presented with a handsome sum of gold, and they spent many happy days together.

Christ our elder brother, with riches untold, stands at the door of every heart, and gently knocks for admittance; if we open unto him he will come in unto us, and bestow untold riches. If we refuse his gentle entreaties, he will refuse to hear our cry when the waters of death overflow us.

Reader, have you responded to his knock of admittance, and thrown wide open the door of your heart, saying, "Come, Lord Jesus." If you have not, may the spirit lead you to do so, and that without delay.

"*Rise, he calleth thee.*" — MARK x. 49.

An old man, past his threescore and ten years, was approached by a Christian one day, who inquired if he had a hope in Christ. The old man answered, in a trembling voice, "No." — "Do you believe the Bible?" asked the man. — "Every word of it," admitted the venerable old man. "Well, does not that book teach us that we must be born again?" — "Certainly, it does." — "Has the Holy Spirit ever knocked at your heart's door?" — "It has done so repeatedly, sir, but I have each time refused Him admittance. Since I became a man, the cares of this world have so taken my time and thoughts that I have had no time to devote to such things." The gentleman asked him if he felt no terrors coupled with the meeting of a just God. He replied,

"I do, but my doom is sealed, my lot is a just one. The Spirit has been refused; now I am reaping the fruits of my sowing."

The old, old story that prompted God centuries ago to say, "I called, but ye refused." Oh! the remorse that sentence may cause you as you stand before the great Judge, "I called, but ye refused." Reader, have you rejected the Spirit's entreaties, oh! so often? I come to you with one more invitation, to open your heart, and bid him come in. I come to say, "Arise, he calleth for thee." He is calling, gently calling; quench not his pleadings, but stand up and say, "Here, Lord, am I."

The story in the illustration is only one in a million almost the same. Youth points to strong manhood, and puts the time there; strong manhood points to old age, and says, "*That* is the appropriate time, when I am too old to let the cares of life disturb me, and when I shall have ample time to attend to such things." As the steps grow feeble, and the mind unsettled, despair comes, and the icy hand of death points to you. "He that seeketh me early shall find me." Therefore, "Arise, he calleth for thee," *now*.

"*I have called, and ye refused.*" — PROV. i. 24.

It is said of Lady Huntington, that as she was being attired in order to be present at a social gathering of friends, that the thought came to her of her soul's welfare. The Spirit came and convicted her of her life of sin and folly. She went to the party, paid her respects, and returned home. When she had closed her chamber door, she fell upon her knees and gave herself to Christ. Peace flowed into her soul like a river, and she devoted her life to the cause of her Master.

The Spirit knocked, and she opened the door of her heart. Reader, have you done so? or have you refused the entreaties? If you have, let me say, resist no longer. You may be in an instant called before the judgment bar of God, and as you endeavor to excuse your unreadiness, be confronted with these words, too plain to be mistaken, "*I have called, and ye refused.*" Now, "depart from me."

Resist not the Spirit. Behold, "I knock at the door, if any man will open, I will come in unto him." Christ is now knocking, will you unlock the door of your heart and greet him with, "Behold the Lamb of God that taketh away the sins of the world?" and may the edict be published this day in the courts of heaven, "I have called, and ye have *accepted.*"

"*I called upon the Lord in distress.*" — Ps. cxviii. 5.

Near the home of my boyhood lived a man known far and near as the most wicked and ungodly wretch in the whole community. When angry, his voice could be heard throughout the neighborhood, cursing and swearing. His slanderous tongue alienated his neighbors. His awful wickedness made his former friends ashamed to be found in his company. A violent fever seized him, and as the awful darkness of the future stared him in the face, he began to call upon God. A minister was summoned, and, when he arrived, an earnest request was made that he should pray for the sick man's soul. The man recovered, and soon fell into the same course of wickedness. "He called upon the Lord in distress;" in health he found no time and no need of calling on him.

How true is this to human nature. Cowardly human nature lives in open defiance and gross wickedness in health; but when danger and distresses come, how pitiful the cry that goes up from our hearts, and how soon, when danger is past, do we relax and fall into the same sinful ways. Oh, kind reader, let me entreat you to seek the Lord while he may be found, and call upon him while he is near. "For it is time to seek the Lord," *now*. "Woe to him that is alone when he falleth."

"*The fierce anger of the Lord may be turned.*"
NUM. xxv. 4.

When Agathocles was going to besiege Carthage, the people saw the extremity to which they were reduced, and imputed their misfortune to the anger of their god Saturn. That a sufficient atonement be made for this, — to them a great crime, — they sacrificed two hundred of the children of their most eminent citizens, hundreds of the inhabitants also voluntarily offering themselves to appease their god's anger.

O thou, reader of these lines, art thou without hope in Christ? The fierce anger of God Almighty rests upon you, because you have rejected the overtures of his patient mercy, and because you have crucified his own beloved Son.

You are trampling the precious blood of the Lamb of God under your feet. You are crying at every step, by your actions, "Crucify him! crucify him!" You are saying, by your life, that you will not have this man rule over you. You are saying, in your guilty heart, "Away with him! away with him!"

Oh, let me hinder your downward course by throwing this in your way. "The fierce anger of the Lord *may* be turned," may be turned *now* by giving your heart to the Lord Jesus Christ, confessing your wayward steps, and trusting him to secure your pardon and reconciliation. This is the way it may be turned.

> "Oh, while thy waiting Saviour's nigh,
> Sinner, to his bosom fly :
> Fly for succor, pardon, rest,
> To that Fount, forever blest."

"*For what shall it profit a man if he shall gain the whole world and lose his own soul? Or what shall a man give in exchange for his soul?*" — MARK. viii. 36-37.

"A wag once halted a traveller, and asked him this question : 'My kind sir, which had you rather be, Crœsus, who possesses great wealth and a vicious spirit, or Socrates, who was as poor as a church mouse, but renowned for virtue?' The traveller replied, true to human nature, "In this life I had rather be Crœsus ; in death, Socrates.'"

In life many of us will give for our souls, a few short years of folly and wickedness. In death, the same man would give a million worlds and all their wealth, were it only in his power to escape one hour of the remorse and dread, that scene presents.

O friend, *now* is the time to lay the foundation of that life which will tide thee over the pending storm, and have the great, strong arm of God with you as you pass through the valley of the shadow of death.

> "*Choose you this day whom ye will serve.*"
> JOSH. xxiv. 15.

"Over the unrecorded death and grave of one of Franklin's Arctic explorers, on the ice-bound shore of Beechy Island, were found these words : 'Choose you this day

whom you will serve." It is told of one, who, in the
Polar zone of death and night, had found the entrance to
an eternal summer in the paradise of God. Looking
over an endless sea of ice, the dying man saw that his
eternity would be according to the choice which he had
made." — *Rev. John Waugh.*

So your eternity may be, dear reader, according to the
choice you make this day. Therefore, " Choose you this
day whom you will serve."

As a lover of your soul and its eternal interests, I
urge an immediate decision. Disaster may choose for
you, if you wait. Your decision to-day will cut off all
the avenues of such liabilities, and tide you triumphantly
over. Therefore, choose Christ Jesus *now*, and enlist in
his glorious service, looking forward to the reward that
God has promised those that serve him.

It is a debt you owe your God and your immortal soul,
to choose *now* whom ye will serve.

"*I am that bread of life.*" — J<small>NO</small>. vi. 48.

In "Pilgrim's Progress" we read of Christian fleeing
from the city of destruction with his fingers in his ears,
crying, " Life ! life !"

This is the only way some of us will ever get away
from our evil surroundings, and find eternal life. Is it
not a very wise thing to flee, before the chains of sin get
a more firm hold upon us ? My unsaved friend, the
longer you remain in your present condition, the harder
it becomes to throw off those chains. The fastenings become rusted, the links become more set, and, after a time,
you will find it almost impossible to release yourself.
Christ is ready *now* to break the fetters, and release you.
He waits at your heart's door. He gently calls you to

come *now*. It matters not how fast sin's clanking chains hold you. Just come as you are, and his great hands will break asunder the great links, and free you. And if Christ "makes you free, you are free indeed."

"*He heard that it was Jesus of Nazareth.*"
MARK x. 47.

A poor, uneducated Greenlander for the first time heard the love and death of Jesus explained, and said, "If this Saviour underwent all this untold suffering, and died for me, from henceforth he shall be my Saviour."

Unsaved soul, would to God that the same cry might go up from your heart *now*.

Did you ever think for five minutes that the shame, the sorrow, the humiliation, the privations, the griefs, the indescribable pain that he bore was for you? And, with this undeniable fact before you, will you not solemnly covenant with your God that you will henceforth and forever take him as your own personal Saviour, and that you will hereby dedicate your mind, your strength, your body, your soul, your very all, to him from this day evermore. It is not performing an act of benevolence on your part; it is a duty, which you owe to your God, to your soul, and to your fellow-man.

"*He was wounded for our transgressions, he was bruised for our iniquities: the chastisement of our peace was upon him; and with his stripes we are healed.*" — ISA. liii. 5.

A gentleman of wealth and social position attempted one day to cross the street while intoxicated; he staggered into the middle of the street just as a carriage was passing. A poor street-sweeper saw his danger, and sprang in front of the team, and rescued the gentleman, though he himself was knocked down, and run over. As he lay there, in the last throes of death, the gentleman saw what he had done to rescue him. The words of our text came to his mind, and he turned from his worldly life to an active service for Christ.

Unsaved friends, did the thought ever come over your mind that you caused the beloved Son of God Almighty to leave his throne on high, and come to earth to bear the insults of men, and finally die a death of shame? You had a hand in this death, my reader, just as much as the Jews of eighteen hundred years ago. You helped to crucify him. Your very actions condemn you. The course of your life supports the accusation.

Now, in view of this fact, coupled with that of a sin-pardoning God, will you not come to the Saviour, and plead pardon, and be reconciled to God through him.

He stands awaiting your decision. Will you "choose *this day* whom ye will serve," and throw yourself wholly and completely upon the merits of a crucified Lord? Your answer to this question may decide your future for all eternity.

CHAPTER XIX.

DANGER IN DELAY.

"HOW LONG HALT YE BETWEEN TWO OPINIONS?"
1 KINGS, xviii. 21.

DANGER IN DELAY.

"*Behold, now is the accepted time.*" — 2 COR. vi. 2.

A minister choosing this as his text had among his congregation a reviler, who was known for his opposition to any religious worship.

Before the preacher had proceeded far with his discourse, the reviler stood up, and said, "I am now almost sixty years old; I remember when a boy of ten hearing the same words; here I stand before you an old man, and feel that I am as safe as fifty years ago."

Before the minister had concluded his sermon, a heavy storm gathered, loud peals of thunder added to the fearfulness of the occasion. The wind became stronger and stronger, until the little church could no longer stand before it. As the few who were unhurt by the disaster ran hither and thither in their efforts to alleviate the sufferings of the injured ones, the minister came to where the poor unfortunate reviler lay wedged between two heavy timbers.

The man of God began trying to release the poor prisoner, who cried out in his agony of soul, "Let my body go; I am too far gone to ever be removed alive. Oh! pray for my soul. Oh! that I had heeded the words long ago. To my soul the future is more terrible than the storm I have just gone through," and as he breathed his last, these words escaped his lips, "The summer is ended, the harvest is past, and I go to eternity *lost! lost!*"

Reader, how is it with you? Are you out of the ark? Remember, there may come an accident that will, without a moment's warning, send you into the presence of the living God without the wedding garment. Let me ask you, as a friend, to meditate five minutes on your own case, and to remember that the decision may govern the eternal welfare of your immortal soul.

"*Escape for thy life.*" — GEN. xix. 17.

"While Napoleon's army occupied Moscow, though the city had been fired by the retreating inhabitants, the French officers were drinking, dancing, and carousing in the midst of their danger.

"A man came rushing into the room, and interrupted the dance. His livid face and frantic gestures stopped even the music. 'The magazine! the magazine!' he cried hoarsely. 'The flames have almost reached the powder.' For a moment an awful silence, like that of the shadow of death, settled upon the gay company. Then one young man, waving his jewelled hand above his head, shouted, 'One more dance, and defiance to the flames!' In their insane hilarity they were hurled into eternity."

Unsaved soul, as you read the above incident, you wonder how men can do thus. But let me say to you, in all love, that Satan has set about your soul a far more destructive magazine, and I warn you solemnly to "escape for thy life" to Jesus Christ the only refuge. If you do not, you are *lost*. You will be hurled into eternity to stand before God.

"*Almost thou persuadest me.*" — ACTS xxvi. 28.

Years ago, desiring to take a boat-ride, a gentleman secured a skiff, and went a little way up the river above the Falls of Niagara; he came floating quietly down the stream, enjoying the beautiful scenery.

Nearer and nearer to the rapids he came. Persons along the shore warned him of his danger, but he shouted back, "Not yet; I will soon turn my course." He floated on, unmindful of his great danger, until a cry of distress told those watching him that he was in the rapids. His boat was carried over, and he was hurled into the surging abyss.

Beloved reader, which way is your bark floating? Is it anchored to Christ Jesus? or are you letting the current carry you at will? Let me warn you that below you is a raging current that is carrying you gradually down, down, and soon the tide will become so swift you cannot turn back. Now you can reach the harbor. "Turn ye, turn ye, why will ye die," with the harbor of safety so near, and whose gates are wide open to admit you.

"For we must all appear before the judgment seat of Christ, that every one may receive the things done in his body, according to that he hath done, whether it be good or bad." — 2 Cor. v. 10.

"A stage driver in California who had been long accustomed to the rough manners of frontier life, one day lay dying. For years he had driven the stage over a very rough and dangerous road. As he observed his breath grow shorter, and his hands becoming colder, he put his foot out of the bed, and began swinging it to and fro, as if in search of something; his attendants asked him what was wanted. He said, 'I am on the down grade, and cannot get my foot on the brake.'"

Dear reader are you on the down grade? Sooner or later you and I will be called into the presence of the

Great Judge to answer for our lives. Will such a summons to you be welcomed? Oh, while not too far down the grade, grasp the brake, and turn your course.

"*Wherefore he is able also to save them to the uttermost that come unto God by him, seeing he ever liveth to make intercession for them.*" — HEB. vii. 25.

Mr. Carl Steinman, who in 1846 made a trip to Iceland, thus describes a visit to the crater of Mount Hecla. On the brink he was prostrated by an eruption of the crater, and held a prisoner by the lava surrounding him. He says, "Oh, the horrors of that awful realization! There, over the mouth of a black and heated abyss, I was held suspended, a helpless and conscious prisoner, to be hurled downward by the next great throe of trembling Nature.' 'Help! help! help! for the love of God, help!' I shrieked in the very agony of my despair. I had nothing to rely upon but the mercy of heaven, and I prayed to God as I never prayed before, to blot out my sins, and not let them follow me to judgment. All at once I heard a shout; and looking around, I beheld, with feelings that cannot be described, my faithful guide hastening down the side of the crater to my relief. 'I warned you!' he said. 'You did!' cried I, 'but forgive and save me for I am perishing.' He reached out his hand, and took me, and set my feet on solid ground. I was free, but still on the very verge of the awful pit."

Reader, is the lava of hell beginning to flow about you? are your feet already being entangled? Oh! make haste to reach out your hand to your Saviour and guide, who is able to set your feet on the solid rock, and to stablish your ways. Oh! that you could see your danger, and seek refuge before it is too late.

"If they hear not Moses and the prophets, neither will they be persuaded, though one rose from the dead."
LUKE xvi. 31.

"A certain nobleman lay on his death-bed, suffering untold agony of body and soul. To those around him he spoke as follows: 'Oh! if the righteous judge would only try me once more; if he would only spare me a little longer, in what a spirit would I spend the remainder of my days. Every means of grace, every opportunity of spiritual improvement should be dearer to me than all the riches, pleasures, and honors of earth. But, alas, why amuse myself with such fond imaginations. I see but a sad, horrible night approaching, bringing with it the blackest of darkness for ever and ever."

The same story has been told for centuries; we are ever ready to form good resolutions when we are so near death that it is impossible to carry them out. "To-day if ye will hear his voice, harden not your hearts."

Oh! soul, why wait? Why put it off until some future time; it is just as easy to believe now as it will be at any future time; the way of salvation is just as plain now as it will ever be, though the angels of heaven come and proclaim it to you. The threadbare excuse of another trial will not relieve your load of remorse one iota in the future world.

If the brethren of the rich man who had Moses and the prophets were inexcusable, surely you are also, who have Christ and the apostles and an innumerable array of witnesses. If the opportunity of a new trial was denied Dives, it stands to reason that the same will be denied you. The choice is at your door. "Choose you, *this day*, whom you will serve."

"But seek ye first the kingdom of God and his righteousness; and all these things shall be added unto you."

MATT. vi. 33.

A young man came to an aged professor of the college he was attending, and with face all aglow, told him his long-cherished wish had been gratified. He had obtained the consent of his parents to study law; he went on telling the professor how he would spare no pains in perfecting his education. The aged man who had been listening with patience and kindness, gently said, "Well, and when you have finished your studies, what do you purpose to do then?"—"Then I shall take my degree," said the young student. "And what then?" asked the venerable professor."—"Then I shall have a number of difficult cases, and attract attention, and win a great reputation."—"And then?" repeated the professor.—"Then I shall be called upon to fill some important office of State," said the student.—"And then?" said the old man.—"Then I shall live in honor, and look forward to a happy old age," replied the young lawyer.—"And then?" repeated the professor.—"And then?" replied the youth, "I shall die."—"And then?" asked the listener.— The student could not answer, but hung his head, and left the professor's presence.

The student was preparing for everything but that which is most important.

My unsaved reader, how is it with *you?* are you following the same course, in direct violation of a great command of Christ, "Seek ye FIRST the kingdom of God?" That is your duty, the duty you owe to God and to your immortal soul. Make that the first and greatest object of your life, and you will be blessed in this life, and find eternal joy in the life that is hid with Christ in God.

"*Oh remember that my life is wind.*" — JOB. vii. 7.

Colonel R. H. Conwell said, while spending some time in China, he was one evening in a gambling den, and saw two men drinking and playing cards. Both were Americans, one past middle age, the other just blooming into manhood. As the elder was shuffling the cards, the young man began humming in a low tone the hymn : —

"One sweetly solemn thought
Comes to me o'er and o'er,
I am nearer home to-day
Than I have been before."

The man threw down his cards, and asked his companion where he had learned that song. The youth replied " at Sunday school." " Come, Harry," said he, " here is what I have won from you. I have played my last game and drunk my last drink ; I am sorry I have mislead you." The two gamblers were reclaimed for Christ through the influence of a little hymn, showing that each setting sun we are one day nearer the gate of eternity.

Dear reader, remember that your life is but as the wind, and may you at once set out to prepare for the coming of the messenger. Remember, you are nearer eternity to-day than you have been before.

"*And what I say unto you, I say unto all : Watch.*"
MARK xiii. 37.

A train running at full speed plunged through the opening of a drawbridge, down, down, into the rushing torrent below. The bridge that had so often stood under the strain of heavy trains was still perfect. No fault could be attached to it. But the watchman, on opening the draw, forgot to put out the danger signal, and as the heavy train hove in sight, the engineer saw the signal, "All's well," and without slackening speed, he sent his train into the chasm with its load of precious freight. The only excuse that could be offered was, the watchman was not watching. The awful result of his carelessness so weighed upon his mind, that he became a raving maniac, and now walks his cell with only one thought, "If I only had been watching."

Reader, how is it with you? Are you *ready* and watching? If not, imagine the remorse you must suffer in the next world, because you did not watch and prepare for your Lord's coming.

"*For thou Lord art good, and ready to forgive: and plenteous in mercy unto all them that call upon thee.*"

Ps. lxxxvi. 5.

An actress was passing through the streets of an English city one lovely afternoon, and was attracted by singing, in a poor cottage near the street. Her curiosity led her to peep in at the open door, where she saw a few earnest souls mingling their voices in praises to God. They were singing that sweet hymn, —

"Depth of mercy, can there be
Mercy still reserved for me."

The words went direct to her heart. She went her way, but they followed her. She sought and found Christ. She went to her manager, and asked him to release her, but he refused. At last he consented, if she would appear once more in a piece in which she was quite popular. She consented, and in the evening appeared at the theatre. The play required her first to sing a song; and when the curtain went up, the orchestra began the accompaniment. But she stood as if lost in thought. The music ceased, and, supposing her to be overcome by embarrassment, the band again commenced. A second time they paused for her to begin, and still she did not open her lips. A third time the air was played, and then, with clasped hands and eyes suffused with tears, she sang, —

" Depth of mercy, can there be
Mercy still reserved for me?
Can my God his wrath forbear?
Me, the chief of sinners, spare?"

The performance suddenly ended. Some ridiculed, but others were led " to consider their ways," and cry for mercy, too. She lived a consistent Christian life, and at length became the wife of a minister.

Rev. E. M. Long.

" Mercy still reserved for thee,
Seek thy pardon now, to-day,
To-morrow thou mayest never see,
Oh, the danger in delay."

" The fool hath said in his heart, there is no God."
Ps. xiv. 1; liii. 1.

A young English lad decided to leave the home of his childhood, and seek his fortune in a far-off land. As his mother planted on his cheek her farewell kiss, she entreated him to hold fast the faith in Christ, which he had so early professed. He turned his face toward a strange country. Ere he had long been settled in his new home, he fell into bad company; evil associates influenced him. He forgot his early training, and went from bad to worse, until he joined a sect called "Familists"; the first principle they sought to instil in his mind was that *there is no God.* The young man was led to commit a crime, whose punishment was death. As he was brought to the place of execution, he requested a few moments in which to warn his friends; and uttered these words. "Say what you will, surely there is a God, loving to his friends, and terrible to his enemies." Then, reader, if there really is a God, permit me to ask you, how can you expect to meet him in peace when your heart is still full of that which he so detests, when your heart is yet unwashed in the blood of the lamb? Was there ever so solemn a question as this, How will you meet God?

There are two ways to meet him. One way is to triumphantly be borne to his presence, and receive the sweet assurance, "Enter thou into the joys of thy Lord." The other, "Depart from me, ye cursed. I called, and ye gave me no answer." Oh, the danger in delaying our preparation to meet God.

"*Escape for thy life.*" — GEN. xix. 17.

"During a fierce gale at sea, a ship which had become unmanageable was hurled with great force against a huge rock and completely wrecked. The force of the shock had landed the captain and his wife on a high rock, not far from shore. The tide was rising, and in a very short time the waves would dash over the rock upon which they stood. There was only one chance for them; if they could spring upon the crest of one of the great waves, they would be borne safely to the shore. The captain explained to his wife that a moment's delay would let them fall where the water was not deep enough to carry them to land. 'The very instant you hear my words, you must spring with all your might,' the captain said to her. He watched until a heavy wave came, and he cried, 'Spring for your life.' She hesitated only an instant, but the wave had passed, and she fell, a helpless, bruised mass, on the rocks below." Oh, how many souls to-day languish in eternal woe, simply because they hesitated to accept Christ until *too late!* Unexpected misfortune overtook them, and they awoke in eternity. Reader, how is it with you?

"*What shall a man give in exchange for his soul?*"
MATT. xvi. 26.

A few years ago a terrible cyclone swept over a small city, and carried death and destruction in its pathway. Scores were taken out of the wreck, maimed, bruised, and dying. Among the number was a lady of great wealth, who saw that her race was run. She requested her attendants to call a minister. When the man of God arrived, she cried out in the agony of her soul, "Oh, pray for my lost immortal soul." As the tender hands sought to relieve her bodily pains, she said, "Oh, let my body alone; pray that my soul may escape the awful doom I see before me. Oh, that I could be spared to make amends for my life of sin; gladly would I devote my life, my wealth, and my all to be spared this awful darkness I am in." She passed to the beyond without a ray of hope in Christ. Oh, my unconverted reader! such a day may come to you, as to the unfortunate lady. Gladly would you give ten thousand worlds to avert the doom awaiting you, but alas! it will be too late! too late!

"*Then shall he say also to them on the left hand, Depart from me, ye cursed.*" — MATT. XXV. 41.

Dr. Chaffee gives us the following illustration: "Two brothers had from boyhood made their homes in a New England town. The elder had won a reputation as an attorney, while the younger had given himself over to evil habits. The younger brother was brought before the bar of justice, and his brother appeared, and plead for him; for his sake the culprit was released. Some time after, the younger brother disobeyed the law, and was brought into court; again the faithful brother appeared, and plead for him. Once more the guilty one was allowed to go free. Years passed, and at last the lawyer ascended the bench. One day they brought again the erring brother, on a criminal charge. But the judge's face was stern. "It is too late," he said. "As an advocate, I could plead for you; as a judge, I cannot. Arise and receive sentence."

Christ is now pleading before the Father for you, unsaved reader, but there will come a time when you will stand before him as a judge. Will it then be too late? Will you reject his offers to secure your pardon, until he ascends the bench, and closes every avenue of mercy that he now holds out to you? I simply ask the question, and leave you to settle it in your own heart.

"*And ye will not come to me, that ye might have life.*"
JNO. v. 40.

A few years ago the department at Washington sent out special messengers to look into the needs of a certain class who had applied for aid through the pension bureau. A messenger came to a certain town, and notified a poor applicant that he was ready to help him in furthering his application for aid. The poor, poverty-stricken fellow thought a day or two would make no difference, and went on about his daily affairs. When he went to meet the messenger, alas! he was too late. The messenger had left the town, and had forwarded the application to the department, with these words written in large red letters, "Failed to appear in his own behalf." The department consigned the paper to the waste-basket, and erased the applicant's name from the pension rolls. Exactly similar is the case of the sinner. Christ has sent to you special messengers to help you in your application for life eternal. You keep deferring the matter, and it may be your name will be erased from "the Book of Life." Remember, reader, God says, "My Spirit will not always strive with man." You may grieve, time and again, the Holy Spirit, but there also may come a time when the Spirit will be withdrawn from appearing in your behalf. Where will you find succor then as you stand before the awful majesty of the Kings of Kings?

There are yet messengers waiting to aid you.

> While the Spirit waits for thee,
> Quickly to thy Saviour flee.

"*Almost, thou persuadest me to be a Christian.*"
ACTS xxvi. 28.

In the Rocky Mountains there is a place called "The Western Divide," a rugged peak towering heavenward, and forming a great mass of overhanging rock, from which fall the most beautiful and sparkling drops of pure water. If the wind comes from the west, the drops are blown to the eastern side of the mountain, and find their home in the stormy Atlantic; but on the other hand, if the wind blows from the east, the drops fall on the western slope, and are carried to the calm and peaceful Pacific. Oh! my undecided friend, it may be that your chances of eternal life hang by a very slender cord. Let me say, resist no more the Spirit's calling, in doing so you may forever decide your future destiny, and go into the presence of your God almost saved, but *lost*.

Halt not between two opinions.

"*Be sure your sin will find you out.*" — NUM. xxxii. 23.

There was a custom among the ancient Egyptians that forbade praises being bestowed upon the dead on funereal occasions, without observing the following conditions: Judges were to be appointed, whose duty it was to examine into the past life of the deceased; if any one had aught against him, he could appear and state his grievances. If the deceased had led a wicked life, the judges condemned his name to perpetual infamy; nor could his relatives erect any monument to his memory. If nothing was brought against the deceased, permission was granted the relatives to proceed with the funeral discourse, which consisted of a recital of the worthy deeds of the dead.

We are told that in heaven there is a record out of which every man is to be judged, according to the deeds done in the body. When a soul is summoned to stand before the judgment seat, and his evil deeds appear against him, then he is to be cast into "outer darkness"; but when his evil deeds have been washed from the heavenly record through the blood of Christ, then he is to be welcomed to the eternal enjoyment of heaven.

Kind reader, how stands your record? has the blood of the Lamb been applied to your page, and made it clean and "whiter than snow"? Oh! that I could impress upon you the awfulness of "falling into the hands of the living God." While it is called to-day, I warn you to flee from the wrath to come, and lay hold on Christ Jesus, for "be sure your sins will find you out," and when you most need some sustaining hand, they will rise up before you and condemn you. As you read these lines, there is a hope for you. "To-day, if ye will hear his voice, harden not your hearts."

"*Go thy way for this time, when I have a convenient season I will call for thee.*" — ACTS xxiv. 25.

I read not long since an account of the execution of a murderer. The friends of the condemned man had made a strong effort to obtain a pardon, but were unsuccessful. They next sought a commutation of the sentence to imprisonment for life. Failing in this, they begged for a brief respite, and presented a petition bearing many names, but it failed to move the governor. The day set for the execution arrived, the preparations for carrying out the sentence were completed, the condemned man was led to the scaffold, his arms pinioned, the rope was carefully adjusted. Suddenly the jail door bell rang. The sheriff supposing that it was the eager mob on the outside, paid no attention to it, but proceeded with his unpleasant duty; the next moment the trap fell, and the poor man's spirit went to his reward. The ringing and knocking at the jail door grew louder and louder, and the sheriff despatched an officer to quiet the mob; the officer quickly returned, bearing a message from the governor. The sheriff read it, and found it to be a pardon, it came only one half minute too late; but it had as well been half a million years too late, so far as it affected the condemned man.

Oh, that piercing cry, "Too late! too late!"

To-day, reader, it may be not too late; to-morrow, this may be your cry of remorse, — too late! I am lost!

"*The redemption of their soul is precious.*"
Ps. xlix. 8.

I once read a very sad story of a young lady who became deeply concerned about the welfare of her soul. She went to her father and mother, but found no words of encouragement or comfort there, they being worldly minded and determined that their daughter should not settle down to the Christian life.

They tried in many ways to win her back to the world. As a last resort Satan interposed, and told them to give a grand party, which suggestion they eagerly grasped, thinking to drown her soul's trouble in gayety and pleasure. They made great preparations, invited the most worldly-minded guests they could find. They provided her an elegant wardrobe, and adorned her with rich jewels. The temptation was too strong, and the young lady thought it no harm to attend this one time, as it was at her own home. She thought for the sake of propriety she must be present. She arrayed herself in all her finery, and was pronounced the belle of the occasion.

But, alas! during the dancing she had become quite heated, and sought a breath of fresh air at an open window. A chilly sensation came over her, though at the time she thought little of it. When the morrow came, she failed to come downstairs to breakfast. A physician was summoned, but to no purpose, the disease had taken such hold, human skill was powerless to arrest its course. In a few days she felt the cold-handed messenger's presence. She called for her mother, who quickly responded. She requested the dress and jewels she wore on the evening of the party to be brought her. As her eyes rested upon them, she said, pointing her finger at the finery, "These are the price of my soul," and sank back cold in death.

Oh! how many wails of remorse are going up to-day from departed and lost souls that were dragged down by the foolishness of this world.

"*Almost thou persuadest me to be a Christian.*"
Acts xxvi. 28.

"ALMOST, BUT LOST."

An eminent resident of a Southern state had an urgent business call to go at once to Europe. He hastened to the port to catch the steamer that sailed the next day. On his way to the port he met some old friends, who proposed to give a great banquet in honor of their guest. The vessel was to sail at 6 P. M. The banquet was to take place at four o'clock the next afternoon. The table was laden with rich delicacies and many varieties of wines. The gentleman became so absorbed in the company of his entertainers, that he quite forgot the hour of his departure. He suddenly was startled by the sounding of the bells of the outgoing vessel. He rushed down to the wharf just in time to see the vessel leaving. Learning that another vessel would sail on the morrow, he returned to his companions to enjoy the banquet. The morrow came, and he took passage on the outgoing vessel, to never more set foot on land. The ship was unseaworthy, and was unable to withstand the tempestuous sea which it encountered. She went down with all on board. The eminent man with such bright prospects found his grave in the deep, simply because he allowed the god of this world to rule him. Similar is the case of the unsaved man; the ship of salvation awaits him, but he is so deeply engrossed with this world that he refuses to go on board, and embarks on an unseaworthy ship that will wreck his immortal soul. Oh, my friend, take passage now on the ship of salvation, with Christ Jesus as captain, and ensure thy safety. Though Satan's tempestuous waves may roll against thy vessel, it will land you safely.

> Safe in the arms of Jesus,
> Safe on His passage to rest,
> There shall my soul find comfort,
> Leaning on his gentle breast.

"*I never knew you, depart from me.*" — MATT. vii. 23.

A gentleman passing along one of the streets of New York one day was hailed by a well-dressed, genteel appearing young man, who grasped him by the hand, and exclaimed, "How glad I am to see you Mr. ———. When did you arrive in the city?" The gentleman looked at him a moment, and said, "Sir, you have the advantage of me. I must confess I never remember seeing you before." The young man tried in vain to introduce himself by referring to a prominent man as his father. Wearied at the young man's attempt, and knowing him to be a confidence man, he said, "Young fellow, the quicker you depart from me, the better for you; I never knew you. I fully understand your game." He hung his head, and walked away.

So it will be with some of us when we stand before

the judgment seat of Christ. "Lord, Lord, have we not prophesied in thy name." "Depart from me, ye workers of iniquity, I never knew you."

"*And the Lord said, my spirit shall not always strive with man.*" — GEN. vi. 3.

A gentleman having a piece of property in another part of the country neglected to pay the taxes on it, and it was sold by the sheriff, but the owner still had a certain time to redeem it. He carelessly waited another period, and then made inquiry about the property. Word came back that the time of redemption had expired, and the property was lost.

My unsaved friend, there will come a time when your time of redemption will expire. There may come a time when you will seek diligently, and not find; there may come a time when you will cry long and loud, but find it not. Now it is within your reach, now the Saviour awaits your coming, now the great advocate is ready to appear for you. But God says, "My spirit will not always strive with man." What will be your hope in the future, when that Spirit is withdrawn?

"*Though I walk through the valley of the shadow of death, I will fear no evil; for thou art with me; thy rod and thy staff they comfort me.*"— Ps. xxiii. 4.

As Addison lay on his death-bed, he sent for his step-son, the Earl of Warwick, and said to him, "I have sent for you that you may see how a Christian can die." Mr. Addison said, in an article that preceded his last hymn, "Among all the reflections that usually arise in the mind of a sick man, who has time and inclination to consider his approaching end, there is none more natural than that of his going to appear naked and unbodied before him who made him."

Kind reader, have you made the necessary preparation to stand face to face with your Creator?

> "When, rising from the bed of death,
> O'erwhelmed with guilt and fear,
> I see my Maker face to face,
> Oh! how shall I appear?"

"*How long halt ye between two opinions?*"
1 Kings xviii. 21.

An anxious teacher in one of our Sunday schools had a class of young men. Intellectually they were above the average; socially, they stood high; but neither of them were Christians.

He had ofttimes earnestly prayed for them, had personally plead with them, but it seemed he would be compelled to despair of ever seeing them brought to Christ. In a neighboring city a gracious revival was in progress, and the thought came to the teacher to invite his class to accompany him thither. They each readily accepted the invitation, and met at the depot at the hour appointed. The evening was warm, and the moon shone brightly. When they arrived at the church, the teacher led the way to the front pew and, after seating his class, gave himself to silent prayer. At the close of the sermon the minister plead with unusual power for sinners to come to Christ. The teacher's heart almost failed him, as he saw no move made by his class to accept the invitation. He started homeward with a heavy heart. The train was so crowded that it fell to the lot of the little company to ride outside on the platform. As they stood there, recalling the scenes of the evening, the teacher led the conversation to the sermon to which they had listened. Each one of the class pronounced it a grand discourse, and freely expressed a desire to become a Christian at some future time. The conversation became more and more earnest as the teacher reviewed the grand opportunity given them to come to Christ. Suddenly the jostling of the train interrupted them, and, in another instant, the car on which they stood went through the bridge into the river, and the young men were killed while halting between two opinions.

Oh, how many poor souls to-day are suffering the torments of eternal woe, because they halted too long!

Reader, let me warn you to decide *now*. "Now is the accepted time." Satan is making you believe the future will abound in opportunities. God says, "To-day, if ye will hear his voice, harden not your hearts. To-day, the "Spirit and the bride say come." Will you come?

" How can ye escape the damnation of hell? "
MATT. xxiii. 33.

A few years ago an evangelist was holding revival services in a town in Scotland, and many were melted by the Spirit's influence, and brought to Christ. Amongst those who attended the meetings was a young farmer. The Spirit convicted him, and strove to turn him to life in Christ. Earnest Christians talked with him; fervent prayers ascended to the throne of grace in his behalf; but to all entreaties he would say, "Not to-night, not to-night." So earnestly did the Spirit strive with him that he left his work, and prayed that God would withdraw his Spirit, and not further strive with him. In a few days all anxiety left him, and he went about his labors undisturbed, until one day a violent fever seized him, which soon terminated fatally. Before he breathed his last he recalled the scene of his prayers, and said, "That sealed my doom." Oh, the countless thousands of poor souls now writhing in hell's torments that were blindly led to their doom by this great lie of Satan's! "Not to-night: plenty of time yet."

Reader, are you trying to persuade yourself that "there's time enough yet?" Are you thus trifling with your immortal soul? Oh! let me say that Satan is leading you, and when middle age comes he will say the same thing. When the time allotted you is almost run, he will say the same thing; when death comes to you, he still will preach the same to you; and when hell's jaws open to receive you, then you will awake to a realization of your condition. "To-day, if ye will hear his voice, harden not your hearts. Now is the accepted time, — NOW is the day of salvation."

"*For it is written, He shall give his angels charge over thee, to keep thee.*" — LUKE iv. 10.

A Christian man once dreamed that he was dead, and had ascended to the pearly gates of the city of God. Before admission into the heavenly city, he was bidden to tarry a moment in the picture gallery; he passed from scene to scene, and every one appeared familiar to him; at last he recognized them as drawn from his own life. He noticed also, that in each picture he was represented as in peril of some kind. But angels sent of God were watching and guarding over him. This scene put his life in a new light. — God's messengers had saved and watched his every breath. In his gratitude of heart he raised his soul in thanksgiving to the God of all mercies, and praised him that he had been kept from harm through in eminent peril.

Reader did you ever think of the peril to which your soul is constantly subjected? Did you ever meditate upon this one question. How shall I meet my God? Herein is where your peril lies. How shall I meet my God? Oh, what danger each hour of your life. The gaping jaws of doom are nigh unto you, the meshes of Satan's web at each breath draws tighter, the emissaries of hell press harder upon you. The cords of sensuality more tightly bind you. The blinding god of this world sways more defiantly the sceptre of his power over thy head; and amid all this, you say you are not in peril.

Dear reader, through all this, God's love has gone out toward you; but he says, My patience cannot always last. "My spirit will not always strive with you." "I have called you, and you gave me no answer." Then will come a time "when ye call, I will not answer."

May the Spirit show you the picture gallery of your life, and may the terrible scene turn you to Jesus Christ, who "shall give his angels charge over thee to keep thee."

"*The Holy Ghost saith, to-day, if ye will hear his voice, harden not your hearts.*" — HEB. iii. 7, 8.

A young man came to the captain of a large ship, and engaged as a seaman. When well out to sea, a severe storm arose, and the youth trembled with fear. As the waves lashed higher and harder, he crept into one corner. and knelt down to pray. About this time, the captain came along, and said, "Get up from there, you coward, say your prayers in fine weather." The young man quickly got up, promising himself if ever he lived to see fair weather he would say his prayers. They soon reached land, but the words of the captain clung to him, and so impressed him that he heard the gospel, and was converted, and became an able minister of Christ. Years after, the captain went into a chapel in New York, and a young man looked at him from the pulpit, and said, "Say your prayers in fine weather." It was the same young man to whom he had some years before given this same advice. Very few people in this enlightened age expect to be lost. Most every one expects at some future time to make his peace with God, and his calling and election sure. The majority look to old age as the time to devote to such things, when they have gotten all the gratification possible out of this world, and as the grave stares them in the face, then they anticipate time for preparation to meet God.

Friend, life hangs by too slender a cord to let any such ideas enter your mind with safety. "While it is fine weather is the time to begin such preparations." "The Holy Spirit of God saith to you, to-day if ye will hear his voice, harden not your heart," to-morrow may be too late.

> To-day the Saviour calls,
>   Oh, hear his voice!
> To-day he bids you come,
>   And make your choice.
>
> The Spirit entreats you, come,
>   Heed thou his cry.
> The blessed Jesus waits,
>   Oh, to him fly! Oh, to him fly!

DANGER IN DELAY. 317

"*To-day if ye will hear his voice, harden not your hearts.*" — HEB. iii. 15.

Some years ago, two young men left home to attend college. During a precious revival, the Spirit convicted them of sin. One of them went to the president of the college, and asked permission for himself and companion to attend the revival services. The companion informed him that he did not care to attend the services, but would walk down the street with him; they soon came to the church, and halted in front of the door; one plead with the other to come in, but he refused, and walked on down the street, while the other went into the church. Before he left, the Lord opened his eyes, and revealed to him the riches of a faith in Christ, and he rejoiced in his Saviour. At the end of their course at college, the two young men separated, one without any particular aim in view, except to gratify present desires; the other with the burden of lost souls resting upon him, and with a fixed determination to devote his life to the cause of Christ. Years passed by. One day as the latter was passing along the street to the church where he was converted, and where he was to preach that day, a voice startled him. He quickly halted, to find by his side a poor, ragged, miserable form of humanity, a true and real picture of a debauched outcast. The minister halted to speak with the tramp, "How can it be possible Mr. —— to see you in such a plight? When I last saw you, you were leaving your college with high honors, and a promise of a useful life before you." The miserable outcast said to him, "Do you recall the day you plead so earnestly with me to go with you into yon church? from that very hour, I date my misery and downfall. From that hour, God withdrew his Spirit, and I have been sinking deeper and deeper into the pit of sin, until now I am at the bottom, without one ray of hope of ever escaping the result of my folly and crimes. God called, but I answered not. Now it is too late; I am forever lost."

The same story has escaped the lips of ten thousand lost souls. Will you not profit by such an experience, and seek the Lord while he may be found?

CHAPTER XX.

PERSONAL APPEALS.

"PREPARE TO MEET THY GOD."
AMOS iv. 12.

PERSONAL APPEALS.

"For the preaching of the cross is to them that perish foolishness; but unto us which are saved it is the power of God." — 1 Cor. i. 18.

A certain author sent to a young lady a copy of a book he had written. The lady carelessly glanced at the contents of the volume, and laid it aside. Not long after, she was requested to give her honest opinion of the book presented to her. She said, "To be candid, I must confess the book is very dry and uninteresting to me." A little later she met the author; the acquaintance ripened into love, and soon she became the bride of the uninteresting writer. She again took up the book, and carefully read it page by page, and found it aglow with interest, until it became her delight to read it; each time new light came to her. How often have we heard worldly-minded people say, "I cannot read the word of God, it is too dry." My dear, lost friend, when the love of Christ dawns on your soul, then you will see with new eyes this precious well of living water springing up unto life eternal. Every page of "sacred writ" will sparkle with a new lustre as you read it. Rich jewels will shine forth from each verse. For all the vicissitudes of life, you will find a complete remedy. You may now see no beauty in Calvary's cross. The empty sepulchre may seem to you no more than a barren rock. Gethsemane may appear no more solemn than the laughing rills of

Galilee. The "upper chamber" may seem to you no more sacred than the judgment hall of Pilate, and why not? may be asked. I answer, because Satan has blinded your sight, and is to-day withholding their glory from your vision. Neither can you comprehend them until Christ opens your eyes, and cuts away these hindrances, and restores your spiritual vision.

Your only hope of relief lies in a simple faith and belief in Him.

"*For where your treasure is, there will your heart be also.*" — LUKE xii. 34.

In the biography of Edward the First, a very touching incident is given us. It said he long had cherished a desire to visit the Holy Land, but ere he could so arrange his life, death came, and claimed him. While lying on his death-bed he ordered his attendants to take his heart after death, and convey it to the place he had so much wished to visit.

You who read these lines, have you made the adorable Christ your heart's treasure, that in the day of his coming you may be found ready to obey his summons to "come up higher." Bear in mind that "where your treasure is, there will your heart be also." If you have chosen this world, then serve it with all your might, for soon you will leave it. If Christ is thy treasure, happy is thy lot, and thrice happy thy eternity.

"*Prepare to meet thy God.*" — AMOS iv. 12.

"A Hungarian king, being sad one day, was asked by his brother the reason of his heaviness of heart. 'I have been a great sinner,' said he, 'and know not how to die, and appear before God in the judgment.' His brother laughed at him. It was the custom in that country for the executioner to sound a trumpet before the door of the man who was to be executed. At midnight the trumpet sounded at the door of the king's brother. He arose and came in great haste to the king, and inquired in what he had offended. The king replied, 'You have not offended me, but if the sight of my executioner be so dreadful, then shall I not, who have greatly offended, fear to stand in judgment before Christ?'"

Reader, have you any fear of that moment when God will say to thy soul, come hither and be judged? Or, can you say, "yea Lord I am ready?"

Such a time will come to you and to me. Will we be prepared to meet it? As I write, a silent prayer goes up that you may be led to seek that preparation.

"But the natural man receiveth not the things of the spirit of God: for they are foolishness unto him."

1 COR. ii. 14.

One of the great mercantile establishments of St. Louis, and with whom I was at one time engaged, found that the expense of the telegrams, that came to them in large numbers every day, was so heavy they could ill afford to bear it. One of the firm hit upon the happy idea of arranging what he called a "Telegraphic Cipher Code," and which consisted of a list of words, each of which was made to represent an entire sentence. They printed a large number of copies, and distributed them among their correspondents. With each book was a key that explained the workings of the book. The idea was a grand success, and made the expenses many times less. No outside party could understand the business transactions of the firm, and a cipher telegram appeared as an unmeaning, foolish mystery. So with many parts of the Bible, to the unregenerate man it seems a mere foolish cipher. But when the blessed spirit of God opens his eyes, then he can use the word as a key to the sweet mysteries of grace which were before as a garden of rich beauty, a fountain sealed and locked.

"I am come that they might have life, and that they might have it more abundantly." — Jno. x. 10.

A short time ago a poor laborer, whose daily toil hardly brought him a sufficiency for the support of his large family, received a letter from his native country, stating that an elder brother had died. When the private papers of the deceased were examined, they found a will bequeathing a portion of the vast estate to him, and that it would be only necessary for him to make a personal application, and the amount would be paid over to him.

Friendly reader, over eighteen hundred years ago an elder brother died, and bequeathed to you untold riches. In order that you may come into possession of this vast wealth, you must make a personal application, and it will be settled upon you. There remains only a short time, and many claims must be settled very soon, or they will forever be debarred. Yours may be among that number; will you not then give your immediate personal attention?

The free gift of salvation by God, through Jesus Christ, unto every one that will apply.

"Behold the Lamb of God, which taketh away the sin of the world." — Jno. i. 29.

Years ago there lived in one of the New England States, a poor Englishman who was feeble in mind and body. He felt that a just God could never pardon his past offences, and save him from eternal destruction. He was a regular attendant upon divine services, and saw his friends and neighbors born into the kingdom; still, all seemed dark to him. He could not perceive how a just God could pardon such a sinner. His sleep became restless and disturbed, his very life became burdensome. At last, one day a Christian man went to talk with him. He began by taking him back to the sacrifices under the law. He told him how a lamb was brought by the guilty one, and laid bound on the altar, and he who had sinned laid his hands upon it confessing his sins, and its blood became the blood of the atonement, and he was thus freed from guilt. His friend then said, "Jesus Christ is our Lamb. He bore our sins on the cross." This was sufficient, the poor man exclaimed, "All is plain now; Christ is the Lamb that takes away our sins," and he went his way, rejoicing in his new-found faith.

Unsaved reader, I to-day point you to the "Lamb of God that taketh away the sins of the world." He stands waiting to turn the scarlet page of your life's record into one of snowy whiteness. Will you come and accept him? "Behold the Lamb of God, that taketh away the sins of the world."

"*All nations before him are as nothing ; and they are counted to him less than nothing, and vanity. To whom then, will ye liken God? or what likeness will ye compare unto him?*" — Isa. xl. 17, 18.

In the early history of the Assyrians, they worshipped the sun and moon. Feeling the need of some object nearer to them, they chose fire as a substitute, and set up Ur, which signifies fire, as their god, and published a challenge to all other nations to stand their gods before

Ur. Vast numbers were brought, but, being made of wood, of course were consumed. Finally, an Egyptian priest hit upon a happy scheme to destroy the reputation of the mighty god of the Assyrians which had so long been the terror of other nations. He made an image of burnt clay, hollow inside, and with holes in the body. He then filled the body with water, and stopped the holes with wax. His challenge to the god Ur was eagerly accepted, and when the fire heated the wax, it melted, letting the water out, and drowned the fire, ruining the reputation of Ur.

Now, every living man has a god, every nation of earth worships some sort of a god. It may be the god of wealth, honor, fame, pleasure, light, heat, wood, stone, metal, or it may be the God of Gods and King of Kings, but I say all worship some god. But "to whom then will we liken our God" who made the heavens and the earth, and who gave life, and who hath power to take it again!

Reader, are you serving some god of this world? Let me say to you to "turn ye, for why will ye die." "Thou shalt have none other gods before Me," echoes the voice of Jehovah down the ages of time.

"*For all flesh is as grass, and all the glory of man as the flower of grass. The grass withereth, and the flower thereof falleth away.*" — 1 Pet. i. 24.

A young college student took his seat one day under a large tree in the college grounds, and soon became deeply engaged with his studies. As he sat there musing over the subject before him, he saw a leaf fall at his feet; he picked it up, and found it apparently perfect in form, its color as green as any on the tree. The thought came to him, "Why did it fall?" The leaf seemed in a still, small voice to say to him, "My hold on life was apparently as good as any on the tree, yet I was cut off in the midst of life, and consigned to the scorching rays of the summer sun. Take heed, young man, your life hangs by a like slender cord. Should that cord by accident become severed, where wilt thou find thy bed?"

Reader, let me ask of thee the same question. Will the scorching rays of God's wrath consume thee? Or will angelic messengers bear thee gently away to heaven's eternal joys? How will you answer?

"*Therefore to him that knoweth to do good, and doeth it not, to him it is sin.*" — JAS. iv. 17.

A father who had five sons, called them to him one morning, and bade them go to a certain field, and do a piece of work in a manner he minutely described to them. In the afternoon he came to where his sons were laboring, and found they had not followed his instructions, but had performed the work in a different way from that outlined by him. He was angry, and chastised them severely, beginning with the eldest. When the youngest son's time came, he excused him, saying, he did not know that which was right from the wrong, and released him. But the elder sons knew perfectly well what was required of them.

Kind friend, God has minutely outlined our course in life, made everything so plain, has bidden you go into his vineyard, and has given you an especial duty to perform. How can you hope to avert his anger by not performing that duty? How can you hope to meet him in peace, with your duty unperformed?

"*God so loved the world, that he gave his only begotten Son, that whosoever believeth in him should not perish, but have everlasting life.*" — JNO. iii. 16.

"At the close of a Gospel meeting, a man came to the speaker in great agony of soul. The rod of conviction smote him heavily, and he inquired the way of salvation. The man of God opened his Bible, and asked the inquirer to read John iii. 16: 'God so loved the world, that he gave his only begotten son, that whosoever believeth in him should not perish, but have everlasting life.' 'Now,' said the speaker, 'go to your room, and take your Bible, and instead of the words, 'world,' and 'whosoever,' just put your own name in the place, and see how it will apply to you.'

"A few days after, this man came again to the Christian, with his face ablaze with the love of Christ, and he said, 'Sir, I am saved. I followed your instructions, and am *now* saved.'"

Oh! thou unsaved one, wilt thou do the same? Will you put your name instead of the two words, and see if there is not a Saviour for you too? "He is able to save to the uttermost all that come unto God by him." *Will you come?*

"*Rejoice, because your names are written in heaven.*"
LUKE x. 20.

Several years ago, Congress enacted a law making every maimed and crippled soldier of the Union a pensioner at the public treasury. Among the thousands of applications made was that of a poor, crippled man, on whom depended the support of a large family. His application was taken up by the proper authorities, but after a long search the army record failed to show his name. Years passed, the poor fellow was struggling along, and had despaired of ever hearing from his application again. One evening as he sat with his family around the humble hearthstone, thinking how hard life was, and what little pleasure the future revealed, his son, who had been to the post-office, handed him a large envelope. He could not imagine who had sent him such a message. He quickly opened it, and read, "After diligent search, your name has been found, and your pension allowed." The poor man was overcome with joy. Sleep left his eyes, he could talk of nothing but the happy times in store for him.

Unsaved friend, have you made application for eternal life through Christ? Do the heavenly records show you as among the blood-washed throng? Oh, the anguish of soul which awaits you when you stand before the Great Judge, and find your name is not recorded; there,

"In the Book of God's kingdom,
Is your name written there?"

"*But every man is tempted when he is drawn away of his own lust, and enticed. Then when lust hath conceived, it bringeth forth sin: and sin, when it is finished, bringeth forth death.*"—Jas. i. 14, 15.

Mr. Spurgeon says that he saw, while on a visit to the gardens of Hampton Court, many trees almost entirely covered, and well-nigh strangled by the huge coils of ivy, which were wound about them like the snakes about the unhappy Laocoon. There is no untwisting the folds; they in their giant grip are fast fixed, and the rootlets of the climbers are constantly sucking the life of the trees. There was a day when the ivy was a tiny aspirant, only asking a little aid in climbing; had it been denied, then the tree need not have become its victim, but by degrees the humble weakling grew in strength and arrogance, and at last it assumed the mastery, and became the destroyer. Just the same with the beginning of sin; the least little act of disobedience, it may be a lie, then another, then something else, and they become alarmingly frequent, and each time a little more wicked until they gain the mastery over us, and overwhelm us, and at last drag our souls down to hell. "Every man is tempted when he is drawn away of his own lusts, and enticed. Then when lust hath conceived, it bringeth forth sin; and sin, when it is finished, bringeth forth death."

Oh! dear young soul, profit thou by the experience of others, and form in thy heart fixed resolutions to resist the first sin, and the second, and learn to trust Jesus for power to do so, and you will escape much of the sorrow and pain that come to some of us that are older.

> When temptations come within,
> Fix your eyes upon Jesus;
> Learn to resist the tiny sin,
> By fixing your eyes upon Jesus.

"*Seek ye first the kingdom of God, and his righteousness; and all these things shall be added unto you.*"
MATT. vi. 33.

It is said of Mr. Samuel Colgate, a trusted servant of God, that when a mere lad he was thrown upon the world to care for himself. Wearied of the slow country life, he directed his steps toward the great city of New York, hoping to realize a larger income from the labor of his hands. He travelled with the driver of the canal team, and when the place was reached where Samuel was to take a different course, the rough and strong hand of the driver grasped him by the hand, and he said, "Samuel, seek ye first the kingdom of God and his righteousness, and all these (temporal) things shall be added unto you." Kneeling, the good man invoked God's blessing on the lad, and they parted. Samuel did seek first the "kingdom of God." He gave himself to Christ. To-day he not only stands among the first business men of the land, but he is noted far and wide as a noble Christian gentleman. It pays every young man and young woman to start out in life with this great truth in mind, to make God first — self, last. God knows the things we have need of, and will freely supply all.

"*Rejoice, because your names are written in heaven.*"
LUKE x. 20.

At the great Centennial celebration in Philadelphia, some years ago, there lay open upon a table near the main entrance, an immense book, said to have been the largest book in the world. In the book was recorded the name of every visitor who cared to make application to the keeper of the great book. More than one laid down the pen with a smile of satisfaction at the idea of having his name written in the largest book in the world, and more than one went home to tell that his name graced the pages of this most wonderful piece of the book-maker's skill.

When the penitent soul comes to Christ, his name is placed upon heaven's records. My friend, is your name written there? When Christ comes with his holy angels will your name be found upon the book of the saved, and will you be invited to take your stand on the right, with the redeemed of God?

"*Mighty to save.*" — Isa. lxiii. 1.

Some years ago there were sad hearts in the homes of a great many New England people. Word came that the great steamer "Atlantic" had foundered off the coast of Newfoundland, and many on board had perished.

"On board was a prominent business man, who was reported as among those who had perished. His place of business was closed, and draped in mourning. Kind friends came to console the sorrowing ones. A telegram came next morning to the business partner, with only one word, '*Saved.*' There was great rejoicing in that sorrowing home. The friends that had mourned with the family now came to rejoice with them."

Dear, unsaved friends, may the joyful news go over the line to heaven that you, who have been so long tossed about on the sea of sin, are at last *saved*, and the glad shout of the holy angels in the presence of God will fill the whole heavens with their praises.

CHAPTER XXI.

TRYING TO SAVE YOURSELF.

"OTHER FOUNDATION CAN NO MAN LAY THAN THAT IS LAID, WHICH IS JESUS CHRIST."
1 Cor. iii. 11.

TRYING TO SAVE YOURSELF.

"*And this is life eternal, that they might know thee the only true God, and Jesus Christ, whom thou hast sent.*" — JNO. xvii. 3.

"When Bishop Beveridge was on his deathbed, a ministerial friend called to see him. He said to him, 'Bishop Beveridge, do you know me?' 'Who are you?' replied the bishop. On being told, he said, 'I don't know you.' Another friend soon came in, and asked the same question; but he replied, as before, 'I don't know you.' His faithful wife then asked him if he recognized her; but he said, 'I don't know you.' Some one in the room said to him, 'Bishop, do you know the Lord Jesus Christ?' Like an electric flash, he brightened up and said, 'Oh, yes, I have known him these forty years. *Precious Saviour, he is my only hope of eternal life.*'"

Reader, this, too, is your and my only hope of eternal life. Satan may tell you that Christ was a mere moral man; moralists may teach you that morality is the only thing necessary to an admittance to eternal life; liberalists may seek to prove to you that God is too loving to let you be lost; but "He that believeth that Jesus is the Son of God shall be saved, and he that believeth not shall be damned." "He that hath the son hath life, and he that hath *not* the son hath *not* life." "Neither is there salvation in any other; for there is none other name under heaven given among men, whereby we must be saved." "He is able to save to the uttermost, them that come unto God by him." "Believe on the Lord Jesus Christ, and thou shalt be saved." "For God sent not his Son into the world to condemn the world; but that the world through him might be saved." Then, unsaved soul, if you are ever saved from the haunting torments of the future world, it must be by coming to Jesus Christ, and confessing your sins, and pleading the merits of him " who came to seek and to save that which was lost." Your morality is but as " sounding brass and a tinkling cymbal," in the sight of God. Will you come ?

"*He that believeth on the Son hath everlasting life: and he that believeth not the Son shall not see life; but the wrath of God abideth on him.*" — JNO. iii. 36.

One bright summer afternoon, some years ago, a little party of ladies and children stood upon the wharf at a fashionable watering-place, awaiting the arrival of a steamer that would bring them husbands and fathers. As they waited there, enjoying the refreshing breeze, their attention was suddenly attracted by a loud splash in the water, followed instantly by a piercing scream. As the startled crowd turned, they saw a young man struggling in the water. He could not swim, and in his frantic efforts to rescue himself, he was at each struggle getting deeper and deeper into the water, and farther from the shore.

The ladies ran hither and thither to find help; they found only one person near, that could render any assistance; he was an old sailor, who was standing motionless, watching the poor man drown before his eyes. The entreaties of the ladies could not move him, until he saw the young man cease trying to save himself. As his hands fell helplessly at his side, his face told plainly that he had given up in despair. As he arose the first time, a feeling of horror came over the little company, who were to be the unwilling witnesses to his death. When all hope was gone, the brave sailor leaped into the water, and, as the drowning man arose for the last time, seized him and bore him safely to shore.

As the ladies gathered around him, he said, "I was compelled to wait until he ceased trying to save himself; for I could save him only when he was without strength."

So the blessed Christ can never save a soul until that soul ceases trying to save itself, and gives up solely to the power of Christ to rescue it from its sin.

Oh, how willingly he then reaches out his great arm, and lifts the soul out of the pit and the miry clay, and tenderly washes and purifies it in the blood of the Lamb, that taketh away every stain of sin.

"*Come unto me, all ye that labor and are heavy laden, and I will give you rest.*" — MATT. xi. 28.

A young man once came to a minister to talk with him about his soul.

The minister bade him tell his story, which ran as follows: "For several years I was a member of a church, and tried hard and earnestly to live a consistent Christian life. I went regularly to church, taught a class in the Sunday school, was prompt in attending the weekly prayer-meetings. I ofttimes heard Christians say it was so easy to live a Christian life and serve God, but I must confess I found it not so, but the very reverse. I found the yoke heavy, the burden hard to carry, and at last, in my despair, I gave up."

"My friend," said the minister, "I do not doubt your statement in the least. There are thousands of professing Christians who, were they as frank as you, would say the same thing. Permit me to ask you if you were not trying to be saved?" "Of course, I was," said the young man. "You put on the yoke with the hope that by wearing it you would at last find eternal life?" "Just so," he replied. "Your mistake, my friend, lies just here. You failed to get the meaning of the whole text. Christ says, 'Come unto me, all ye that labor and are heavy laden, and I will give you rest'; then he adds, 'Take my yoke upon you.' Did you ever experience the sweet rest he gives, and the blessed assurance of salvation through simple trust in his name?" "I never did, sir," the young man replied. "Then no wonder the yoke galled your neck."

"If a soul," says one, "is put upon a course of doing, in order to be saved, instead of believing, it is pursuing an unfinished work, and therefore can never have rest." Meanwhile eternity, because hidden, seems afar off, and earth with its attractions are near. The weary one necessarily turns to that which is seen and temporal, for the rest he seeks. The hungry one receives no satisfaction from a Christ not yet found, and turns to the very husks the swine do eat, for the food he craves.

"*The son of man is come to seek and to save that which was lost.*" — LUKE xix. 10.

In a Southern city, a few years ago, lived a wealthy gentleman and wife. The gentleman had been successful in business, and had erected for himself an elegant home. One day he came home as usual at the dinner hour, and found his wife sick. He immediately summoned a physician, who informed him that he could do nothing for her. A change of climate was proposed, and the anxious husband started at once for a trip to the North. They had hardly reached the point of destination ere the dread disease was fully developed, and it was plain to both that death was very near. The wife expressed a desire to see a Christian. In order to gratify her wishes, her husband sent a note to a Christian gentleman near by. As he entered the door, the dying woman fixed her eyes on him, and said, "I am dying, and oh, I do want to be saved! I can't pray." Her words told the godly man her spiritual condition, and he asked her if she had ever tried to pray. "Oh, yes," she replied, "for twenty years I have tried hard to be a Christian." — "In what way have you tried?" asked the man of God. "I have gone to church, read my Bible, and done the best I knew how," she said. "Still you are unsaved?" asked the Christian. "Still unsaved," she said in a low voice. "What else can you do?" he said. "I do not know," she replied. "I have sent for you to tell me." He opened his Bible, and read of the saving power of Jesus Christ. She listened with intense eagerness, and at last she exclaimed, "I thought I had to pray to be saved. I see now how it is, I only have to trust Jesus, and he will save me." New light shone into her heart, and she rejoiced in Christ Jesus.

"*Come unto me, all ye that labor and are heavy laden, and I will give you rest.*" — MATT. xi. 28.

"A pastor was one day summoned to the bedside of a dying lady. He soon found that she had imbibed infidelity through the influence of her teacher at school. He argued with her to no effect, and finally left her, to call the next day. When he arrived, the lady turned her face to the wall. 'Lucy,' said the pastor, 'I have not called to argue with you, but will ask the privilege of reciting one verse of a precious hymn to you.' The lady granted his request, and he repeated, with much emphasis,

> 'Just as I am, without one plea,
> But that thy blood was shed for me,
> And that thou bid'st me come to thee
> O Lamb of God I come, I come.'

"The pastor left her, and after several days called again. Taking his seat beside her bed, she turned to him, and repeated the verse, 'Just as I am,' and added, 'Oh, sir, I've come, I've come,' and soon afterwards peacefully folded her hands, and passed away."

Dear friend, are you trying to save your own soul? Is Satan misleading you by making you believe your own efforts will save you? Let me in all sincerity tell you, that you are throwing your time away. You can of yourself do nothing more than come "just as you are, without one plea, but that Christ's blood was shed for thee." This is the only way you can ever be found in the kingdom of the redeemed. This is the only means of escape, this is the only avenue by which you can leave your sinful life, and find peace with God. Take this experience of one who was in your position, and apply it to yourself.

> "I struggled and wrestled to win it,
> The blessing that setteth me free,
> But when I had ceased from my struggling,
> His peace Jesus gave unto me."

"*By grace are ye saved.*" — EPH. ii. 8.

At the close of one of Mr. Moody's meetings he noticed a young lady, who had for several evenings accepted his invitation to remain at the after meeting. Mr. Moody went to her, and asked her what her soul's trouble was. She frankly confessed her great desire to become a Christian, and briefly telling of her efforts to find Christ, until she had almost concluded that she was beyond the power of Christ to save. Mr. Moody opened his Bible, and turned to one of those passages that so strikingly portrays the lost sinner, read to her, then he turned to the great sacrifice Christ had made for her. Closing his Bible, Mr. Moody said to her, "I see wherein lies your difficulty, you don't believe the Bible." She quickly said, "You are wrong, sir, I do believe it." He turned to Luke vii. 50, and asked the young lady to read. She read, "And he said to the woman, thy faith shall save thee." Mr. Moody quickly looked up, and said, "Can't you read?" A flush of anger came to her face as she informed him that she was a graduate of —— institute. She took the book once more, and read the same verse, "He said to the woman, thy faith *hath* saved thee; go in peace." The book fell to her lap, and a joyful light shone on her face, as she exclaimed, "Oh! I see how it is. I see all clearly now. The woman was not trying to be saved, she was simply trusting Christ to save her." She arose, no longer trying to save herself, but rejoicing in the Saviour who had saved her.

CHAPTER XXII.

SATAN'S DEVICES

"LEST SATAN SHOULD GET AN ADVANTAGE OF US: FOR
WE ARE NOT IGNORANT OF HIS DEVICES."

2 COR. ii. 11.

SATAN'S DEVICES.

"*Without me ye can do nothing.*" — JNO. xv. 5.

In my father's field stood a stately walnut tree, very beautiful to behold, and in whose shade I often sat down to rest. Yet around that tree the grain never matured. It was puny and sickly from the start, and each year at harvest time we never stopped to gather it; long before maturity, the blades withered and died. So it is in this life. Satan blinds us by offering us a shade in which to rest, and when Christ comes in his magnificent glory, we too will be left standing as worthless in the garner of his Father. "Nothing but leaves, nothing but leaves." Fortunate is he who early learns to centre his hopes and affections on Christ, and who can have his abiding presence to outshine the shady nets of Satan. Let us remember we can do all things through Christ, which strengthens us, and without *him* we can do nothing.

"*Whoso diggeth a pit shall fall therein.*"
PROV. xxvi. 27.

A certain king ordered one of his subjects to make for him a chain. Not surmising the use to which his master would put it, the poor fellow made a chain of great strength, and appeared before the king, who expressed his admiration of the workmanship, and, turning to his servants, bade them bind the man, and cast him into prison.

This is often the case with the sinner out of Christ. Satan makes him dig a pit, and, when it is done, he pulls him into it. Oh, blind, deluded, unsaved one, why let the old deceiver drag your immortal soul to perdition? Why not come out bravely and throw off your allegiance to him, and flee to Jesus, who is able to keep you from falling, and to present you spotless before the court of heaven? Greater is he that is for your eternal welfare, than he who is for your everlasting destruction. Will you take him?

"*And who is he that will harm you, if ye be followers of that which is good?*" — 1 Pet. iii. 13.

During a precious revival, some years ago, when hundreds were crying out for mercy, a young man became earnest about his soul. A Christian man took him by the hand, and asked him what the trouble was in his heart. With faltering voice the young man replied, "I want to give my heart to Christ. I know that I am lost, but if I should do such a thing, the men in the shop would harass me to death. I would be compelled to quit my position. I could not endure the taunts and sneers of five hundred men, and I do not care to make a start, and fall back to my old ways."

The gentleman opened his Bible, and read, "He that is for you is greater than he that is against you," and, turning to 2 Peter ii. 9, read, "The Lord knoweth how to deliver the godly." — "Will he do it?" asked the young man. The gentleman assured him it was God's personal promise to him, and God could not lie. "I will! I will!" cried he, "take Christ as my Saviour, and trust all to him."

The next day the young man went to his place in the

shop, as usual, and, as he passed by his fellow laborers, he thought their look more soft than before, and many were the kind words on every hand that greeted him.

Reader, Satan is ever trying to pull you back by telling you that you will be sneered at by your old associates. "Remember, he that is for you is greater than he that is against you. And those that would thrust a straw in your way are worthy to be let alone, and discountenanced as bosom friends.

"*I am thy shield, and thy exceeding great reward.*"
GEN. xv. 1.

An American citizen in a Spanish city violated some of their laws. He was tried, and sentenced to be shot on a certain day. The American consul was appealed to, and did all in his power to save the condemned man. He called the representative of the British government to his aid, but the day on which the execution was to take place was so near at hand, it rendered an examination of the case out of the question.

The condemned man was led forth to the place of execution. The two consuls appeared on the scene, and, in order to stay the proceedings until they could collect evidence to clear the man, they each wrapped about the prisoner the flag of his country. The soldiers stood with their muskets levelled, and waiting for the order to fire, but the captain dare not give the order, and desecrate the flags of two powerful nations.

Just so it is with us. Satan may so get us in his power that we are almost ready to fold our hands in despair, but that moment we apply to Christ, he throws around us the seal of his protection, which defies Satan and hell to approach it.

"*For man also knoweth not his time: as the fishes that are taken in an evil net, and as the birds that are caught in the snare; so are the sons of men snared in an evil time, when it falleth suddenly upon them.*" — ECL. ix. 12.

A gentleman relating to me his success in hunting geese on one of the great Western prairies, told me had killed many thousands of them. I asked him, "How did you manage to kill so many?" He replied, "I dug a long ditch, and placed bait on the bottom the entire length of the trench, then I fixed a net so it could, by pulling a cord, be made to fall over the ditch, and all I had to do was to walk along and slaughter them."

Beloved friend, this is exactly what Satan is doing to thousands of our fellow-men to-day. Can it be you are one that he is leading into the ditch? Oh! let me say, step not therein, for they who follow his cunning devices shall reap the fruits of their folly.

"*He that maketh haste to be rich shall not be innocent.*"
PROV. xxviii. 20.

Some years ago a Savings Bank was started in Philadelphia, that promised an unusual interest on deposits. Thousands of poor working people flocked to the counter, and laid down their hard-earned dimes and dollars to be placed on interest. When the bank had succeeded in getting a great sum of money in its vaults, its doors were closed, and the officers fled, carrying with them both principal and interest, and leaving many poor families in want.

Such are the investments Satan offers to-day to win us away from heaven, and when the end comes we will find both principal and interest gone, and our hopes in eternity a wreck. "Lay not up for yourselves treasures on earth, where moth and rust doth corrupt, and where thieves break through and steal; but lay up for yourselves treasures in heaven, where neither moth nor rust doth corrupt, and where thieves do *not* break through nor steal."

How is it with *thee*, friend?

"*The fool hath said in his heart, there is no God.*"
Ps. xiv. 1.

Some years ago a young man came to one of our New England colleges; he was the son of infidel parents, and possessed no religious or moral principles. His sole object was to seek his own present pleasure. The rules of the college compelled each student to be present each morning at the chapel prayer service. As this young man listened to the venerable President, when he addressed the Invisible Being, he would say within himself, "There is no God. Why all this foolishness?" One day while attending these services, a still small voice whispered these words to him, "It may be you are mistaken, it may be there is a God." His mind became troubled. The thought of the possibility of a hereafter clung to him. He went to the President of the college, who urged him to banish past ideas from his mind, and to accept Christ as a real and personal Saviour. The arrow of conviction sunk deep into his soul, the spirit enlightened his heart, and he felt that truly there is a God. At the next chapel services he with difficulty restrained his emotions until the prayer was ended, after which he publicly confessed his faith in a real God and Saviour, and became a faithful Christian.

How many poor souls are trying to educate their consciences to the belief in no God. Many do so simply to evade the responsibility of a Christian life. Some do so to be odd; others, because the teachings of God's word are so different from their lives that it would cause them to make too great a sacrifice to forsake their worldliness for the Gospel truth; so they accept the easiest way out of the dilemma, and say, "There is no God." Friend, there is a God, before whom you will stand, and give an account of your life here on earth. Are you prepared to meet Him?

"*For they have digged a pit to take me, and hid snares for my feet.*" — Jer. xviii. 22.

There is a story about how the hunters capture elephants, which gives us a useful illustration of the cunning devices old Satan uses in ensnaring unguarded souls. The hunters tell us that they dig a large pit, and first cover it with small sticks, then they lay a thin layer of dirt, upon which they place the sod. For a few days they pour water on the sod, and cause the grass to grow more rapidly, and present a better appearance, which soon attracts the great beasts, who come along and step on the trap door, which lands them at the bottom of the pit.

How eagerly Satan watches for our weak points, and makes the temptations more enticing that he may ensnare us. But, thanks be to God, through Christ we can say, "Get thee hence, Satan," and he leaveth us.

"*But they that will be rich fall into temptation and a snare, and into many foolish and hurtful lusts, which drown men in destruction and perdition.*" — 1 Tim. vi. 9.

When Rome was besieged, it is said of the daughter of its ruler, that she saw the golden bracelets on the arms of the enemy, and sent word to them that she would betray her city, and deliver it into their hands, if they would give her their bracelets. They readily accepted her proposition, and before sunset the daughter had secretly opened one of the gates to the city, and as the enemy entered they threw upon her their golden bracelets, and also their shields, until the great weight crushed her to death.

How many, many poor souls to-day are striving to gain that which will, in the end, prove the means of their everlasting death. Reader, can it be that you are one of that number? can it be that you are out of Christ, and lost? If so, let me urge you to immediate action in seeking first the kingdom of God and His righteousness, and these things, so far as you have need, *shall* be added unto you.

CHAPTER XXIII.

THE BLOOD.

"WITHOUT SHEDDING OF BLOOD IS NO REMISSION."
HEB. ix. 22.

THE BLOOD.

"*Without shedding of blood is no remission.*"
HEB. ix. 22.

It is asserted by historians that there is not a nation mentioned in history, the blood of whose citizens has not been poured out on its altars as an atonement for their sins, or to propitiate their deities. Even in this nineteenth century, it is said that there is a custom, carefully kept secret by Mussulmen, which shows that they believe that, "Without shedding of blood is no remission of sin." In time of great trouble and sorrow, when dreading the death of a favorite child, it is their custom to secretly kill a lamb, and sacrifice it, crying, "Allah, take the life of this lamb for the life of my child." The flesh of the lamb is then carefully removed, and given to religious beggars, while the skeleton is buried without breaking a bone.

Christ shed his precious blood that we might be brought back to God, and rescued from our degradation. By the shedding of his blood, the way of eternal life was made perfect, and an invitation went forth to all the earth to come and partake of that sacrifice.

"*In the day when God shall judge the secrets of men by Jesus Christ according to my gospel.*" — ROM. ii. 16.

A traveller crossing the frontier had to pass the custom house. The examining officers said to him, "Have you any contraband goods?"—"I don't think I have," he replied. "But we cannot allow you to pass until we have examined you," said the officers in charge. After he was examined he said to the officers, "Gentlemen, will you permit me to tell you what thoughts this examination has brought to my mind? We are all travellers to an eternal kingdom, into which we cannot take any contraband goods. By these forbidden things I mean deceitfulness, anger, pride, lying, covetousness, and all such offences, which are an abomination in the sight of God Almighty. For all these, every man that passes the boundary line of the grave is searched far more strictly than you have searched me. God is the great searcher of hearts, and from him nothing is hid that shall not in that day be revealed."

We can conceal nothing that will not be revealed in that great day. The all-searching eye of God will bring to light all our evil deeds. But "the blood of Jesus Christ his Son cleanseth us from all sin."

"*The blood of Jesus Christ his Son cleanseth us from all sin.*"— 1 Jno. i. 7.

A gentleman one day asked a little girl, "Are you a sinner?" She promptly replied, "No, sir." Somewhat amused at such an answer, he asked, "Have you never done anything wrong?"—"Oh, yes," she replied, "a great many times."—"How then do you say you are not a sinner?"—"It is *taken away*," she said. "I have trusted Christ whose blood cleanseth us from all sin."

Not simply from the grosser sins, but from *every sin* both great and small, the crimson tint, and the scarlet hue, all are made whiter than snow, through the blood of Jesus Christ his Son.

Reader, think not that your sins are too great to be washed away; for just such as you, his blood was shed on that dark day when the sun veiled its face in shame. For just such hearts as yours, the weary, bleeding feet of Christ trod the stony paths of the highways of Judea. For just such lost, helpless creatures as you, his strong arm reaches down, and rescues from the pit of despair.

On the other hand, don't think your sins are too few, and too insignificant to cause any anxiety; Satan may say this to you, but you can never prove it to God. "Ye must be born again." "Repent and believe." "Except ye be converted, ye cannot see the kingdom of God." "He that hath the Son hath life, he that hath not the Son hath not life." "Believe and thou shalt be saved." For "the blood of Jesus Christ, his Son, cleanseth us from all sin," and sets our feet in the path that begins at Mount Calvary, and ends at the pearly gates of heaven. Will you then not come with this simple prayer in your heart? — "Oh! Lord Jesus, in view of the fact that I am a wretched, lost soul, swiftly passing to the beyond, a mountain of iniquity behind me, the gaping jaws of hell before me, the chains of sin holding me fast, may thy strong arm rescue me, and may thy blood cleanse me; and thy name shall have the praises of my heart and life."

"*And they overcame him by the blood of the Lamb, and by the word of their testimony.*" — REV. xii. 11.

Rev. Edwin M. Long, in his "History of Hymns," tells the following incident illustrative of the power of the blood of Christ to reach to the lowest depths of degradation, and rescue the most hardened sinner from the pit of sin. He said, "While preaching in Maryland, I was told of a thief who was then and there rejoicing that the fountain for sin was still open.

"The evening before the execution of a murderer, a devoted Christian lady felt herself constrained before retiring, to prolong her devotions on his behalf. In her importunate prayer she mentioned thieves, and similar characters, as those for whom the atoning blood had been efficacious in apostolic times. Her soul was so stirred with sympathy that she could not sleep for a long time. Toward midnight she thought she heard a noise beneath her bed. At length she saw the head of a thief appear. Being alone, and not near any of the family to whom she could call for help, she closed her eyes in silent prayer, and calmly trusted in divine aid for protection. The thief trod softly along the bedside, to see if she was asleep. He bent over her pillow, coming so near that she felt his breath upon her face. He then quietly descended the stairway, and endeavored to get out, but he could not find the key to the door, as that was kept in a secret place. While he was engaged in trying to escape, this Christian heroine awoke a brother, and told him that there was a thief in the house, who was trying to get out. Getting a lamp, they descended the stairs, when the light fell upon the face of the intruder, who was a man from the village whom they knew. He confessed that he came there to steal. Being unable to meet a note due the next day, of three hundred dollars, he knew that this lady had that amount, and, supposing she kept it in her bedchamber, he concealed himself under her bed, intending to search for it when she was asleep, but her prayer for thieves so completely disarmed him, and so convicted him of sin, that he resolved to seek pardon in the blood of the Lamb. After hearing his confession, the sister was so impressed with the genuineness of his contrition, that she told her brother to get the money, and loan him the amount. He afterward not only repaid the money, but became an earnest Christian, and at the time of my visit was superintendent of the Sunday school of the village."

"The blood of Jesus Christ, His son cleanseth us from ALL sin." What encouragement to the poor, lost soul. No matter how low in sin, the blood cleanseth from *all* sin. No matter how deep in iniquity, no matter how degraded, Christ's blood can cleanse all.

"*Though your sins be as scarlet, they shall be as white as snow: though they be red like crimson, they shall be as wool.*" — ISA. i. 18.

There is a story told of a man who carried about with him a book with only three leaves in it, and not a word on any one of them. The first leaf was black as jet; the second, red as scarlet; the third, as white as the driven snow. Some one asked him one day what it meant. He replied, "The black leaf represents my sin; the red leaf, the precious blood; the white leaf represents my soul as washed in the precious blood of Christ, and made white as snow."

While not a word was written in the three-leaved book, yet it teaches us a plainer truth than the largest volume ever written, aside from the Bible. "The blood of Jesus Christ his Son cleanseth us from *all* sin."

"*The blood of Jesus Christ his Son cleanseth us from all sin.*" — 1 JNO. i. 7.

Martin Luther said the devil once appeared to him perched upon the foot of his bed, with an immense scroll in his hand, which he began to unfold, showing at each turn some gross sin of his life. Satan asked him if he could be a Christian, with all these black deeds recorded against him. Luther replied, " Unroll all; I want to see it all, awful as it is." As the last roll unwound, Luther saw the whole page crossed with great red marks, and he exclaimed, "The blood of Jesus Christ his Son cleanseth us from all sin."

Precious and inspiring thought! to know that however black our past life has been, we can come to Christ, and be made pure with his righteousness, and our imperfections made perfect through him.

"'Tis Jesus Christ, the first and last;
He saves, and he alone."

" *The blood of Jesus Christ his Son cleanseth us from all sin.*" — 1 Jno. i. 7:

A missionary was travelling from one station to another one day, and found a poor heathen man by the wayside, dying. After doing everything in his power to relieve his bodily pains, he asked him if he had a hope of heaven. The poor man looked up, and, in a faltering voice, repeated, "The blood of Jesus Christ his Son cleanseth us from all sin." As he finished the sentence, he breathed his last. The missionary saw he held, tightly grasped, a piece of paper; he took it, and found it a leaf of the New Testament, containing the first chapter of 1 John, on which was printed our text, — "The blood of Jesus Christ his Son cleanseth us from *all* sin."

Did you ever read carefully this verse? Observe how complete it is: *all* sin; not only the sins of commission, but the sins of omission. Yea, *all* sin, and leaves the heavenly record one great white page, **even** whiter than snow.

You may ask me, "How can these things be?" I answer, because "God so loved the world, that he gave his only begotten Son, that whosoever believeth should not perish, but have everlasting life." Then, *he that believeth* and comes to the Son finds pardon and forgiveness of sin, is washed and cleansed by the blood of Christ his Son, who died to redeem a condemned race, thereby paying the penalty and reconciling an offended God.

Therefore, dear friend, there is ample provision made, and all that stands between you and that provision is your sin; and "the blood of Jesus Christ his Son cleanseth from all sin."

The course for you to pursue is to come right now, this moment, to Christ, and say, "Dear Saviour, I am a lost sinner. The clanking chains of hell hold me fast. I can of myself do nothing. Except thou help me, I must go down. My sins are too heavy: I cannot longer carry them. Thou hast said, 'Come unto me, all ye that labor and are heavy laden, and I will give you rest,' and 'He that cometh, I will in no wise cast out.' I come, O Lamb of God, I come! For such as I, thou hast said, 'I came to seek and to save.' I must plead, my Saviour, *thy* merits, for within my own heart I find nothing to plead. I, therefore, throw myself, body and soul, at thy feet: 'tis all that I can do. I believe that thou canst save me, and save me wholly. Help my unbelief."

Dear friend, if you come in this spirit, your Saviour will meet you with outstretched arms, and draw you unto him; and while the glad shout of angels resounds throughout the heavenly courts, Jesus washes away your sins, and presents your soul in spotless purity before the throne of God and the Lamb. This is the way you must come, and the only way, "for other foundation can no man lay than that is laid, which is Jesus Christ."

"The blood of Jesus Christ his Son cleanseth us from all sin." — 1 Jno. i. 7.

"Sister," said a dying girl, "please do get the Bible, and read for me that passage about the blood which cleanseth from sin, for I am afraid some of my sins are too great to be forgiven. Do look whether it says, '*all sin*,' or only '*sin*,' for I don't remember." — "Yes," replied the sister, "these are the exact words: 'The blood of Jesus Christ his Son cleanseth us from *all* sin.'" — "Oh, that is sweet!" said the girl, whose fire of life was almost out, "for now there is pardon for *all my sins*."

O thou blessed God Almighty! I thank thee for this glorious fount, wherein my guilty soul may be cleansed and purified of all its filth, and made fit for that blest abode which thou in thy mercy hast prepared for those that love thee. Grant that when I hear thy voice saying, "Come up higher," and as I stand before thy throne, my soul may reflect the spotless purity of this cleansing stream; and, as I sit at thy feet, thy matchless name shall have the praise. Amen.

INDEX TO SCRIPTURE TEXTS.

	Page
Genesis 6:3 — "And the Lord said, My Spirit shall not always strive with man"	311
Genesis 15:1 — "I am thy shield, and thy exceeding great reward"	347
Genesis 19:17 — "Escape for thy life"	294, 302
Exodus 4:12 — "Now, therefore, go, and I will be with thy mouth, and teach thee what thou shalt say"	126, 174
Exodus 15:11 — "Who is like unto thee, O Lord, among the gods? Who is like unto thee, glorious in holiness, fearful in praises, doing wonders"	158
Exodus 20:8 — "Remember the Sabbath day, to keep it holy"	77, 87
Numbers 10:29 — "We are journeying unto the place of which the Lord said, I will give it you: come thou with us, and we will do thee good"	174
Numbers 25:4 — "The fierce anger of the Lord may be turned"	285
Numbers 32:23 — "Be sure your sin will find you out"	306
Deuteronomy 11:18 — "Therefore, shall ye lay up these my words in your heart and in your soul . . . and ye shall teach them your children, speaking of them when thou sittest in thine house, and when thou walkest by the way, when thou liest down and when thou risest up,"	172
Joshua 24:15 — "Choose you this day whom ye will serve"	286
I. Samuel 16:7 — "The Lord seeth not as man seeth, for man looketh on the outward appearance, but the Lord looketh on the heart"	137
I. Kings 17:14 — "For thus saith the Lord God of Israel, the barrel of meal shall not waste, neither shall the cruse of oil fail"	49
I. Kings 18:21 — "How long halt ye between two opinions"	312
Job 6:24 — "Teach me, and I will hold my tongue"	26
Job 7:7 — "Oh, remember that my life is wind"	299
Job 13:15 — "Though he slay me, yet will I trust in him"	53
Psalms 5:11 — "But let all those that put their trust in thee rejoice: let them ever shout for joy"	74
Psalms 9:9 — "The Lord also will be a refuge in times of trouble"	24
Psalms 14:1 — "The fool hath said in his heart, there is no God"	301, 349
Psalms 16:11 — "In thy presence is fulness of joy"	42
Psalms 17:5 — "Hold up my goings in thy paths, that my footsteps slip not"	22
Psalms 17:15 — "I shall be satisfied when I awake with thy likeness"	160
Psalms 19:12 — "Cleanse thou me from secret faults"	86
Psalms 23:2 — "He leadeth me"	45

Psalms 23:4 — "Though I walk through the valley of the shadow of death I will fear no evil, for thou art with me; thy rod and thy staff they comfort me" 39, 311
Psalms 25:14 — "The secret of the Lord is with them that fear him" . 43
Psalms 31:2 — "Be thou my strong rock, for an house of defence to save me" 211
Psalms 32:8 — "I will guide thee with mine eye" 19
Psalms 37:5 — "Commit thy way unto the Lord" 198
Psalms 49:8 — "The redemption of their soul is precious" 308
Psalms 51:17 — "A broken and a contrite heart, O God, thou wilt not despise" 198
Psalms 55:17 — "Evening and morning and at noon will I pray" ... 147
Psalms 59:16 — "Yea, I will sing aloud of thy mercy in the morning" . 143
Psalms 62:6 — "He only is my rock and my salvation" 206
Psalms 73:28 — "It is good for me to draw near to God" 106
Psalms 77:12 — "I will meditate also of all thy work, and talk of thy doings" 121
Psalms 86:5 — "For thou, Lord, art good, and ready to forgive; and plenteous in mercy unto all them that call upon thee" 300
Psalms 91:9-11 — "Because thou hast made the Lord ... thy habitation, there shall no evil befall thee, neither shall any plague come nigh thy dwelling; for he shall give his angels charge over thee to keep thee in all thy ways" 46
Psalms 96:1 — "O sing unto the Lord" 69
Psalms 103:13 — "Like as a father pitieth his children, so the Lord pitieth them that fear him" 75
Psalms 107:2 — "Let the redeemed of the Lord say so" 69
Psalms 115:1 — "Not unto us ... but unto thy name give glory" .. 18
Psalms 118:5 — "I called upon the Lord in distress" 284
Psalms 119:18 — "Open thou mine eyes" 268
Psalms 119:42 — "For I trust in thy word" 43
Psalms 119:114 — "Thou art my hiding-place and my shield" 279
Psalms 119:135 — "Make thy face to shine upon thy servant" 25
Psalms 119:162 — "I rejoice at thy word, as one that findeth great spoil," 169
Psalms 145:5 — "I will speak of the glorious honor of thy majesty, and of thy wondrous works" 135
Proverbs 1:10 — "My son, if sinners entice thee, consent thou not" .. 78
Proverbs 1:24 — "I have called, and ye refused" 280, 283
Proverbs 11:30 — "He that winneth souls is wise" 131
"He that is wise winneth souls." — Revised version.
Proverbs 18:24 — "There is a friend that sticketh closer than a brother," 5
Proverbs 22:6 — "Train up a child in the way he should go; and when he is old he will not depart from it" 32
Proverbs 26:27 — "Whoso diggeth a pit shall fall therein" 345
Proverbs 28:13 — "He that covereth his sins shall not prosper" 95
Proverbs 28:20 — "He that maketh haste to be rich shall not be innocent" 348
Ecclesiastes 9:12 — "For man also knoweth not his time: as the fishes that are taken in an evil net, and as the birds that are caught in the

INDEX TO SCRIPTURE TEXTS.

snare ; so are the sons of men snared in an evil time, when it falleth
suddenly upon them" 348
Ecclesiastes 11: 1 — "Cast thy bread upon the waters ; for thou shalt find
it after many days" 120, 120
Ecclesiastes 11: 6 — "In the morning sow thy seed, and in the evening
withhold not thine hand" 117
Isaiah 1: 18 — "Come now, and let us reason together, saith the Lord" . 184
Isaiah 1: 18 — "Though your sins be as scarlet, they shall be as white as
snow ; though they be red like crimson, they shall be as wool " . . 360
Isaiah 5: 20-21 — "Woe unto them that call evil good, and good evil ; that
put darkness for light, and light for darkness ; that put bitter for
sweet, and sweet for bitter."
"Woe unto them that are wise in their own eyes, and prudent in
their own sight" 164
Isaiah 25: 4 — "A refuge from the storm, a shadow from the heat" . . 216
Isaiah 29: 19 — "The poor among men shall rejoice in the Holy One of
Israel" 251
Isaiah 30: 15 — "In returning and rest shall ye be saved" 250
Isaiah 40: 17-18 — "All nations before him are as nothing ; and they are
counted to him less than nothing and vanity. To whom, then, will ye
liken God ? or what likeness will ye compare unto him " 325
Isaiah 41: 10 — "Fear thou not, for I am with thee ; be not dismayed, for
I am thy God" 197
Isaiah 42: 16 — "I will make darkness light before them " 28
Isaiah 50: 4 — "The Lord God hath given me the tongue of the learned,
that I should know how to speak a word in season to him that is
weary" 130
Isaiah 53: 5 — "He was wounded for our transgressions, he was bruised
for our iniquities" 213, 265, 288
Isaiah 53: 6 — "The Lord hath laid on him the iniquity of us all" . . . 234
Isaiah 55: 1 — "Ho everyone that thirsteth, come ye to the waters, and
he that hath no money come ye ; buy and eat, yea, come ; buy wine
and milk without money and without price" 241
Isaiah 55: 11 — "So shall my word be that goeth forth out of my mouth,
it shall not return unto me void, but it shall accomplish that which I
please, and it shall prosper in the thing whereto I sent it" . . . 70, 138
Isaiah 63: 1 — "Mighty to save" 230, 332
Jeremiah 15: 2 — "Thou shalt tell them. Thus saith the Lord" . . . 118
Jeremiah 17: 10 — "I the Lord search the heart ; I try the reins, even
to give every man according to his ways, and according to the fruit
of his doings" 27
Jeremiah 18: 22 — "For they have digged a pit to take me, and hid snares
for my feet" 350
Jeremiah 21: 14 — "But I will punish you according to the fruit of your
doings, saith the Lord" 224
Jeremiah 31: 16 — "Thy work shall be rewarded " 164
Lamentations 3: 33 — "For he doth not afflict willingly, nor grieve the
children of men" 17
Ezekiel 20: 47 — "I will kindle a fire in thee" 58

Daniel 12:3 — "And they that be wise shall shine as the brightness of the firmament; and they that turn many to righteousness as the stars for ever and ever" 131
Hosea 14:8 — "From me is thy fruit found" 61
Amos 4:12 — "Prepare to meet thy God," 322
Malachi 1:10 — "I have no pleasure in you, saith the Lord of hosts. Neither will I accept an offering at your hand" 7
Malachi 3:3 — "He shall sit as a refiner" 4
Malachi 3:7 — " Return unto me, and I will return unto you" . . 221, 253
Matthew 5:16 — "Let your light so shine" 21, 72, 137
Matthew 5:44 — "But I say unto you, Love your enemies, bless them that curse you, do good to them that hate you, and pray for them which despitefully use you and persecute you" 96, 151
Matthew 6:6 — "But thou, when thou prayest, enter into thy closet, and when thou hast shut thy door, pray" 147
Matthew 6:15 — "But if ye forgive not men their trespasses, neither will your Father forgive your trespasses" 96
Matthew 6:19–20 — "Lay not up for yourselves treasures upon earth, where moth and rust doth corrupt, and where thieves break through and steal; but lay up for yourselves treasures in heaven, where neither moth nor rust doth corrupt, and where thieves do not break through nor steal" 199, 204
Matthew 6:24 — "No man can serve two masters" 33
Matthew 6:33 — "But seek ye first the kingdom of God, and his righteousness, and all these things shall be added unto you" . . 104, 298, 330
Matthew 6:34 — "Take, therefore, no thought for the morrow, for the morrow shall take thought for the things of itself" 17
Matthew 7:1 — "Judge not that ye be not judged" 153
Matthew 7:5 — "Thou hypocrite" 33
Matthew 7:8 — "To him that knocketh, it shall be opened" 210
Matthew 7:13 — "Broad is the way that leadeth to destruction" . . . 209
Matthew 7:20 — "By their fruits ye shall know them" 61
Matthew 7:21 — "Not every one that saith unto me, Lord, Lord, shall enter into the kingdom of heaven; but he that doeth the will of my Father which is in heaven" 194
Matthew 7:23 — "I never knew you, depart from me" 310
Matthew 8:11 — "Many shall come from the east and west, and shall sit down with Abraham, and Isaac, and Jacob, in the kingdom of Heaven" 125
Matthew 9:6 — "But that ye may know that the Son of Man hath power on earth to forgive sins" 259
Matthew 10:8 — "Freely ye have received, freely give" 58
Matthew 10:22 — "He that endureth to the end shall be saved" 107
Matthew 10:27 — "What ye hear in the ear, that preach ye upon the housetops" 66
Matthew 10:28 — "Fear not them which kill the body, but are not able to kill the soul: but rather fear him which is able to destroy both soul and body in hell" 52
Matthew 10:32 — "Whosoever, therefore shall confess me before men, him will I confess also before my Father which is in heaven" . . . 122

Matthew 10 : 33 — " But whosoever shall deny me before men, him will I
  also deny before my Father which is in heaven " 8
Matthew 10 : 37 — " He that loveth father or mother more than me is not
  worthy of me " 186
Matthew 11 : 28 — " Come unto me all ye that labor and are heavy laden,
  and I will give you rest " 260, 261, 337, 339
Matthew 13 : 46 — " When he had found one pearl of great price, went
  and sold all that he had and bought it " 212
Matthew 16 : 24 — " If any man will come after me, let him deny himself,
  and take up his cross and follow me " 105
Matthew 16 : 26 — " What shall a man give in exchange for his soul " . . 303
Matthew 17 : 7 — " And Jesus came and touched them, and said, Arise,
  and be not afraid " 11
Matthew 17 : 20 — " If ye have faith as a grain of mustard seed . . . nothing shall be impossible unto you " 15
Matthew 19 : 29 — " And everyone that hath forsaken houses or brethren,
  or sisters, or father, or mother, or wife, or children, or lands, for
  my name's sake, shall receive an hundred fold, and shall inherit everlasting life " 68, 119
Matthew 23 : 33 — " How can ye escape the damnation of hell " 313
Matthew 24 : 46 — " Blessed is that servant, whom his Lord, when he
  cometh, shall find so doing " 12
Matthew 25 : 29 — " For unto everyone that hath shall be given, and he
  shall have abundance " 114
Matthew 25 : 32 — " And before him shall be gathered all nations, and he
  shall separate them one from another " 207
Matthew 25 : 36 — " Naked and ye clothed me. I was sick and ye visited
  me, I was in prison and ye came unto me " 151, 157, 228
Matthew 25 : 40 — " Verily, I say unto you, inasmuch as ye have done it
  unto one of the least of these my brethren, ye have done it unto me," 14
Matthew 25 : 41 — " Then shall he say also to them on the left hand,
  Depart from me, ye cursed " 304
Mark 1 : 41 — " And Jesus, moved with compassion, put forth his hand,
  and touched him, and saith unto him, I will : be thou clean " . . . 243
Mark 4 : 19 — " And the cares of this world, and the deceitfulness of riches,
  and the lusts of other things, entering in, choke the word, and it
  becometh unfruitful " 107
Mark 5 : 19 — " Tell them how great things the Lord hath done for thee,"
  61, 128, 132
Mark 8 : 36, 37 — " For what shall it profit a man if he shall gain the
  whole world and lose his own soul ? Or what shall a man give in exchange for his soul " 286
Mark 8 : 38 — " Whosoever, therefore, shall be ashamed of me and of my
  words in this adulterous and sinful generation, of him also shall the
  Son of Man be ashamed when he cometh in the glory of his Father
  with the holy angels " 6
Mark 9 : 42 — " And whosoever shall offend one of these little ones that
  believe in me, it is better for him that a millstone were hanged about
  his neck, and he were cast into the sea " 73

Mark 10:23—"How hardly shall they that have riches enter into the kingdom of God" 227
Mark 10:47—"He heard that it was Jesus of Nazareth" 288
Mark 10:49—"Rise, he calleth thee" 282
Mark 11:13—"And when he came to it he found nothing but leaves" . 57
Mark 11:26—"But if ye do not forgive, neither will your Father which is in heaven forgive your trespasses" 159
Mark 13:37—"And what I say unto you, I say unto all, Watch" ... 299
Mark 16:16—"He that believeth ... shall be saved" 48
Luke 4:10—"For it is written, He shall give his angels charge over thee, to keep thee" 314
Luke 6:38—"Give and it shall be given unto you; good measure, pressed down, and shaken together, and running over" 29
Luke 9:23—"And he said to them all, if any man will come after me, let him deny himself, and take up his cross daily, and follow me" 103
Luke 9:60—"Go thou and preach the kingdom of God" 139
Luke 10:20—"Rejoice, because your names are written in heaven" . 328, 331
Luke 11:9—"And I say unto you, ask and it shall be given you; seek, and ye shall find; knock, and it shall be opened unto you" 195
Luke 12:34—"For where your treasure is, there will your heart be also," 322
Luke 12:37—"Blessed are those servants whom his Lord, when he cometh, shall find watching" 7
Luke 14:17—"Come; for all things are now ready" 252
Luke 14:23—"Go out into the highways and hedges, and compel them to come in" 113
Luke 14:33—"So likewise, whosoever he be of you that forsaketh not all that he hath, he cannot be my disciple" 28, 32
Luke 15:18—"I will arise and go to my father" 246
Luke 16:31—"If they hear not Moses and the prophets, neither will they be persuaded, though one rose from the dead" 297
Luke 19:10—"The Son of man is come to seek and to save that which was lost" 201, 272, 338
Luke 22:40—"Pray that ye enter not into temptation" 143
Luke 23:26—"On him they laid the cross" 180
John 1:11—"He came unto his own and his own received him not" .. 232
John 1:12—"As many as received him, to them gave he power to become the sons of God, even to them that believe on his name" .. 254
John 1:29—"Behold the Lamb of God which taketh away the sin of the world" 324
John 3:16—"For God so loved the world that he gave his only begotten son, that whosoever believeth in him should not perish, but have everlasting life" 179, 248, 328
John 3:36—"He that believeth on the Son hath everlasting life" . 269, 336
John 4:13, 14—"Whosoever drinketh of this water shall thirst again. But whosoever drinketh of the water that I shall give him shall never thirst, but the water that I shall give him shall be in him a well of water springing up into everlasting life" 257
John 5:39—"Search the Scriptures, for in them ye think ye have eternal life" 172, 176

INDEX TO SCRIPTURE TEXTS. 369

John 5: 40 — " And ye will not come to me, that ye might have life " . . 304
John 6: 37 — " Him that cometh to me I will in no wise cast out " . . . 255
John 6: 47 — " He that believeth on me hath everlasting life " 251
John 6: 48 — " I am that bread of life " 287
John 8: 12 — " Then spake Jesus again unto them, saying, I am the light of the world; he that followeth me shall not walk in darkness, but shall have the light of life " 31, 193, 202, 208
John 8: 36 — " If the Son therefore shall make you free, ye shall be free indeed " 203, 259
John 9: 5 — " I am the light of the world " 196
John 10: 10 — " I am come that they might have life, and that they might have it more abundantly " 324
John 10: 27-28 — " My sheep hear my voice, and I know them, and they follow me. And I give unto them eternal life; and they shall never perish; neither shall any man pluck them out of my hand " 47
John 12: 32 — " And I, if I be lifted up from the earth, will draw all men unto me " 196, 207
John 13: 15 — " For I have given you an example, that ye should do as I have done " 11
John 14: 2 — " In my Father's house are many mansions " 163
John 14: 6 — " I am the way, the truth, and the life " 217
John 14: 27 — " Peace I leave with you, my peace I give unto you; not as the world giveth, give I unto you " 235
John 15: 3 — " Now ye are clean through the word which I have spoken unto you " 171
John 15: 4 — " As the branch cannot bear fruit of itself, except it abide in the vine; no more can ye, except ye abide in me " 116
John 15: 5 — " For without me ye can do nothing " 109, 345
John 15: 6 — " If a man abide not in me, he is cast forth as a branch, and is withered " 115
John 15: 7 — " If ye abide in me, and my words abide in you, ye shall ask what ye will, and it shall be done unto you " 9, 16
John 15: 13 — " Greater love hath no man than this, that a man lay down his life for his friends " 180, 185, 187
John 15: 27 — " Ye also shall bear witness " 13
John 16: 23 — " Whatsoever ye shall ask the Father in my name, he will give it you " 116
John 17: 3 — " And this is life eternal, that they might know thee, the only true God, and Jesus Christ, whom thou hast sent " 5, 335
Acts 3: 6 — " Silver and gold have I none; but such as I have, give I thee," 246
Acts 5: 29 — " We ought to obey God rather than men " 84
Acts 5: 32 — " We are his witnesses " 65
Acts 16: 30 — " What must I do to be saved " 270
Acts 24: 25 — " Go thy way for this time, when I have a convenient season I will call for thee " 307
Acts 26: 28 — " Almost thou persuadest me " 21, 294, 305, 309
Romans 2: 6, 7 — " Who will render to every man according to his deeds: To them who by patient continuance in well-doing seek for glory and honor and immortality, eternal life " 16

INDEX TO SCRIPTURE TEXTS.

Romans 2: 16 — " In the day when God shall judge the secrets of men by Jesus Christ according to my gospel " 355
Romans 8: 18 — " For I reckon that the sufferings of this present time are not worthy to be compared with the glory which shall be revealed in us " 30
Romans 12: 10 — " Be kindly affectioned one to another " 158
Romans 14: 7 — " For none of us liveth to himself, and no man dieth to himself " 77
Romans 14: 10 — " For we shall all stand before the judgment seat of Christ " 271
Romans 14: 12 — " So, then, every one of us shall give an account of himself to God " 267
I. Corinthians 1: 18 — " For the preaching of the cross is to them that perish, foolishness; but unto us which are saved, it is the power of God," 321
I. Corinthians 2: 14 — " But the natural man receiveth not the things of the Spirit of God: for they are foolishness unto him " 323
I. Corinthians 5: 6 — " A little leaven leaveneth the whole lump " . . . 98
I. Corinthians 6: 19, 20 — " And ye are not your own, for ye are bought with a price: therefore glorify God in your body, and in your spirit, which are God's " 187
I. Corinthians 10: 10 — " Neither murmur ye, as some of them also murmured, and were destroyed of the destroyer " 49
I. Corinthians 14: 19 — " I had rather speak five words with my understanding, that by my voice I might teach others also, than ten thousand words in an unknown tongue " 144
I. Corinthians 15: 3 — "How that Christ died for our sins " 265
I. Corinthians 15: 33 — " Evil communications corrupt good manners " . 71
I. Corinthians 15: 58 — " Therefore, my beloved brethren, be ye steadfast, unmovable, always abounding in the work of the Lord " 59, 134
I. Corinthians 15: 58 — " Your labor is not in vain in the Lord " 134
II. Corinthians 5: 10 — " For we must all appear before the judgment seat of Christ, that every one may receive the things done in his body, according to that he hath done, whether it be good or bad " 295
II. Corinthians 5: 19 — " God was in Christ, reconciling the world unto himself " 221
II. Corinthians 6: 2 — " Behold, now is the accepted time " 293
II. Corinthians 6: 17 — " Wherefore come out from among them, and be ye separate, saith the Lord " 67
II. Corinthians 12: 10 — " Therefore I take pleasure in infirmities, in reproaches, in necessities, in persecutions, in distresses for Christ's sake, for when I am weak then am I strong " 51
II. Corinthians 13: 5 — " Examine yourselves; whether ye be in the faith," 51
Galatians 5: 9 — " A little leaven leaveneth the whole lump " 72
Galatians 5: 26 — " Let us not be desirous of vainglory, provoking one another, envying one another " 152, 157
Galatians 6: 7 — " Whatsoever a man soweth, that shall he also reap " . 226
Galatians 6: 17 — " I bear in my body the marks of the Lord Jesus " . 103, 108
Ephesians 2: 8 — " By grace are ye saved, through faith, and that not of yourselves; it is the gift of God " 254, 340

INDEX TO SCRIPTURE TEXTS.

Ephesians 6 : 11 — " Put on the whole armor of God, that ye may be able
to stand against the wiles of the devil " 44, 83, 93
Ephesians 6 : 13 — " Take unto you the whole armor of God " 45
Ephesians 6 : 17 — " Take the helmet of salvation, and the sword of the
Spirit, which is the word of God " 87, 173
Philippians 3 : 13 — " Forgetting those things which are behind, and
reaching forth unto those things which are before " 223
Philippians 4 : 13 — " I can do all things through Christ, which strength-
eneth me " 50
Colossians 3 : 2 — " Set your affections on things above, not on things on
the earth " 205
I. Thessalonians 5 : 17 — " Pray without ceasing " 144
I. Timothy 3 : 16 — " Without controversy, great is the mystery of godli-
ness " 14, 19
I. Timothy 5 : 24 — " Some men's sins are open beforehand, going before
to judgment; and some men they follow after " 273
I. Timothy 6 : 9 — " But they that will be rich fall into temptation and a
snare, and into many foolish and hurtful lusts, which drown men in
destruction and perdition " 350
Titus 2 : 14 — " Who gave himself for us, that he might redeem us " . . 182
Hebrews 3 : 7, 8 — " The Holy Ghost saith, to-day if ye will hear his voice,
harden not your hearts " 315
Hebrews 3 : 15 — " To-day, if ye will hear his voice, harden not your
hearts " 317
Hebrews 4 : 1 — " Let us therefore fear, lest a promise being left us of
entering into his rest, some of you should seem to come short of it " . 20
Hebrews 4 : 9 — " There remaineth therefore a rest to the people of God," 165
Hebrews 4 : 12 — " For the word of God is quick and powerful " . 170, 173, 175
Hebrews 4 : 16 — " Let us therefore come boldly unto the throne of grace,
that we may obtain mercy, and find grace to help in time of need " . 40
Hebrews 7 : 25 — " He is able also to save them to the uttermost that
come unto God by him, seeing he ever liveth to make intercession for
them " 236, 242, 296
Hebrews 9 : 22 — " Without shedding of blood is no remission " 355
Hebrews 9 : 28 — " So Christ was once offered to bear the sins of many " . 268
Hebrews 10 : 24 — " And let us consider one another to provoke unto love
and to good works " 71, 123
Hebrews 10 : 31 — " It is a fearful thing to fall into the hands of the living
God " 228
Hebrews 12 : 1 — " Let us lay aside every weight, and the sin that doth so
easily beset us, and let us run with patience the race that is set before
us " 97
Hebrews 12 : 2 — " Looking unto Jesus " 3
Hebrews 12 : 6 — " For whom the Lord loveth he chasteneth, and scourg-
eth every son whom he receiveth " 27
Hebrews 12 : 14 — " Follow peace with all men, and holiness without
which no man shall see the Lord " 156
Hebrews 13 : 2 — " Be not forgetful to entertain strangers, for thereby
some have entertained angels unawares " 154

James 1:12 — "Blessed is the man that endureth temptation; for when he is tried he shall receive a crown of life, which the Lord hath promised to them that love him" 83
James 1:14, 15 — "But every man is tempted, when he is drawn away of his own lust, and enticed. Then when lust hath conceived, it bringeth forth sin; and sin, when it is finished, bringeth forth death" .. 329
James 2:7 — "Do not blaspheme that worthy name by the which ye are called" 23
James 2:10 — "For whosoever shall keep the whole law, and yet offend in one point, he is guilty of all" 98
James 3:5 — "Behold how great a matter a little fire kindleth" 115
James 3:6 — "The tongue is a fire, a world of iniquity" 152
James 4:6 — "God resisteth the proud, but giveth grace unto the humble," 25
James 4:7 — "Resist the devil, and he will flee from you" 86, 108
James 4:17 — "Therefore to him that knoweth to do good, and doeth it not, to him it is sin" 327
James 5:16 — "The effectual fervent prayer of a righteous man availeth much" 145
I. Peter 1:8 — "Whom having not seen, ye love" 211
I. Peter 1:24 — "For all flesh is as grass, and all the glory of man as the flower of grass. The grass withereth, and the flower thereof falleth away" 326
I. Peter 2:21 — "Christ also suffered for us, leaving us an example, that ye should follow his steps" 30
I. Peter 2:24 — "Who his own self bare our sins in his own body on the tree, that we, being dead to sins, should live unto righteousness," 233, 258
I. Peter 3:8 — "Be ye all of one mind, having compassion one of another: Love as brethren, be pitiful, be courteous" 155
I. Peter 3:10 — "He that will love life, and see good days, let him refrain his tongue from evil, and his lips that they speak no guile" 154
I. Peter 3:13 — "And who is he that will harm you if ye be followers of that which is good" 346
I. Peter 5:7 — "Casting all your care upon him, for he careth for you," 53, 200
I. Peter 5:8 — "The devil, as a roaring lion, walketh about, seeking whom he may devour" 85, 88, 215
II. Peter 2:9 — "The Lord knoweth how to deliver the godly out of temptations" 48
II. Peter 3:18 — "But grow in grace, and in the knowledge of our Lord and Saviour Jesus Christ" 105
I. John 1:5 — "God is light, and in him is no darkness at all" 239
I. John 1:7 — "The blood of Jesus Christ ... cleanseth us from all sin" 356, 359, 360, 362
I. John 1:9 — "If we confess our sins, he is faithful and just to forgive us our sins, and to cleanse us from all unrighteousness" ... 224, 231, 245
I. John 2:9 — "He that ... hateth his brother is in darkness" 222
I. John 4:10 — "Herein is love" 181, 183, 188
I. John 4:17 — "Herein is our love made perfect" 127
I. John 4:18 — "There is no fear in love" 41, 156
I. John 5:17 — "All unrighteousness is sin" 60

Revelation 2: 10 — "Be thou faithful unto death, and I will give thee a crown of life" 34, 118
Revelation 3: 8 — "Behold, I have set before thee an open door" . . . 214
Revelation 3: 15 — "I know thy works, that thou art neither cold nor hot. I would thou wert cold or hot" 58
Revelation 3: 20 — "Behold, I stand at the door and knock" 281
Revelation 5: 9 — "For thou wast slain, and hast redeemed us to God by thy blood" 65, 248
Revelation 12: 11 — "And they overcame him by the blood of the Lamb, and by the word of their testimony" 357
Revelation 14: 13 — "Blessed are the dead which die in the Lord" . . . 76
Revelation 21: 6 — "I will give unto him that is athirst, of the fountain of the water of life freely" 124
Revelation 22: 15 — "For without are dogs, and sorcerers, and whoremongers, and murderers, and idolaters, and whosoever loveth and maketh a lie" 274
Revelation 22: 17 — "Whosoever will, let him take the water of life freely" 235, 244, 249

www.ingramcontent.com/pod-product-compliance
Lightning Source LLC
Chambersburg PA
CBHW022334230426
43664CB00040B/631